Santeria from Africa to the New World

Santeria from Africa

Blacks in the Diaspora
Darlene Clark Hine, John McCluskey, Jr., and David Barry Gaspar
GENERAL EDITORS

to the New World THE
DEAD SELL MEMORIES

George Brandon

Indiana University Press | Bloomington and Indianapolis

The paper used in this publication meets the minimum requirements of American
National Standard for Information Sciences—Permanence of Paper for Printed
Library Materials, ANSI Z39.48-1984.

∞

MANUFACTURED IN THE UNITED STATES OF AMERICA

Library of Congress Cataloging-in-Publication Data

Brandon, George, date
    Santeria from Africa to the new world : the dead sell memories /
George Brandon.
        p.   cm.—(Blacks in the diaspora)
    Includes bibliographical references and index.
    ISBN 0-253-31257-4 (hard : alk. paper) ISBN 0-253-21114-X (pbk.)
    1. Santeria (Cult) I. Title. II. Series.
BL2532.S3B73   1993
299'.67—dc20   92-24251

     4   5   6   7   01   00

For

Iyalosha Oshunfunke,
Iyalosha Olurde,
Mwedogi, Ewe Babalawo of the village of
    Kissema, Ghana—be he living or dead,

and to the memory of

Thelonious Monk (1917–1982) and
Vera Mae Green (1928–1982),
    Ibaiye Tonu.

Contents

Illustrations follow page 31 and page 120.

Acknowledgments

This book has had a long and tortuous history. Much of the material was gathered in the course of writing my Ph.D. dissertation on Santeria for the Department of Anthropology at Rutgers University. That was in 1983. The dissertation itself proved to be so massive that it was certainly unpublishable as it was. It became clear that what I had was two books rather than one. One of the books, this one, was an historical study, albeit with heavily anthropological overtones; the other book was an ethnography, which remains to be put into a new and publishable form.

The first year of the research on which this book is based was conducted with the assistance of an award from the National Fellowships Fund of the Ford Foundation in 1980. The bulk of the dissertation research, however, was carried on during my tenure with the Inner-City Support Systems (ICSS) Project of the University of Medicine and Dentistry of New Jersey from 1980 to 1982. I cannot adequately express the debts that I owe this remarkable group of people. Even though I pursued my dissertation research independent of ICSS, the end result would have been very different had I not worked there. Dr. Vivian Garrison was instrumental in securing me entry into what proved to be my most valuable network of informants. Her long acquaintance with Espiritismo was also invaluable, as were our long hours of conversation, which, gratefully, continue up through the present. Other members of the ICSS team who were helpful along the way were Ana Hernandez, Carol Weiss, and Judy Podell.

Some of the things I uncovered through the historical study and field research I had done threw much of what I had learned to accept as anthropological theory into question. Following out the implications of this in general terms and putting together the beginnings of an appropriate framework for understanding and presenting what I had found consumed many hours of meditating on and reworking of this material during the succeeding years and continues to this day. Much of this work took place at the University of Maryland Baltimore County, where I was employed as assistant professor of African American studies from 1982 to 1989. I could not have asked for a more supportive and collegial environment than the one provided during those years by Daphne Harrison, Robert Hall, Jonathan Peters, Chezia Thompson-Cager, and Willie Lamouse-Smith. A National Endowment for the Humanities Fellowship allowed me to attend the 1985 Princeton University Summer Institute on African American Religious Studies and to rethink some of my materials and ideas within the broader context provided the other fellows under the direction of Albert Raboteau and David Wills. It also allowed me to reconnect with the inspiration of Charles Long, who was my first mentor in African religious studies nearly thirteen years before at the University of Chicago.

My library and archival research benefited from the services of the Center for Cuban Studies, the Schomburg Center for Research in Black Culture, the Northwestern University Archives, the staffs of Rutgers University's Dana and Alexander Libraries, the Library of Congress Africa Section, the Alvin O. Kuhn Library of the University of Maryland, the Milton Eisenhower Library of the Johns Hopkins University, and the National Museum of Lagos, Nigeria.

Many individuals deserve mention because of their assistance, but there is scarcely space to name them all or to tell of the variety and graciousness of their help: Andres Perez y Mena, Verna Gillis, Joe Falcone, Lenny Lopate, Clarence Robbins, John Mason, Kwabena Perry, Kelly Royal, Tufani Rafua, Edward Tivnam, Eric Plasa, Dele Fan, Samy Gardner, Jose Alicea, Maria Rivera, Mikelle Smith-Omari, Margie Baynes Quiniones, Angela Fleming, Rosa Levya, Petra Lomar, Nana Yao Opare Dinizulu, Oba Osejiman Adefunmi I and the residents of Oyotunji Village in South Carolina, David Brown, Elio Torres, Babatunde Olatunji, Chief Olu Akaraogun, Joseph Holloway, Lionel Tiger, William Powers, Patricia Womack, and the anonymous manuscript reviewer at Indiana University Press whose comments were so helpful.

Santeria from Africa to the New World

I.

Introduction

For a variety of reasons, anthropologists traditionally carried out their studies with the assumption that for each society there was but a single culture. Clearly the model for this kind of assumption was the study of a relatively simple, relatively isolated, small-scale "primitive" society on one hand and the marginal, nationally based, culturally distinctive ethnic group on the other. To assume that these monocultural societies and groups were culturally uniform as well was entirely consistent with that point of view. Multicultural societies could only be seen, then, as somewhat exceptional cases. Yet cultural struggle and the fusion and separation of peoples and civilizations are part and parcel of the whole history of humans on the planet. In the Americas, and particularly in Afro-America, the cases are especially intricate and compelling. For here Amerindian, African, Asian, and European peoples were all brought together under an economic system dominated and controlled by Europeans. In the great forced migration to the Americas that was the slave trade, Africans were scattered across the vastness of the Atlantic world. Slavery and indentured servitude were not conditions that favored the calm dissolution of cultural differences or the formation of homogeneous monocultural societies. The United States, the Caribbean, Central and South America all received millions of Africans through the slave trade, but it has been in the Caribbean Basin and in northeastern Brazil that African cultures have remained most evident as distinct and identifiable heritages. Nowhere have these traditions continued to exist without change. Intact preservation of the lifeways of the homeland was not possible for any of the groups—dominant or subordinate, oppressor or oppressed. Continuity and discontinuity, persistence and disruption, survival, disintegration, and death have marked and scoured them all. This has been especially true of the religions of the numerous African peoples and the specific religious tradition with which this study is concerned: Yoruba religion and one of its present embodiments, Santeria.

To put Santeria into a proper perspective we have to place it into several contexts simultaneously: global, New World, and local–national.

In global context Santeria belongs to the transatlantic tradition of Yoruba religion, a religious tradition with millions of adherents in Africa and the Americas, and should be seen as a variant of that tradition, just as there are regional and doctrinal variants within the Christian, Buddhist, and Islamic religious traditions. Santeria is a New World neo-African religion with a clear dual heritage. Its component traditions include European Christianity (in the form of Spanish folk Catholicism), traditional African religion (in the form of orisha worship as practiced by the Yoruba of Nigeria), and Kardecan spiritism, which originated in France in the nineteenth century and became fashionable in both the Caribbean and South America.

In having this kind of a dual heritage, Santeria is not unique. It is but one of the series of related Yoruba-based religious forms that exist in the Caribbean, in Central and South America, and now in the United States as well. Santeria is the Cuban variant of this tradition. Shango in Trinidad and on Grenada, Xango and Candomble in Brazil, and Kele on St. Lucia are other examples. Yoruba religion also entered Haiti to compose there, along with Kongo-Angolan and Dahomeyan practices, the kaleidoscope that is the religion of Vodun. Santeria should also be viewed, then, in relation to its kindred New World forms.

In regard to the local–national context, I must point out that Santeria was not the only African-based religious group I found during my fieldwork in New York. Far from being an isolated instance, Santeria is in fact only one—though possibly the largest—part of an extensive African occult underground in New York, Philadelphia, Chicago, Los Angeles, Washington, Miami, and probably other cities across the United States. When placed within this context Santeria looks far less exotic and atypical.

In relation to the United States, Yoruba religion and Santeria—and really the greater part of this whole African occult underground—involve not the retention of African tradition but rather the convergence of the reintroduction of African tradition by immigrants from areas where African religions have been retained with greater influence and greater fidelity, with the purposeful revitalization of that tradition by U.S. blacks and Puerto Ricans. In this context the issue of Africanisms in the United States becomes not only an historical one but contemporary as well and concerns processes of culture change that can be observed in the present and over the very recent past.

What I would like to do in these chapters is to take the reader along one path of what this transatlantic tradition of Yoruba religion has come to be—the path from Africa to Cuba to New York City. Other paths could have been, and ultimately must be, chosen and researched by scholars in the future. So this book talks about one line, one path among the many, and its focus is mainly on the structures and rhythms of Santeria's history and on problems of collective memory and syncretism. As a result, this work draws on the literature of African, Spanish, and Cuban history; African religious studies; primary and secondary sources on Santeria; and my own fieldwork undertaken in Ghana (1974), Cuba (1978), the New York metropolitan area (1979–81), and Oyotunji Village, South Carolina (1981).

The Processual Framework

I see the development of Yoruba religion–Santeria falling into five phases, and it is these phases which determine most of the plan of presentation. In each phase, if followed out long enough, I believe we would find three stages: a formative, a persisting, and a transformative period.

In terms of religion, a formative period is when a religion is beginning to assume a different physiognomy than previously, through exposure to other religions, internal developments, economic or political catastrophe, and so forth. What marks this period is exposure, innovation, recoil, or seeking, and these are seen in a number of processes which do not necessarily eventuate in a coherent direction of change. Eventually, though, these developments eventuate in a period of conflict over a small number of alternatives, followed by a taking of positions and the working out of these alternatives until one or more of them becomes a major direction of change. Those alternatives that survive assume a form which is recognizable and whose recognizability can be successfully and consistently reproduced. When this happens it constitutes a period of persistence, and the new form is repeatedly reproduced within a range of variation that assures its uniqueness and coherence. The transformative stage is simply another version of the formative stage, with the form that exists during the persisting stage as its point of departure.

That is a macrolevel portrait of the processes involved. The picture at lower levels, as we shall see, may appear to be quite different. These lower-level processes, of which the macrolevel phases are the interactive products, include processes of regularization (whose effect is to ensure the reproduction of some existing and persisting structure), processes of situational adjustment (in which people try to manipulate aspects of the situation in which they find themselves so that they obtain results closer to what they desire), and an ever-present tendency toward indeterminacy and leveling, which can be actual or latent, willfully incorporated or vigorously opposed by conscious effort, planning, or ideological assertion. These ideas can be readily applied to the periodization of Santeria.

Phases of Religious Development

The progression of development of Santeria that I have conceptualized has five phases: Phase I, the African and Pre-Santeria period; Phase II, Early Santeria (1760–1870); Phase III, Santeria (1870–1959); Phase IV Branch I, Persisting Santeria and Santerismo; Phase IV Branch 2, Persisting Santeria and Early Orisha-Voodoo; and Phase V, Orisha-Voodoo.

Phase I, African and Pre-Santeria period. This phase (chapters II and III) includes the formation of the Yoruba people, Yoruba religion, and the

Yoruba city-states, as well as the coming into being of mutual influences between the Yoruba kingdoms of Benin and Dahomey, a confluence of powers radiating in different but parallel directions from the city of Ife in Nigeria. This phase also includes the beginnings of the involvement of these states in the Atlantic slave trade. The deepening involvement of Africans in the slave trade and the economic and political changes that result are only part of what signals the end of this period. What also demarcates this period for our purposes is the appearance of slaves from the Bight of Benin area in the slave trade to Cuba.

The first two phases of religious and cultural development were intersected by a rhythm of economic development in Cuba: the occurrence of two periods of booming plantation economy with a lengthy interregnum in between. This pattern of development had a significant impact on the character of race relations and national culture in Cuba and on the development of Yoruba religion and Santeria.

The first boom period began right after the Spanish conquest of the islands. For three quarters of a century afterward, imported African slaves and the remaining Amerindians worked the sugar mills. This early boom was followed by a rapid and prolonged economic decay as Spain shifted its money, interest, and immigrant population toward mainland areas that gave more promise of delivering gold. Free Africans and slaves, Amerindians and whites took advantage of the open spaces located inland to establish farms far from the coast and far from the overseas control which was vested in the cities and their urban elites. The result was a characteristic rural economy and the birth of a peasantry. A relatively homogeneous creole culture and a system of racial relations which functioned without either fixed color lines or group endogamy were other products of the first boom period and the following interregnum.

Cuba's second boom came in the 1760s, when sugar production became again the centerpiece of economic production. This boom continued through the nineteenth century and required the massive importation of African slaves, Chinese contract laborers, and Amerindians from the Yucatan Peninsula. When immigration became the order of the day, the newcomers were absorbed into a national culture and a system of racial and ethnic relations that had already become set during and after the first boom. But the number of African slaves imported drastically shifted the racial composition of the island's population, as did later black immigration from the British West Indies and Haiti. The eastern areas of the island not given over to sugar cane retained the socioracial structure of the earlier period; but in the west, where the sugar zones were located, the racial continuum began to polarize. The newcomers—slave and free, African, Amerindian, European, and Asian—had an impact through sheer numbers and through importing new influences and institutions. The incorporation of diverse groups into a starkly yet fluidly class-structured society produced a great deal of cultural variation. Whether in the form of political divisions, economic inequality and poverty, ethnic group stereotypes, or racial and religious hostility, difference and division became fundamental.

Phase II, Early Santeria (1760–1870). Phase II (chapter III) represents the formative period of Early Santeria leading to a persisting phase of Yoruba Afro-Catholicism. I see this period as extending from about 1760 through the 1860s. It includes the appearance in Cuba of significant numbers of slaves from the Bight of Benin, the beginning of the sugar boom, and the foundation of sugar, coffee, and tobacco estates. During this period we have evidence of the attempts of Catholic churchmen to guide religious change within the African population. This is undoubtedly the period when Santeria was forming, particularly in the western urban areas in Cuba. The initial syncretism between the Yoruba deities and the Catholic saints had taken place by this period, and the Catholic Church and Spanish government adopted shifting, inconsistent policies toward the new Afro-Catholic religion. To understand what occurred in this period it is necessary to understand the way Catholicism was used as a component of cultural hegemony within Spain as well as within Cuba.

Phase III, Santeria (1870–1959). This is the transformative phase (chapter IV) leading to a phase in which the religion assumes the form of a predominantly Yoruba-spiritist-Catholic amalgam. Cuban slavery persisted through 1880 and was abolished only by degrees, so this period includes the final abolition of slavery and the migration of many ex-slaves to Cuba's urban areas. This convergence eventuated in three major trends. First, Spiritism became an influence on the religious system of Early Santeria, bringing it into the main forms in which it persists today. Second, this period saw the suppression of the legal Afro-Cuban religious organizations and the cessation of the Catholic Church's protection of them. With independence from Spain the middle and ruling classes of Cuba took a variety of stands in relation to the Afro-Cuban religions. As the island slipped more and more out of political independence and into economic underdevelopment at the hands of the United States, racial and ethnic relations within Cuba became more tense, aggravated at once by economic and political instability and by the racialist influences of North Americans. Programs of assimilation, persecution, and avant-garde artistic appropriation reflect the complex dynamics current in Cuba in the early part of this century as the society grappled with the place of the Afro-Cuban religions in the island's national culture and identity in the context of crosscurrents from Europe and the United States. The general direction of this pattern altered only with the Cuban Revolution of 1959. Phase III ends, therefore, with Fidel Castro's revolution and the exodus of Cubans to the United States. After a discussion of the condition of

Santeria under Cuban socialism, the focus shifts from Cuba to the United States and to developments in New York City and the surrounding area (chapter V).

The final two phases, i.e., all the variants of Phase IV and Phase V, should be thought of as occurring as a form of multilinear evolution rather than in a strictly unilinear fashion or as entirely separate. Despite the evident changes which have occurred and are occurring, all these variants exist in differing degrees of tension, relationship, conflict, or dominance with each other, but they also all now exist simultaneously in differing contexts in New York or elsewhere.

Phase IV involves the importation of Santeria in New York and its rebirth and persistence here since 1959. Two new religious forms have arisen here which bear important relationships to Santeria. Both can be seen as offshoots of it to some degree, even though their relationships to Santeria are quite different.

Phase IV Branch 1, Persisting Santeria and Santerismo. This branch represents the formative stage of Santerismo in which some preexisting forms of Puerto Rican Espiritismo encounter and absorb some aspects of Santeria. I believe that Santerismo has not yet passed through this stage to a persisting form. Santerismo began to appear in New York in the middle 1960s as a variant of Puerto Rican Espiritismo which exhibits the influence of Santeria. This variant continues to exist there presently, especially in the South Bronx.

Phase IV Branch 2, Persisting Santeria and Early Orisha-Voodoo. Orisha-Voodoo represents a fusion of Santeria with black nationalism in New York. In this early period the people who eventually became Orisha-Voodooists were highly dependent on the Puerto Rican and Cuban Santeria priesthood. Their efforts at African revitalization, including the expunging of Christian influences, brought them into increasing dissonance with the Santeria establishment. For a variety of reasons, the leadership of the movement left New York and the movement itself went on an independent trajectory. The time was roughly 1959 to 1969.

Phase V, Orisha-Voodoo. This phase sees the consolidation of Orisha-Voodoo as a movement through the founding of Oyotunji Village, a commune devoted to the practice of African religion. It also sees increasing reliance on Nigerian priests, the initiations of the movement's founder in Nigeria, and a conscious broadening of the group's ritual and ideological bases to include elements of Fon religion, Haitian Voodoo, Bini religious motifs, and elements of the Egyptian mystery system. The fundamental base of the movement, however, remains Yoruba religion, which most of the leadership and followers initially contacted in the form of Santeria. Phase V is roughly 1970–71, the period of the founding of Oyotunji Village, to the present. Phase IV encompasses the formative phase of Orisha-Voodoo, while Phase V encapsulates its persisting form at present. Since we are primarily concerned here with developments which took place in New

York, I will reserve more detailed treatment of Orisha-Voodoo's persisting phase for another publication.

Continuity and Change

The dialectic of continuity and change in Santeria is the subject matter of chapter VI. The focus is historical but anthropological as well. It is historical in the sense that it is concerned with the past. However, it does not discuss specific historical events so much as the structures, processes, and mechanisms by which the past was retained, reconstituted, and reproduced while incorporating change.

The key notions in the first part of chapter VI are religious tradition and collective memory. Halbwachs's writings on collective memory have never been fashionable outside of France and for the most part remain untranslated into English. To many anthropologists his idea seems initially to reek of a kind of metaphysical slipperiness or to be akin to Jung's notion of the collective unconscious. This is not the case. My own use and elaboration of his concept has been greatly influenced by Roger Bastide's use of it in his treatment of Afro-Brazilian religion and the more recent uses of the concept by Phillip Connerton and the Haitian anthropologist Michel Laguerre (Bastide 1978a, Connerton 1989; Laguerre 1987). Although I introduce ethnographic data as examples and illustrations, the intent of this chapter is ethnological rather than ethnographic.

While the first part of chapter VI examines how the African religious tradition in Cuban Santeria remained the same while changing, the second part looks at how it changed while remaining the same. Here the central problem is syncretism. I think that the concept of syncretism hides more than it reveals about Santeria while revealing more about Western conceptions of religion and culture than about the cultural reality they are supposedly trying to explain. The phenomenon of syncretism was an important theme of Bastide's studies of Afro-Brazilian religion, and though I was originally inspired by his work on syncretism, I have come to regard it as inadequate overall and in some sense even misdirected. While I have been able to build on his treatment of collective memory to some extent I have had to propose an alternative perspective and a model very different from his to look at syncretism and what has been called syncretism in Santeria.

In the modern world what has been called syncretism revolves around the more general problem of the organization of cultural diversity in multicultural, multiethnic, and multiracial societies. Contemporary linguistic research on creole and pidgin languages has provided one key to the nature of the organization of that diversity in the form of the concept of a cultural continuum or intersystem. To my knowledge the concept of the cultural continuum or intersystem was first applied to nonlinguistic aspects of culture in Lee Drummond's analyses of Guyanese ethnicity and ritual

(1980). In the second part of chapter VI I attempt to extend its use and apply it to the development of an Afro-Cuban religion.

In a society such as Cuba's in which the cultural traditions of Africans could neither be continued entirely intact nor be smoothly integrated into a harmonious national culture, what evolved was an intersystem or cultural continuum (ibid.:353). In a cultural continuum the recognition of socially and culturally significant differences in thought and behavior derives from a shared pool of common ideology, history, myth, and contemporary experiences. Into this shared pool fall racial and ethnic concepts, stereotypes and images, and the relationships between symbols and economic and political power on one hand, and group traditions and self-identity on the other. Nevertheless people relate differently to this shared pool because of their place in society and on the cultural continuum. It is because of this that social and cultural differences that are seen as meaningful can be used as a way for people to represent themselves to others and as emblems of group and personal identity. In such a situation the systematic nature of culture resides in the relationships which, through a series of gradations, transformations, bridges, and situational adjustments, link one end of the cultural continuum with the other or one intersystem with another (353, 370).

While Drummond's 1980 paper provided the inspiration for the model I present in this chapter, I go beyond seeing the cultural continuum as one way that groups within a multiethnic, multiracial society organize its cultural diversity at a particular time to presenting the cultural continuum as a temporal and historical process as well. This shifts the orientation from the fusion of formerly separate religious traditions toward the analysis of cultural variation and the fate of Yoruba religion in a multiethnic, multiracial Cuban society in which the ideological, ethnic, racial, and economic conflicts were all expressed through a small shared set of religious symbols, concepts and categories.

My approach here, while making use of anthropological concepts and data, is still primarily historical. A second complementary volume in preparation is an ethnographic study of Santeria in New York. It will describe Santeria belief, ritual, and social organization and will contain detailed comparisons with traditional African beliefs and practices. While I expect that the second volume will be of interest primarily to scholars, believers, and specialists in African and African-American religious studies, I hope that both volumes will find a wider readership as well.

II.

Africa

I cannot but admire the incuriousness of so
many travellers who have visited Dahomey
and have described its Customs without an
attempt to master, or at least explain, the
faith that underlies them. Their excuses must
be the difficulty presented by the incorporation of manifold elements, and the various
obstacles to exploring a religion which every
man, to a certain extent, makes up for himself. "Perhaps," said a Dahomean officer to
Captain Snelgrave, the first European who
visited his country (1727), "that God may be
yours who has communicated so many extraordinary things to white men; but as that
God has not been pleased to make himself
known to us, we must be satisfied with this
we worship."

Captain Sir Richard Burton,
Mission to Glele, King of Dahomey

A complex web of political interaction, trade, and cultural influence linked
large areas of the Western Sudan, and the fortunes of three of the major
kingdoms of this region—Benin, Dahomey, and the Yoruba city-states (especially Oyo)—were intricately entwined with each other and with the slave
trade that brought thousands of Africans from this region to Cuba.

I often think of these kingdoms as being in a sense brothers, and in spite
of the differences among them, there are good reasons for thinking so.
The kings of Benin, Dahomey, and the Yoruba city-states all trace their origin back to Odua (Oduduwa), creator of the earth and progenitor of the
Yoruba people. Odua began his work at Ile Ife, which therefore has the
status of a holy city in all of these regions (Egharevba 1936:7; Herskovits
1938:vol. 1, 206; Bascom 1944:21–22). Benin's first Oba is also linked by a
myth to the first Alafin of Oyo. The first king of Benin was born to a Bini
woman, but his father was Yoruba: Oranmiyan, a son of Oduduwa, who
would later go on to found Oyo and be its first ruler. The Yoruba orisha
Ifa, Shango, Ogun, Eshu, Olokun, and Ifa have their counterparts in the
religions of Dahomey and Benin, and while the deities that are the focus of
greatest attention in Dahomey are called voduns, the Bini deities are called
by the same term by which the Yoruba deities have become known, orisha

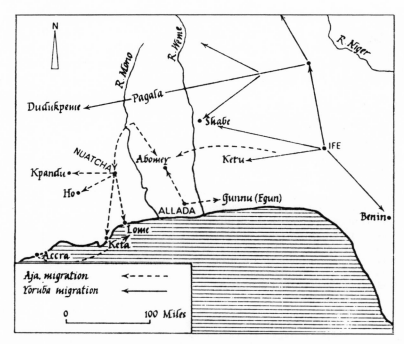

MAP 1. The migrations of Yoruba and Aja peoples. Reproduced from *Dahomey and Its Neighbors, 1708–1818*, by I. A. Akinjobin, p.12. Courtesy of Cambridge University Press.

(Egharevba 1972:36–37, 38, 45; Herskovits and Herskovits 1933; Bascom 1944:38). There are, however, additional reasons for considering the three kingdoms brothers.

The African scholar Akinjobin has written of an ancient constitution, the Ebi theory, which, though unwritten, served as the basis for monarchical government before the advent of Europeans and bound the monarchs of the principal kingdoms, cities, and towns into a great family stretching throughout the Yoruba-Aja commonwealth (1967:14–17, 81, 177, 204). What bound the kingdoms together was acceptance of the claim that all the kings of the major kingdoms were descendants of the same great ancestor.

The smallest unit within the state was not the individual but the family (the lineage), including the living, the dead, and the unborn generations. People regarded the state as a larger version of the family. The king was in relation to his subjects as a father to children. The father-king of each family-state looked on his neighbors in a particular familial relationship, and all father-kings of family-states looked on a particular king as father. Each kingdom had duties, and nonperformance of these duties would offend the souls of the ancestral dead and bring disaster on the whole country. In the Yoruba territories, as already noted, all the kings claim descent from Oduduwa either directly or indirectly. The kings of Allada, Whydah, and Dahomey claim descent from a single prince. The king sitting on the throne of the original ancestor was regarded as the "father" of all the other kings and all the other kings regarded themselves as "brothers." This father-son relationship between the king occupying the throne of the original ancestor and the other kings formed the basis of the constitution of the Yoruba-Aja territories, including both Dahomey and Benin. All this was based on a claim of kinship rather than force. It derived from descent, not conquest, and was a social bond founded on blood relationship, not security or economic interest.

The Old Religion

The religions of the three brother kingdoms were not revealed religions. They arose through generations of imagination, observation, and reflection by which their peoples gradually built up a coherent orientation toward the facts of human existence. It was an attempt to include everything that was visible, all that aroused emotion, and all that contained a seed of significance from the perspective of human beings into a framework for human action. Individuals, particularly those in influential positions or those with powerful personalities, contributed their reflections and ideas over the millennia, but there was no guarantee that they would be either accepted or transmitted to succeeding generations. Some ideas spread to other individuals, groups, and peoples and were retained; some were forgotten; some were not consonant with other ideas; and others were rejected. These continuing processes of accumulation, renewal, discarding, modification, and borrowing form a part of a religious history about which we know little. These reflections and ideas and the practices that were based on them were not subjected to a uniform or orthodox systematization. Nonetheless they came to permeate the society as a whole rather than existing within it as a separate and isolable institution. Their expression takes many forms whether in artistic production, mythology, proverbs, rites, symbols, interpersonal relations, economics, and government or in relations with the natural world. To understand African religion on its own terms, then, means not to look at it as a body of beliefs, doctrines, and rituals but rather as the ongoing manifestation of a basic attitude toward life which is expressed in a variety of ways and a variety of contexts.

PLACES OF WORSHIP

Worship took place in temples and at shrines. Temples were houselike buildings which, while too small to enclose large numbers of people, could contain the images and paraphernalia associated with the deities and had enough room remaining for the priests and priestesses to enact their rites. The laity had little involvement in worship at the temples except as an audience that could congregate outside. Unless the ritual was public and took place in front of the temple, the laity never saw it.

Each temple was dedicated to one of the large number of deities worshiped. Several temples to the same deity might exist in the same city or town, but each temple had a separate priesthood with its own separate altar dedicated to that deity. Sometimes temple exteriors were colorfully and elaborately decorated with tall carved doorposts, geometric patterns, and paintings of humans and animals enacting scenes from mythology. Inside, symbolic objects (emblems, statuary, and ritual paraphernalia) functioned as altar images and indicated the presence of the deity. Although some of the altar images were in the form of human icons, most of them were not. Instead they were usually common ordinary objects, such as pots, cowrie shells, pieces of iron, gourd bowls, stones, tree limbs, and branches. These things would be selected because of their symbolic association with the deity or function they were to serve. After ritual treatment and placement within a sacred context, they would become religious icons and representations of the deity. Beyond being a place for the gathering of the priesthood and for performing secret rites, the temple served the main function of housing these objects.

It was the empowered objects that were important, not the physical structure of the building or even the existence of one. Neither temples nor shrines had to be permanent structures. Wherever a collection of the empowered objects of a deity could be brought together and a place could be found that expressed the attributes of that deity, a shrine or temple came into existence. So there were shrines in the marketplaces, at the boundaries of towns, along roads, at the riverside, and in fields. Most worship took place in homes rather than at the temples, and among the laity one found shrines in the rooms and yards of compounds, tiny shrines for deities in front of houses, and objects hung up as charms and protective devices over doorways.

THE ORGANIZATION OF WORSHIP

Worship was organized on several levels. These levels can best be described in terms of the four levels of priests and priestesses. At the bottom of the hierarchy was the household level with the household or compound head as priest. Above this were the temple priesthoods, each with its internal hierarchy or system of rank. Hierarchy and ranking were characteristic of Yoruba social life at every level. Within the temple groups, members were ranked according to their order of initiation into a particular grade. Elders were deeply respected, and their relative rank was shown by addressing them with special titles and honorific pronouns and by obeisance and prostrations (Bascom 1942, 1951; Morton-Williams 1967:51; Eades 1980:54). The temple priesthoods all came under the responsibility of a village or town priest, who was in turn responsible to the priesthoods of the national or royal cults.

Worship took place in a daily, weekly, and annual round, with daily worship centered for the laity in their compounds. Weekly worship gathered

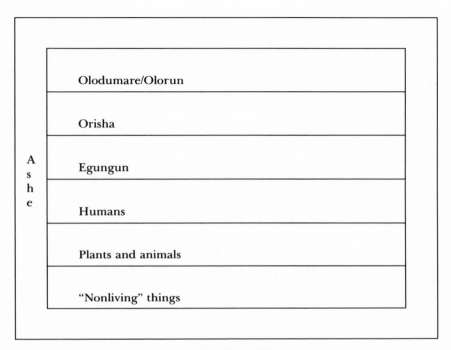

FIGURE 1. Hierarchy of beings in Yoruba religion.

together those who worshiped the same deity. The annual celebrations, commemorating each major deity worshiped in the area, were communitywide festivals.

COSMOLOGY AND PANTHEON

Since there has been no attempt by the Bini, Yoruba, or Dahomeyans at either sustaining or creating a systematized, orthodox body of belief and doctrine, it is to be expected that there would be a great deal of controversy and disagreement among scholars attempting to present these religions as if there were one. This is especially evident in the varying models through which Yoruba religion has been described. I have no wish to add to these controversies and disagreements, and the reader should take Figure 1 not as the model of Yoruba religion but rather as the first of a series of diagrams which will allow him or her to grasp visually what has continued and what has changed in the course of the evolution to be described in these chapters. The idea is not that this very simple model of a complex and multidimensional phenomenon is adequate or even necessarily correct in detail but that it should facilitate both the exposition and an easy comprehension of the path that lies ahead.

One way of looking at Yoruba, Bini, and Fon religions is as constituting a hierarchy of the powers and beings which compose the universe and have a variety of relationships to each other. From this perspective they form a common set of cosmological categories: the supreme being, the spirits, humans, plants and animals, and "nonliving" things. I will look at this with specific reference to Yoruba religion and start from the top of the diagram and work down.

The supreme being. In Yoruba religion this is Olodumare, the creator and sustainer of the universe, who nonetheless is remote from humans and has neither priesthood nor temples. Olodumare is never represented pictorially and has no human attributes, although references make use of anthropomorphic imagery and titles and praise names picture Olodumare as a male. Among Olodumare's other names is Olorun, meaning "owner of the skies or heavens."

The spirits. These superhuman beings are objects of worship through temples and shrines and secret societies. In this category belong the orisha and the egungun. Some of the orisha (such as Obatala, Oduduwa, and Orunmila) appear to have been around before the creation of human beings and are therefore emanations directly from Olodumare. They came from heaven. Others were once human beings and died remarkable deaths. They sank into the ground or rose into the heavens on chains; they committed suicide and did not die; they turned to stone. Their death was not an end but the occasion for their metamorphosis into an orisha. It should not be thought that the concept of orisha is readily verbalized or even needs verbalization when it is so much a part of the presumed background against which life takes place. The orisha are the guardians and explicators of human destiny. It is they to whom people turn for help, aid, and advice in the great and small problems of life.

When William Bascom was able to get two high priests to give him accounts of the conception of the orisha which underlay their worship, they told him that

> an orisha is a person who lived on earth when it was first created, and from whom present-day folk are descended. When these orishas disappeared or "turned to stone," their children began to sacrifice to them and to continue whatever ceremonies they themselves had performed when they were on earth. This worship was passed on from one generation to the next, and today an individual considers the orisha whom he worships to be an ancestor from whom he is descended. The tradition is accepted by all groups of the Yoruba tribe, and apparently in a modified form in Benin and Dahomey. (1944:21)

Worshipers of an orisha are spoken of as being its children. The idea of descent was translated into secrecy by excluding from some part of an orisha's ceremonies all those who were not themselves children of the orisha (69).

While some orisha are widely worshiped throughout the Yoruba territories and even into areas west and east such as Dahomey and Benin, others have a purely local following, and there is much variation in the rituals
and mythology of the deities in the different regions. As a result some orisha are associated with specific places or regions. In some places the worship of an orisha can be traced back to a stranger who brought it there from
another place. Myth names the city of Ife as the birthplace of most of the
orisha, which means that for Ife residents most of the orisha are of local
origin. For residents in other places, the orisha worshiped there originated
elsewhere. The wide spread of the worship of deities closely associated with
Oyo—such as Shango, Oya, Oba, Yemoja, Oshosi, Orisha Oko, and
Erinle—is undoubtedly the result of both the centralizing influence Oyo
wielded as the dominant Yoruba city-state over several hundred years and
the dispersal of Oyo's population after the city fell to conquest.

Although the orisha may be regarded as ancestral by its worshipers, it is
not in the same category as a person's immediate ancestors or the founder
of the compound in which one lives. These latter are the egungun, who
receive separate veneration at shrines within the household and compound. At the village level there was a secret society of male maskers, the
Egungun Society, which impersonated the ancestors of the community as a
whole at major festivals. Ancestor veneration also existed at the national
level in terms of the cult of the royal ancestors. While the orisha are concerned with the minutiae of individual destinies, the ancestors are concerned with the moral and social order of society and with adherence to
public norms. Within Yoruba, Bini, and Dahomeyan society, social rules
and injunctions were continuously phrased in the idiom of kinship (as we
have already seen in relationship to the ties among the kingdoms and the
theory undergirding it and in relationship ties between the orisha as
sources of power and their devotees). The role of the ancestors was not to
ensure individual achievement and satisfaction, although they remained
interested in the fates of their descendants; it was to undergird the continued existence of society and of a just social order at all levels. This was true
at the level of the household and compound in which the bodies of the
dead were frequently buried, and the ancestors therefore were close at
hand, and it was true at the level of the royal dynasties whose ancestors
were central for the national identity of the kingdom and whose guardian-
ship of fundamental moral and social values undergirded kingship. The
king was at once a link in a long chain of powerful ancestors, a living ancestor himself, and a deputy of the orishas on earth.

As manifestations of the communal ancestors, the Egungun maskers
embody a moral force still resounding from the time when all human institutions first came into existence. Since their word is law, they can medi-
ate and judge disputes and cleanse the community of illness and witchcraft
(Lawal 1977:59). More than anything else they embody the conquest of

death by the techniques and rituals of immortality and the return of the dead from their world to renew their strong bonds with those they still love. For this reason they are welcomed at their annual festivals with great joy.

Humans. This category includes those living people who are visible and those about to be born. Among them are kings, witches, priests, and twins, all of whom are believed to have special powers for both good and evil.

Plants and animals. These constitute the environment in which humans exist and their means of survival and nourishment. In turn they depend on humans as well. Plants in particular are sources of both healing and food, while knowledge of the individual characteristics of animals, birds, and insects is important to hunter and farmer alike. Plants, animals, insects, and humans all ultimately depend on the bounty of the earth, which is deified as Onile and has an important secret society, the Ogboni, connected with it.

"Nonliving" things. Things such as stones, clouds, rivers, and pieces of iron, which we might regard as not having biological life, are seen as being alive, as having will, power, and intention, just like persons. The sky with its stars, sun, thunder, lightning, meteors, and moon was the residence of Olorun and the deities. Much of what goes on there is a counterpart of what goes on on earth. It is simply the land of the dead and the orisha with a vast population which usually sees everything from its own vantage point on the other side of the visible sky.

Encircling this whole hierarchy of beings is an encompassing energy, ashe, which permeates the entire universe. All of the powers (the orisha, the ancestors, the forces and actions of nature, perhaps even the supreme being itself) are manifestations of this absolute and indefinable power. It is ashe which ties together all of the entire ontology and embraces the interpenetration of all beings. Pierre Verger, a longtime student of Yoruba and Dahomeyan religion, has described it best.

> The ashe of the forces of nature are part of the orisha, because the cult of the orisha is directed to the forces of nature—though not to their unbridled and uncontrolled aspect. The orisha is only a part of such forces, the part that is disciplined, calmed, controlled, the part that forms a link in the relations of mankind with the indefinable. Another link is made up of the human being who lived on earth in olden times, and who was later deified. The latter was able to establish control over a natural force, and to make a bond of interdependence with it by which he attracted toward himself and his people the beneficent action of the ashe, and sent its destructive force upon his enemies. To achieve this he made offerings and sacrifices to the tamed aspect of the force as were necessary to maintain the potential of the ashe.
>
> The orisha cult is addressed jointly to the tamed natural force and to the deified ancestor, both of these links being considered as a unity. This alliance is represented but not materialized by a witnessing object, which is the support of the ashe. (Verger: 1966:37)

It becomes the responsibility of the orisha's human descendants to transmit to subsequent generations the objects and the secrets that give them a measure of control over the orisha. The objects become the material support of that orisha's ashe, and everything that went into forming the object, from leaves, earth, and animal bones to the incantations that praised and coerced the power to lodge in one place, becomes part of its secret.

It is ritual which allows humans to traverse all the categories of being through the manipulation and communication of ashe. The various forms of divination allowed people to have access to the accumulated wisdom of the deities and the dead as the paradigms for solving current problems. Offerings of food, objects, song, money, or the blood of animals in sacrifice all revivified the ashe of the orisha and directed it toward specific ends. In ceremonial spirit possession, the link between the orisha and its descendants became palpable as, in ceremonies held in its honor, the immaterial being came down from on high and took over the body of one of its children, communicating to the assembly in a visible, physical, human form. Last but not least, it is the ashe in the priestess and the herbs, in the blood of the animal and the chants of praise and supplication, that heals the sick and forestalls death in rituals of affliction.

RELATION TO HUMAN BEINGS

Human beings exist at the center of the universe. Their ability to carry out ritual gives them an awesome responsibility because it is unique. Only humans can carry out rituals on behalf of all other beings; only humans can sacrifice and empower objects with ashe. It is only humans, then, who have the ability to create and sustain the harmony, freshness, and balance that ought to exist in the universe.

To some extent humans were seen as being like priests for the other beings of the earth. But their religion was not concerned primarily with Olodumare or with the orisha or other beings or nature; it was concerned primarily with humans and how the forces and beings and things present in the universe could be used for the good of human beings and their lives. The religion, therefore, contained a strong instrumental strain and was concerned with using religion in the context of the practical exigencies of everyday life, especially medicine and healing.

Although humans are at the center of the world, this does not make them its master. A mystical bond links living and nonliving things in an intricate web of influence and interdependence. To attain his or her ends, the human being had to depend on the orisha and the ancestors. The human had to depend on the environment for subsistence and had to live in harmony with the natural world. Humans also had to depend on each other and ensure the harmony of their communities by conforming to the moral and religious order of government, kinship values, taboos, and interaction with the dead. As a result divinity and the sacred were closely associated with ecology and with human relationships.

OPENNESS TO CHANGE

The basic orientation which evolved out of the accumulation of centuries of reflection, imagination, and observation represented a set of eternal relationships structuring process and change in the world. Within it a great deal of change could occur and be accommodated without distorting its essential architecture. Powerful personalities could have far-reaching impact, even to the point of changing certain ideas and practices or through ultimately receiving worship as orisha and being incorporated into the structure themselves. New elements and ideas could be absorbed—as was always happening anyway—whether from indigenous sources or foreign ones. New forms of expression were carried from place to place through the migration and dispersal of peoples and through conquest. Africans frequently see other religions as supplementing rather than replacing traditional religious practices. As a result many items of rite and belief have diffused out of Yoruba territories to their neighbors, and many have diffused into Yoruba religion as well (see Ojo 1976 for an excellent historical and ethnographic essay on this interaction). Islam and Christianity have made great inroads; the number of people who are practitioners of the old religion alone dwindles, and the temples fall into disrepair or are abandoned. Still the old religions are seen as ethnic traditions, the property of specific peoples, and even if they are closely related and very similar in so many respects it still makes sense to speak of a Yoruba, a Bini, or a Fon religion.

Three Brothers Quarrel, and Their Homes Are Invaded by Strangers

The old religion was not separated from African society, and if we want to understand it fully, the history of religion cannot be separated from the study of society either. To appreciate the full significance of the changes that happen in the later history of the African religions in the Americas it is necessary to know something about the similarities and differences among the African societies in which they evolved.

The kingdoms of the Yoruba city-states, Benin, and Dahomey existed within what is best thought of as a field of social, cultural, and political forces that continually expanded and contracted in response to internal and external tensions. They were characterized by complex interlocking of fields of power rather than well-defined frontiers between sovereign states (Bradbury 1964:147).

All three kingdoms shared a common economic foundation in the practice of slash-and-burn agriculture. The hoes and axes that made this cultivation possible were made by castes of ironworkers, as were the swords and spears that were necessary for war. Other artisans manufactured a large variety of craft goods that flowed through an internal network of marketing and exchange and outward into trade with other areas, including Europe.

Kinship, in the form of lineage organization, controlled access to land and to other important resources. Lineages were groups of people tracing descent to a common ancestor. These groups were thought of as continuing corporations, as ever-growing groups containing the living and the dead and those about to be born. As such they extended directly back into the distant past and were expected to continue intact into the distant future. The religious manifestation of all this was the various forms of ancestor veneration, which were such an important part of the daily lives of the people. The economic functions of these lineages went beyond controlling access to land. Indeed, in these societies it was not land that was a scarce commodity but labor. Since rights to labor were encysted in kinship arrangements, a major responsibility of lineage elders was control of the reproductive powers of women and the lineage's relations with other lineages through managing marriages and bridewealth.

Another source of rights over labor was slavery. Almost by definition slaves were persons who had for one reason or another been separated from their lineage. There were three major ways in which this could happen. As payment of a debt a person might be given over as a possession to someone in another lineage for a specified period. In this case the person was merely pawned and his separation from the lineage was not permanent. The person was a debt-slave and could return to the home lineage when the debt had been fulfilled. Capture in warfare also cut lineage ties. Prisoners of war were passed over whole to their captor or to whomever the captor designated as the slave's owner. The slave's labor and whatever other capacities the slave might possess were then transferred over to the owner's kin group. Infractions of kinship obligations offended not only the living relatives but the ever-present ancestral dead as well. Some of these infractions merited perhaps the most severe punishment imaginable in societies like these short of capital punishment: severance from the lineage. A person could also end up as a slave, then, as the result of a judicial decision before a local court. Since the person was no longer seen as being within the lineage, he or she could be sold as a slave to another lineage. The slave would be a functioning member of the domestic group where he or she resided but might never be a member of that lineage either. Slave offspring, though, could be adopted into the lineage. A relatively autonomous local social and economic system developed out of the continuing interaction of lineages with each other, trade, the practice of slavery, and the agricultural economy on which they all depended.

Above this local level there was a more extensive system of power topped by a divine king. The myths and traditional charters of these kingships linked them with the major sources of supernatural power. While land and labor remained under the control of local lineage-based groups, other resources, both economic and military, came to be concentrated at the royal court. If the divine king established control over commodities such as gold, slaves, iron ore, and salt or over external trade and warfare, a more complex system arose which depended on the development of elite groups of warriors and traders and the consolidation of local lineages around a royal capital. Together with the group of elite lineages related to the king's lineage and the elite groups of warriors and traders, there was also a ritual and religious elite connected to the court and the cult group centers of the capital. Together with the trading elite, the elite priesthoods and their cult groups served to link the concerns of the court with the concerns of the local lineages and their elders.

The dynamics of these kingdoms could be extremely fluid over long spans of time. The development of a key monopoly could expand a kingdom's resources and depth of control, while the expansion of long-distance trade in familiar goods might expand its reach and influence and lead to intensified warfare against neighbors to extend its land base. The formation of rival power centers outside the capital could also lead to secession, thus reducing the kingdom in size and extent. The encroachment of other kingdoms, biting off larger and larger pieces at the kingdom's edge, could accomplish the same thing. The kingdoms could be destroyed by the infiltration of lineages and peoples who later rose up in revolution and seized power. Or, finally, they could be conquered outright, as they all were, by foreign powers intent on the exploitation of their lands and peoples.

The Yoruba city-states. The Yoruba appear to have entered southern Nigeria before A.D. 1000. They came with only crude tools, but eventually they evolved an urban social life, a distinctive language, artistic traditions which have gained international fame, monarchical government, and a pattern of religious belief and practice which has become a diasporic tradition with millions of adherents in the Americas.

The Yoruba are among the most urban of African peoples. Town and city life is a traditional trait of the Yoruba, dating back long before European contact. The oldest traditional cities were farming centers with belts of farms on their peripheries. People commuted from the towns out to their farms in the countryside, often staying for weeks during peak periods of farm labor. Along with sedentary hoe farming, which formed the basis of life, craftwork and trade were dominant sectors of the economies (Bascom 1969b:3–4, 18.)

Fage suggests that the first Yoruba kingdoms were established by the twelfth century (1969:11). The Yorubas split into two groups, one in the savannah (Oyo region) and one in the forest (Ife and Ijebu), and each differentiated into subgroups (Murphy 1972:168). While the earliest stages of a distinctively Yoruba culture are linked with the city of Ife, the Yoruba kingdoms became associated with the Igala to the east and Benin to the southeast. A number of preexisting groups also actually became Yoruba under the influence of the founders of Yoruba cities. Among these were some groups of Egba, Egbado, Nago, Aja, Ewe, Adangbe, and Ga (Fage 1969:42.)

The founding of the Yoruba city-states initiated a chain reaction that propelled a general westward migration of peoples. Yoruba subgroups now extend from southwestern Nigeria through the modern Republic of Benin (formerly Dahomey) and Togo and on into some areas of Ghana (Fage 1969:42; Parrinder 1949). Eades (1980) estimates the total present-day Yoruba population at about fifteen million.

While the Yoruba did evolve a common language and culture, they never constructed a common political state. Instead various cities and kingdoms developed separately, interacting with each other over the centuries but each with its own dialect, history, and variations in religion, political structure, and general culture. By the beginning of the nineteenth century the largest of these Yoruba city-states, the most populous and most centralized, was Oyo. Oyo, a true empire, came closest to integrating all of the Yoruba peoples under a single influence—that of the Alafin, Oyo's king. Egba, Dahomey, Borgu, Porto Novo, and parts of Nupe all paid tribute to Oyo.

The political system of Oyo was complex. The Alafin, theoretically an absolute ruler and divine king, lived secluded in a palace. Surrounded by ritual restrictions, he administered through a corps of eunuchs and titled slaves. Seven principal nonroyal chiefs formed the Alafin's council, the Oyo Mesi. The Oyo Mesi also administered the nonroyal wards and descent groups of the capital city.

Religion played an important role in both social and political life. Each cult group was organized around a hierarchy of priests, some of whom were also significant political officials. Though the Alafin was said to "own" all the cult groups, he did not have unrestricted power over them. Each cult group, however, did communicate with the Alafin before performing any ritual affecting the interests of the community as a whole (Morton-Williams 1967:58). The most important of these cult groups, in political terms, were the Ogboni cult and the cult of Ifa. The Ogboni cult of the earth, restricted to powerful old men, mediated between the Alafin and the Oyo Mesi. The Ogboni also had important judicial functions (Morton-Williams 1960a, 1967:59). Divination played an important part in government, and the Alafin had constant recourse to a diviner, a chief priest of Ifa, to interpret events and the will of the gods and to advise him in decision making.

Benin. Descriptions by Portuguese who visited Benin City in the sixteenth century register it as an impressive metropolis with great streets and neat houses, palace courtyards and galleries, brass figures and elaborate carvings (Barros 1552; Cadamosto 1937; Fernandes 1951). The later observations of Dutch and British explorers paint a similar picture (Bosman 1967). Benin and the Yoruba states were clearly the results of long development and were well differentiated from each other from the times to which Bini oral traditions refer. In Benin a person became rich by holding a fief and judiciously extending patronage. Long-distance trade was another way to wealth, and a large number of associations of traders and titleholders existed throughout the state, serving as a means by which commoners could advance in status. Aside from war, raiding, and internal trade, there was an overseas trade which was strictly controlled from Benin City by its king, the Oba. Great fortunes also lay in warfare and in raiding for slaves, for regardless of the means by which they obtained their wealth, rich Bini invested it mainly in slaves to farm for them in the villages.

Benin was a centralized state only insofar as its provinces rendered tribute to the Oba at Benin City. Outside of Benin City the state consisted of relatively self-governing communities. The state of Benin seems to have expanded and contracted according to the degree of authority and control the Oba was able to exert from the capital. Theoretically, Benin's king was an absolute monarch. The reality was something different. In practice the Oba was the apex of a hierarchy of titled nobles whose ability to wield power depended more or less on the personality of the Oba himself. Some of the titleholders were also important state officials, but all of the untitled nobles were members of a council which the Oba consulted on major questions of state.

It was the traders' and titleholders' associations that eventually came to control trade routes between the coast and the markets that lay inland. In periods of prosperity these associations broadened the basis of the king's support throughout the state. But in periods of economic decline the allegiance of these associations could become brittle. The associations would then take their place alongside the royal retainers, the powerful men who had inherited their titles, and the religious authorities of the common people and become just one more part of a skein of conflicting interests focused toward the Oba.

The actual degree of control which the Oba exercised over his subjects' ability to trade seems to be a matter of dispute, but it is certain that considerable quantities of European goods came into Benin (Anene 1972:274). It was not uncommon for the Oba to embargo trade with the Europeans and Itsekiri. Visiting ships always had to pay a heavy toll, and certain exports could only be traded by the king and his cohorts. Bini traders exchanged ivory, vegetable gums, palm oil and palm kernels, and slaves for European guns, powder, cloth, and salt. At the beaches on the southwest edge of the kingdom they received goods direct from the Europeans or through Itsekiri middlemen and took them inland through specified trade routes. State control had two major aims: reproducing the economic power of the ruling elite and ensuring the continuing security and integrity of the kingdom. The latter was achieved in part through control over the ownership and distribution of guns and ammunition.

The history of Benin reads as a succession of alternating periods of prosperity and profound disturbance. In between the fratricidal civil wars over rival claims to the throne, Benin seems to have been able to recover remarkably well. The wars, however, were ruinous (Anene 1972:270; Bradbury 1957:94).

Dahomey. In many ways it is remarkable that a major state ever arose in the region of old Dahomey. It has one of the poorest coastal areas in West Africa. The poor savannah with its frequent droughts and famines seems an unlikely place for a powerful and wealthy kingdom, yet in the seventeenth century several Aja states existed in the region under the dominance of Allada, which in turn was subject to the Yoruba state of Oyo. In fact it was Oyo that upset the delicate balance that kept this network of states together. When Oyo invaded the coastal Aja states and introduced the slave trade there, the preexisting social, economic, and political organization began to weaken (Akinjobin 1972:256). By the middle of the seventeenth century the coastal Aja states were rebelling against Allada's control.

Into these shifting currents leapt Agadja, king of Abomey from 1708 to 1732. Agadja took advantage of the power vacuum created by the coastal rebellions and subordinated all the other Aja states to his rule. In 1724 he invaded Allada and destroyed and conquered his neighbors; by 1730 he had completed his revolution. Agadja and his successors eventually drew so much power into the kingship that Dahomey truly became an absolute monarchy. An extensive governmental bureaucracy uncoiled throughout the kingdom from Abomey. The king appointed and dismissed all state officials, ministers, and chiefs; military officers received their appointments from him; and the king monopolized all the forces of a standing army, a civilian militia, and a legendary corps of female warriors. History, too, became a royal monopoly as the traditions concerning royal clans and lineages were confided only to certain royal relatives. Within the city of Abomey the king even selected the heads of lineages (Lombard 1967:79). The entire governmental apparatus was designed to exact obedience directly from individual subjects to their king. It is not surprising, then, that it should have been riddled with royal spies, part of a permanent system of espionage directed from the capital city (Lombard 1967:79–80; Webster and Boahen 1967:112; Fage 1969:103).

If the Dahomeyan king's power in the judicial, political, and military spheres was absolute, it was only slightly less so in the field of religion. The chief priests of all religious societies came to the king for licensing. As high priest of the state religion, the king confirmed the election of the priests of the national cults and supervised their activities. Throughout the neighboring regions of West Africa the secret society remained, and remains, an important socioreligious institution. In Dahomey the king forbade secret societies as a possible threat to royal power (Lombard 1967:75–80; Webster and Boahen 1967:112). Furthermore, all cults and worship, whether national or local, communal or domestic, indigenous or incorporated from conquered peoples, were subordinated to the cult of the mystic leopard Agassu, the cult of the royal ancestors. In these ways Dahomey was as different from the previous Aja states as it was from Oyo and Benin.

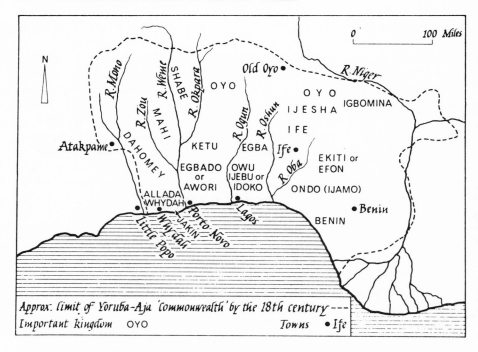

MAP 2. The Yoruba-Aja "commonwealth" in the seventeenth and eighteenth centuries. Reproduced from *Dahomey and Its Neighbors, 1708–1818*, by I. A. Akinjobin, p. 10. Courtesy of Cambridge University Press.

WARFARE AND THE SLAVE TRADE

The expansion of the slave trade in Benin seems to have taken place without the use of firearms—one of the prizes of the trade in slaves on the African end—and there is no evidence that in Benin proper the trade in slaves was ever extensive in absolute numbers (Graham 1965:319–20, 331). This is not to deny that sizable numbers of slaves were exported from the Bight of Benin; rather it is to point to the laxness of state control and the lack of intervention by the Oba in the slave-trading activities of the outlying provinces. The European slave trade may well have increased the autonomy of the Benin kingdom's outlying provinces. "It is probable, in connection with the state's role in the slave trade, that the European factors, from the very beginning, dealt more directly with the individual communities than with the Oba" (ibid.:320).

In the fifteenth century Benin had been a well-established state. Over the next four hundred years the tranquillity and cohesiveness of the Benin empire were shaken by the rise of Oyo, the Atlantic slave trade, the Nigerian civil wars, and disputes within the royal house of Benin itself. Its large and far-flung army had, by the sixteenth century, pushed the borders of the Bini kingdom out into the territories of the eastern Yoruba and the western Ibo, enfolding these peoples in its influence. The seventeenth century was the period of expansion for Benin. During this period the kingdom expanded to Bonny and engulfed the Yoruba city of Lagos. Benin was a major source of slaves. By the end of the century, though, the slavers had shifted their focus further west, and the economic benefits of the slave trade from Benin declined.

The next two hundred years also saw the amount of land under Benin's power shrink. The area from which Benin could conscript troops dwindled, vassal territories broke off and no longer paid tribute, and eventually the Oba was unable to guarantee security in all the areas supposedly under his control. Whatever vitality there was left within the system was strangled by state control and by the fruitless search for a security that was never to be found.

Even more ominous were the incursions of the British, Europeans who were no longer looking to Benin for slaves but rather for possession of the people and the land itself. Their presence and inland penetration represented a creeping and irreversible threat as the Oba lost control of the outlying territories and former vassals became enemies.

> The Oba was undoubtedly suspicious of the actions of the white men on the coast. He was also vaguely aware that somehow the presence of the white men in his kingdom would upset religious practices cherished in Benin for centuries. The white men who now condemned slavery could not countenance the mass slaughter of slaves for religious observances and funeral rites. In the meantime, the British agents who were operating in the neighborhood of the Benin River were fed with the stories of dark happenings in Benin by the Itsekiri middlemen who were anxious to exploit the economic resources of Benin. (Anene 1972:274)

The latter half of the nineteenth century spelled the tragic end to this anxiety. Out of the north came Nupe-Fulani raiders to bite away at the northern border of the Benin kingdom. The Bini, who had once exacted tribute, now had to watch as northern Bini were forced to pay tribute to the Muslim Emir at Bida. Both on the east and on the west the Oba was losing control of his subjects. European traders made their way farther inland through Lagos and up the Niger River into the regions that had formerly been trading preserves.

In 1897 the Oba of Benin seems to have known what was coming, but he made no attempt to pull together a military defense at the capital or throughout his remaining territories. Indeed the Oba seems to have lost control of his own palace. The immediate cause of Benin's fall was the attack of the British Punitive Expedition which was dispatched to revenge the ambush of an earlier exploratory party. The Oba, in fact, had wanted to receive this pioneer mission but had been overruled by his titleholding councillors. The mission was snuffed out instead. On the advice of his priests the Oba had many slaves sacrificed in a futile attempt to ward off the impending British attack. Ralph Moor's lurid account of Benin after the Punitive Expedition is typical of the shocked reactions of the invaders to the slaughter they had provoked.

> The city presented the most appalling sight, particularly around the king's quarters. . . . Sacrificial trees in the open spaces still held the corpses of the latest victims. . . . One large space, two hundred to three hundred yards in length, was strewn with human bones and bodies in all stages of decomposition. (Quoted in Anene 1972:275)

The account of R. H. Bacon, commander of the British invasion, was equally sensational.

> Crucifixions, human sacrifices and every horror the eye could get accustomed to, to a large extent, but the smells no white man's internal economy could stand. . . . Blood was everywhere; smeared over bronzes, ivory, and even the walls. (Quoted in Graham 1965:317)

It was this image which was carried into the West after Benin's conquest as the image of what Benin had always been, when in fact the opposite was the case. Benin was in a desperate condition and its fortunes at a low ebb when the British conquered it in 1897.

> The impression which the members of the expedition carried away from Benin town, as the City of Blood, was no doubt largely due to the number of corpses seen by them in the Arho Ogiuwu . . . which they thought were the bodies of slaughtered victims, whereas they were really those of executed criminals and of persons who had died from infectious disease, etc., to whom decent burial was denied. If also, as stated, all the human sacrifices consisted of criminals, these would probably have preferred death as an offering to the gods or ancestors than in any other form. . . . The most abhorrent to modern ideas were the sun and rain sacrifices in which the victims were tied to trees, but it must be remembered that these were always wizards and witches, and so guilty, in native eyes, of the worst possible crime. The idea of Benin rule, therefore, as one of blood-stained despotism appears at variance with the truth. (Talbot 1926:90)

Westward, in Dahomey and the Yoruba territories, turbulent events were also occurring. Between 1726 and 1730 Agadja completed his revolution and established the Alladaxonous dynasty as the rulers of Dahomey. Having just established his new state, Agadja was now being pressured front and back. To the south were the troublesome Europeans. They seemed interested only in trading slaves and not at all in keeping treaties or showing a modicum of respect to a new monarch. When Agadja forbade them the slave trade in his kingdom, they promised one thing but did another. For this betrayal he burned up the European trading houses (Akinjobin 1972:258). On the other side, toward the northeast, was an Oyo reluctant to relinquish possession of the region to an upstart. Oyo invaded Dahomey four times in order to contain and control the revolt and the new kingdom. In this threatened position, Dahomey was forced to became tributary to Oyo. The rulers of Abomey and Oyo City exchanged daughters as brides, Dahomey paid an annual tribute, and the court at Dahomey increasingly absorbed Yoruba religious and cultural influences from 1730 onward.

In the last quarter of the eighteenth century King Kpengla of Dahomey set up slave-worked plantations, and the centralization of power became even more pronounced than before. At the same time, however, Dahomey became more and more dependent on the Atlantic slave trade and owed its rise and splendor to its profits. As a result its status depended a great deal on the effects of external forces. The head tax levied on slaves transported from or through the territory was a major financial support of the Abomey kingdom (Webster and Boahen 1967:115). Oyo exported slaves out of Porto Novo rather than through Abomey so that Oyo paid no taxes on the slaves as did England. When England abolished its slave trade in 1808, the court at Abomey was greatly affected.

Historians are divided on their views of the eighteenth-century political conflicts that led to the collapse of the kingdom of Oyo. Akinjobin (1966) believes it resulted from a factional struggle between the Alafin and his council over expansion of the kingdom, with the Alafin wanting to develop trade and increasingly exploit the areas they already held, while the Oyo Mesi held a more expansionist position. R. C. Law (1971), on the other hand, sees the conflict as centering, on one hand, on raw power for the control of resources garnered by Oyo's growth and, on the other, on Oyo's increased involvement in the Atlantic slave trade through the seventeenth and eighteenth centuries.

When Alafin Abiodun died in 1789, the Oyo empire began to fall apart. It disintegrated with astonishing rapidity into a plethora of autonomous war leaders beholden only to their followers and the expediency of their slippery, rapidly shifting alliances. By 1840 Oyo had completely collapsed. While it lasted, old Oyo's power and prestige had prevented major wars in its territories and on its frontiers; its collapse precipitated the civil wars and jihads that made the nineteenth century for Nigeria a century of warfare. Civil wars broke out in the southern Yoruba territories. New states founded in the 1820s and 1830s tried to fill the vacuum left by Oyo's process of decline. Oyo's own population shifted south to the fringes of the forests after the empire's death. Attacks on travelers and kidnapping became commonplace, and such events led up to the Owu and Egba wars (1820), the first of the Nigeria civil wars stretching out through the nineteenth century.

The period between about 1820 and 1878 saw the final fall of Oyo, the outbreak of the Owu War, the overthrow of old Oyo city by the Muslim Fulani, migration southward out of the war zones, and the building of new towns, including a new Oyo city. It also saw resumption of warfare and slave raids into Yoruba territories launched from Dahomey (Akinjobin 1972). The leopard had not changed its spots.

FROM SLAVES TO PALM OIL

In 1818 Gezo of Dahomey seized the throne and declared Dahomey's independence from Oyo. Gezo took advantage of Oyo's collapse and fragmentation and annexed some territories and towns formerly under Oyo's control. While Oyo was involved in a civil war with Ilorin, Dahomey ceased paying tribute and began aiming slave raids at Yoruba towns.

Independence from Oyo did not solve Dahomey's economic problems. Dahomey had continued to sell slaves to the Portuguese and Brazilian traders who persisted in coming after Britain had abandoned and then banned the trade. But eventually the slave raiders exhausted their slave raiding grounds. The court split over a debate about the direction of the economy: to continue in the dwindling and embattled Atlantic slave trade or go into large-scale palm oil production. By the 1850s the direction became clear as Dahomey increasingly became a slave society—not a society based on the trade in slaves but a society based on large-scale production by slaves. More and more the catch from slave raids was diverted from export into labor on palm oil plantations in the service of the African elite. Raids shifted farther north, up into the Yoruba palm oil belt, but they were not particularly successful. In the 1850s the slave trade from Dahomey to the Americas sank into insignificance (Webster and Boahen 1967:116). By the 1870s Dahomey had completed the transition from an economy centered on slave trade to one centered on slave production of palm oil (from slave trade to protoindustrial slavery).

Though a considerable number of slaves had passed through Oyo in the eighteenth century, the Yoruba themselves were not enslaved in large numbers before the Owu and Egba wars (Eades 1980:28). These wars were a turning point in Yoruba history for three reasons. First, they began the chain of civil wars and thus a century of fratricide. Second, they were distinctive among Yoruba wars for their use of firearms manufactured by Europeans. Finally, they were particularly brutal in that they employed, for the first time in Yoruba history, the tactic of total war in which whole towns would be razed and their populations enslaved en masse. As it became more dangerous and less profitable to obtain slaves from farther north in Nigeria, slaves of Yoruba origin appeared on the market in increasing numbers.

It was the trade in slaves that helped bring about British intervention and later British control of the Yoruba territories. In 1808 the British prohibited English ships from engaging in the slave trade and patrolled the Guinea coast as an international policeman trying to suppress the trade of other countries in black cargo. They also tried to make treaties with African kings. While these were ostensibly to be pacts for the suppression of the slave trade in their territories, the treaties were also meant to serve as a prelude to developing trade in other goods between England and West Africa. The English were not always successful in doing this, nor always welcomed with open arms.

When, in 1851, negotiations between the British consul and the king of Lagos proved fruitless, the British were fired upon as a reward for their persistence. On the third attempt to complete their mission, one of the British ships set off a rocket after being fired upon by Africans on the shore. The rocket exploded a munitions magazine on shore and started a fire that burned the Yoruba city of Lagos to the ground. The British consul eventually got his treaty anyway, but it was a treaty signed by a king he had installed himself in 1852. In 1861, though, the slave trade was still going on in Yoruba territories and the British forced the king of Lagos to sign a treaty ceding the city to England. This was the beginning of the end. From then on there was more and more British intervention into the interior of Nigeria. The year 1865 saw the first intervention by Britain into the civil wars when the West India Regiment was sent in to battle the Egba to free toll roads so the British could use them as trade routes into the interior. The remainder of the century saw the expansion of British colonialism until Nigeria assumed its present national boundaries in 1914. England remained in control, ruling indirectly through indigenous authorities, until Nigeria became an independent nation in October 1960.

Certainly West Africa was not moribund or asleep, waiting for Europeans to arrive. The region of the Yoruba, Benin, Dahomey, and its neighbors in the western Sudan, was complex and dynamic. I have sketched the nature of the states in the region, and we have seen that the differences among them existed within a similar overall pattern. Societies and religions were evolving and in contact. Interaction in politics, trade, warfare, and religion contributed to the internal variation in each society. Fluid, shifting ambitions and alliances pitted the great kingdoms of the area against each other at the same time as they were being penetrated by powerful external groups: by Christian missionaries; Muslim armies, traders, and clerics; Dutch, Portuguese, English, and French explorers; and the explorers' progeny, the traders in guns, slaves, oils, and cloth. They were the products of long development, development which was continuing at the time of their conquest. This development was not only social, political, and economic but religious as well.

A basic religious idiom, which I have tried to sketch, existed throughout the region. While it was built up and practiced in local areas, it had spread and been absorbed to varying extent in the different states. There was varying worship of some of the same or similar deities throughout, while others were limited to specific states, towns, temples, even specific households.

The African religions of the area are human centered but possess an idiom embracing all of life. The happy, prosperous passage of humans through this world and the spectacle of curing and immortality are their major concerns, not salvation. They sanctify nature, cultural production, and human relations as modes and means of divinity. Integral and diffuse, they penetrate everyday life with a distinctive attitude toward existence. Kinship played a key role in religion and in social life as a whole. It was through kinship that the Africans articulated their personal relationships and organized the relationships between the living and the dead, humans and their deities, commoners and kings, and king and king.

The tendency in all of the kingdoms was for conquerors to absorb the deities of their newly acquired territories while they set up and established temples, priesthoods, and cults of their own. So the relatively long stability and centralizing influence of the Yoruba kingdom of Oyo allowed the spread of Oyo's own deities to other areas. Oyo's stability also permitted free and safe migration through the areas under its control, so other cults or forms of rite also spread from one area to another. The West African religions were open to change, incorporating deities and borrowing myths and rites without losing the integrity of their world view. The religions had evolved and were evolving. Their history, which uses rites, myths, masks, statues, dances, poems, and migrations as the engines of memory, is only beginning to be mined.

The contradictions that exist between what people believe and what they do give the historian many opportunities to moralize, for the opportunities increase with distance, hindsight, and the passage of time. One is tempted to moralize on the fact that the kingdoms broke Ebi, the ancient family ideology and constitution governing the relations between states and kings. True, none killed their father and Ile Ife remained inviolate, but the brothers quarreled and warred on each other. While they were distracted by duplicity and power, the stranger with whom they traded people entered from behind and became their conqueror. It would be easy enough to see this as a kind of moral retribution for their part in the iniquity of the Atlantic slave trade, but it would also be mistaken and short-sighted. Slavery was not the only reason for the warfare between the kingdoms and their neighbors. Yoruba slaves were being exported from the Dahomeyan port of Whydah as early as 1698, and the warfare that fed the supply dates from that period (Bascom 1969b:12). But the cessation of Dahomey's involvement in the Atlantic slave trade did not end the warfare. It continued up to the 1890s, when the French army finally conquered Dahomey. The kingdoms had other interests than the slave trade, political and economic interests of their own unrelated to Europe. Although the trade in slaves was an entryway for the Europeans, it was not the only one. Nonetheless the outcome was tragic. The Yoruba civil wars and the Dahomeyan invasions of Yoruba territories caused great destruction and loss of life, and for a time they fed the slave traders' markets well.

From the fifteenth century on through the latter part of the nineteenth, an enormous black wave swept out of Africa. The effect was like dropping a pebble into a still lake, then following it with another and another and another. But this wave rippled out into the sea, faster and faster and more turbulent, until it became a seamless rush, a powerful black tide, that mounted and curled and finally broke up against the farther shore of the Atlantic with a silent but incredible force.

I can visualize the anger of the ancestors as their descendants were severed from them. For the descendants, death lay ahead, not behind. It would not be a gradual slipping into another world, a change of position welcomed with rejoicing, but a sudden wrenching into voidness, into nakedness, into emptiness. It was not the ancestors but the descendants of the enslaved who would really be dead. In the future, when the long genealogies that invoked the living and the dead through their names were spoken, the lost ones, the enslaved ones, were as if vanished beyond the horizon of life and death, and their descendants, if they had any, had names that were not known.

The farther shore, however, only received those that still breathed. All along the way, strewn in the wake of that black wave, were the bodies of the dead. They lay on the battlefields and sacrificial grounds. They lay scattered along the slave routes to the African coast and in the cemeteries of the coastal forts. They expired in chains in the holds of the ships and they lie, even now, at the bottom of the sea where they have long ceased being food for the fishes.

PLATE 1. Decorations on the front of a Vodun shrine. Dahomey, 1930s. Photograph by Melville Herskovits. Herskovits papers courtesy of the Schomburg Center for Research in Black Culture.

PLATE 2. Shrine to Orisha Oro (Oro Society House). Photograph by William Bascom, Nigeria, 1940. Herskovits Collection courtesy of Northwestern University Archives.

PLATE 3. Worshipers assembled outside a shrine to the Vodun. Dahomey, 1930s. Photograph by Melville Herskovits. Herskovits Papers courtesy of the Schomburg Center for Research in Black Culture.

PLATE 4. Inside a shrine to the Orisha Osanyin, the master of herbs and medicinal plants; a view of the altar. Nigeria, 1940. Photograph by William Bascom. Herskovits Collection courtesy of Northwestern University Archives.

PLATE 5. Inside a shrine to the Orisha Shango in Oyo, Nigeria. Note the dark smooth stones in both the lower and the raised containers. Photograph by William Bascom, Nigeria, 1940. Herskovits Collection courtesy of Northwestern University Archives.

PLATE 6. Inside a shrine to the Orisha Oshumare, the rainbow serpent, Nigeria, 1940. Photograph by William Bascom. Herskovits Collection courtesy of Northwestern University Archives.

PLATE 7. "Witnessing objects": sacred pots from a shrine for the Orisha Obatala. Photograph by William Bascom, Nigeria 1940. Herskovits Collection courtesy of Northwestern University Archives.

PLATE 8. Candidates for initiation into the priesthood seated on a mat behind their sacred pots. Note the strings of cowrie shells in the sacred pots. Dahomey, 1930s. Photograph by Melville Herskovits. Herskovits Papers courtesy of the Schomburg Center for Research in Black Culture.

PLATE 9. Procession of initiates bearing their sacred pots on their heads and strings of cowrie shells hanging from their mouths. Dahomey, 1930s. Photograph by Melville Herskovits. Herskovits Papers courtesy of the Schomburg Center for Research in Black Culture.

III

Cuba: Pre-Santeria and Early Santeria (1492–1870)

Virgin of Charity
who from a cove of copper
givest hope to the pauper
and the rich security.
In your creole pity,
Oh Mother, I believe;
therefore, I ask of thee
(if thou with me wilt cope)
give the rich man hope
and security to me.
    Nicholas Guillen, *Tengo*
        (trans. Richard Carr)

When Columbus landed in Cuba he found the island already inhabited. The Ciboney, a northern Amerindian group which was slowly being pushed southward by the Arawaks and Caribs, had preceded him there. The Ciboney were the first human beings to reach Cuba. They were also the first Amerindians to have contact with Europeans, and this was to lead to their eventual extinction.

After "discovering" Cuba, Spain settled it with a government and a resident labor force. This became more difficult after the dream of Cuba as a perpetual gold mine evaporated into thin air and economic realities bleakly stared the colonizers in the face. For more than two hundred years the peninsular government made strenuous efforts to entice Spaniards to settle there. Promises of land grants, tax rebates, free farm animals and buildings, prizes for crop innovation—Spain tried everything to attract enterprising farmers, merchants, and adventurers to this beautiful but peripheral link in its chain of colonies but was not very successful.

As if this were not bad enough, Spanish emigration policy languished under severe restrictions, which were in part self-imposed and in part a real acknowledgment of Spain's ethnic and religious problems. The great physical and cultural diversity of the population and the strength of group ties to different regional traditions posed intricate problems for the integration of Spain as a nation. The central government chose to deal with this by imposing Roman Catholicism as state religion, as an ideology which would unify the population and consolidate the cultural and political dominance of the province of Castile. Queen Isabella put this policy into effect with two edicts issued in 1492 and 1502. In essence what these edicts declared was that in the matter of religion, Moors and Jews, as the major non-Christian groups in Spain, had two alternatives: they could convert to Catholicism or face exile from Spain. Under no circumstances would the Crown compromise with Islam or Judaism. The Spanish monarchs expected to use the Catholic religion as an integrating ideology in the New World just as they were already using it in Spain, and no Moslem or Hebraic influence was to be allowed to spoil the future Catholic purity of the Indies. Moors and Jews who converted to Catholicism publicly but persisted in practicing clandestine non-Christian rites were simply asking for their turn under the knife of the Inquisition. By 1505 most Moors and Jews still residing in Spain had at least gone through the motions of conversion, yet their orthodoxy and the sincerity of their beliefs remained highly suspect.

The Conquest Culture

The Spanish conquest of the Western Hemisphere exhibited a purposeful philosophy of guided culture change which was consistent, logical, and sustained. For three centuries Spain pursued the goal of extending an "ideal" system of social life, culture, and values to its New World colonies. But any "ideal" culture is somewhat artificial. And the "ideal" culture propagated to the colonies was a distillate of the wealth of regional variations existing in Spain. It was simplified as the result of a deliberate selection of those traits and institutions containing the basic premises of Spanish culture and those systems by which both colonizers and colonized could be controlled. It was, to use George Foster's term, a conquest culture (1960:11). Its axioms were clear, simple, and pragmatic: the inherent superiority of this version of the Spanish way of life; Spain's military, economic, and political control over its subject peoples; and the use of this control to bring about planned changes in these peoples' culture, consciousness, and behavior.

The apparatus through which the conquest culture was assembled lay within the formal decisions of the state and the church. Through these decisions the cultural forms deemed desirable for diffusion were selected, many traditional elements discarded, and new forms created. Formal processes in Spain governed the creation of Indian villages in Cuba, governed the island's trade and commerce, regulated emigration and the treatment of slaves, and controlled Cuban land tenure, the pace of urbanization, and the introduction of a theologically "ideal" Catholic doctrine and rite to the island. In this project the Spanish Catholic Church—by the sixteenth century already distanced from Rome—was no mere follower but an active participant, a vigorous prop of the social order. The blending of the sacred and the profane was a hallmark of the age, and Christian baptism ushered the newborn child into both the church and Spanish citizenship. In the ab-

TABLE 1. Arrival of Cuba's Most Influential Families

Century	Number (%)
1600s	35 (7.8)
1700s	114 (25.3)
1800s	189 (42.0)
1900s	112 (24.9)

Source: Knight 1977a:235.

sence of any civil register, baptism functioned as the real birth certificate of new citizens (Ortiz 1971:207, 209).

The promotion of a conquest culture, however, requires a cadre of agents for transmitting it, for practicing it, and for controlling it in the colony, a colonial elite. In the case of Cuba it is possible to know who these people were and how their influence waxed and waned under the pressure of changes within and beyond the colonial society. Franklin Knight, drawing on a sample of 450 of Cuba's most influential, wealthiest, and most prestigious families, was able to trace their origins and their time of arrival (see table 1).

The vast majority of these families could be traced back to Spain, France, Portugal, Ireland, and the Low Countries (428, or 95.1 percent) and had attained social importance before arriving in the New World. They belonged to exclusive military orders and sided with the right people in monarchical disputes, or had been raised to nobility from service as imperial bureaucrats. They fulfilled the criterion of *limpieza de sangre* ("cleanliness of blood," i.e., no Jewish or Moorish blood on either side for four generations back), and they were staunch, unfailing Roman Catholics for as many generations (Knight 1977a:235). The high rate of intrafamily marriages in this group reinforced their already evident tendencies toward aristocracy, and genetic conservation went hand in hand with the accumulation of wealth and property (Martinez-Alier 1974). Through selectivity in arranging marriages and control of property this group of "old" families marked themselves off from the future generations of "new rich" as well as the subsequent waves of new arrivals. From this pool of privileged aspirants the Crown might select the royal governor, the treasurer and accountants, and the customs and military officials of the island. These were all royal appointees. Colonials were excluded from these offices, and creoles, those born on the island, were to have some control of the local economy but no political or social power (Klein 1967:17–21).

Other groups besides the hegemonic white elite and the few free white Catholic settlers and adventurers the state was able to attract contributed to the labor force of early Cuba. A mixed labor force came into being during this first phase of the island's history as Spain drew on the diverse populations under its control. These included Amerindians, the full range of Spanish slaves, free Africans, and ladinos residing in Spain and slaves direct from the African continent.

When the system under which Spain gave land grants to the conquistadors was abolished in 1550, there were nearly three times as many Arawaks and Ciboney on the island as Spaniards, but the Arawak and Ciboney populations had dropped to between one or two thousand from the sixty thousand estimated to have been there when Columbus landed (Guerra y Sanchez 1952:138; Rouse 1963a:519; Wright 1916:194). That same year the Spanish freed the remaining Indian slaves and settled them in autonomous communities just outside the principal Cuban towns. Despite their initial social isolation the Indians prospered, and during the eighteenth and nineteenth centuries they spread out into the eastern and central regions of Cuba. They were, therefore, in constant contact with the Spanish, intermarrying with them, adopting their language, and assimilating into the version of Spanish culture prevalent on the island.

If we set aside the small number of sub-Saharan Africans that the Moors brought with them when they invaded the Iberian peninsula in A.D. 711 and the small cargoes of black African slaves that the Spanish Christians imported from Tunis and the Barbary Coast after the eleventh century, we can date the appearance of sizable numbers of Africans in Europe from about 1440. By 1462 the Portuguese were supplying Africans as slaves to Spain on a regular basis (Rout 1976:15). Africans were not the only slaves in metropolitan Spain. Jews, Moors, Egyptians, Syrians and Lebanese, Greeks, Russians, and some Spanish Christians all participated in fifteenth-century Spain's multiracial system of slave labor. The decrees regulating slavery applied equally to all these groups regardless of race or ethnicity. Besides the enslaved Africans present in Spain, a class of free Africans was there also whose condition was not that much different from Africans in bondage. Like their enslaved brothers and sisters, they were domestics, stevedores, miners, and agricultural laborers for the most part. They too were harassed by police and forbidden to bury their dead where other people buried theirs. But free Africans in Spain also found their social and economic advancement blocked by the racism of the craft guilds, which refused to admit people of African descent. The majority of the few Africans to attain any prominence in Spain were mulattoes of mixed Spanish-African descent. The ladinos—Christianized, Spanish-speaking blacks and mulattoes, slave or free—would seem to have been an appropriate population for peopling the overseas colonies. There were attempts to do this, but there were problems.

Slave or free, the ladinos were expensive to attract and expensive to buy, and they did not adjust well to their new circumstances in the Indies—at least not well enough for Spanish tastes. Many ladinos were urbanites unused to working as farm hands and miners. In many locales, even in the early history of Cuba, the ladinos outnumbered whites. They could easily escape into the uninhabited interior, where they would establish small communities of their own or team up with the Indians with often calamitous results for the Spanish settlers. The Christianized Africans were not above establishing a common cause against the whites with the Muslim *jelofes*, African slaves imported to Spain from ports between Sierra Leone and the Senegal River. They even joined with pagan Africans imported directly from the continent and could incite them all to insurrection. When such a rebellion actually occurred in Santo Domingo in 1522, the shock waves felt on the opposite side of the Atlantic were so strong that Spain altered its policy on who should go to labor in the New World. Ladinos and jelofes were the prime suspects in the Santo Domingo rebellion, and the Crown decided that they would never have a second opportunity to hurl such a frightening blow at white supremacy in the Spanish West Indies. In 1532 and 1540 royal decrees came down prohibiting the export of any white, Moorish, Jewish, or ladino slaves to the Caribbean colonies. This process of elimination left only *bozales*—"raw", un-Christianized slaves direct from the African continent—as an additional labor force to be bought and caught and shipped to a new life in the New World.

This mixed labor force of whites, Indians, and Africans—all interacting and influencing each other—formed the basis of the racially mixed population which evolved out of Cuba's early days and from which the elite strove to isolate itself. Parallel to the mixed work force, then, was intermixture at the level of sex, marriage, and biological reproduction. Along with this a creole culture soon evolved which formed the substratum on and over and through which many subsequent developments in the island's culture took place. To clarify what I mean by creole culture, and because some aspects of it seem to have varied over time while others did not, it will be necessary here not only to describe it as a type of situation but also to anticipate the developments of later periods. This is necessary because a creole culture's real nature is processual and is only truly revealed by the way in which it unfolds in time.

The creole culture which began to emerge in Cuba was cultural intersystem combining elements from several sources. In the early stages of settlement, when the population was very small, it was also very diverse and atomized. There were people from a wide range of ethnic and racial groups, but each group was present in such small numbers that its continued existence as a distinct group was unstable, and culturally the result must have been chaotic, undifferentiated, and mercurial. Eventually a set of distinctions arose classifying the main cultural groups and trends in the society into two: Spanish and African. The roots of this process are in the period 1492–1790.

The intersystem evolved, however, combining elements from Spanish and other European, Islamic, West and Central African, and Amerindian sources. It later came to include input from populations originating in

Haiti, Jamaica, China, and the Yucatan Peninsula. Nonetheless the creole culture was seen as poised between the poles of Africa and Spain. The emergence of these poles out of the previous entropic situation was the result of the hegemonic strategies of the Spanish state and church and the increase in the numbers of Africans as well as their persisting physical and cultural distinctiveness. On the other hand the Ciboney, the Arawak, and the products of their intermixture with the Spanish were regarded as Indians by the general public in some contexts, but in official terms and in relationship to Cuban marriage law, they were regarded as white. The census takers of 1770 treated the Indians as whites for their purposes, and ever since then they have never been reckoned, officially, as a separate racial category (Martinez-Alier 1974:81; Thomas 1971:21). This was true even when there were visible physical differences between them and Spanish folk. (In some instances, though, the Ciboney and Arawak were even lighter in color than the Spanish.) What they contributed as Ciboney and Arawak to the cultural intersystem, and particularly in terms of religion (ritual use of tobacco, fumigation with tobacco smoke as a healing technique, herbalistic knowledge) was absorbed into the cultural intersystem in various ways but ceased to be regarded as Indian. Racially Indians were classified as whites; in relation to the Spanish–African cultural polarity, then, they were most likely to be Spanish.

Nonetheless the creole culture represented by the continuum that evolved out of the social relations among the groups in the population became the first and native culture for those born on the island in the succeeding generations regardless of their ethnic or racial origins and to varying degrees at all class levels. This was not the case for people who were imported to Cuba as adults from other places, including those places considered the source systems of the continuum. The repositories and exemplars of the source systems were the Spanish-born elite (the *peninsulares*) and particularly the female aristocracy, on one hand, and the imported African elder (the old *bozale*), on the other. But it was the creole culture, the continuum, which became the native, the popular, and the most widespread type of culture. The area between the two poles—the complex of intermediate forms that was the intersystem and expressed the heterogeneity of the diverse backgrounds of the populations of the colony in its variations and mixtures—was where most people were. While the creole culture became popularly dominant, it did not become socially dominant. It was not linked to the colonial cultural institutions or to political power deriving from Spain and was without formal social legitimization or prestige.

Even in the earlier undifferentiated pioneer phase of European controlled settlement it was clear that Spanish culture was to dominate everything else, bridge all the fragmentary groups, and be linked to the sources of political and economic power. Still, this did not obliterate the differences within the population as a whole or keep new ones from evolving. The creole continuum was Spanish dominated but was also mixed and hence internally syncretic. The nature and process of the creole culture itself had varied over time from being undifferentiated and atomized at one point to assuming a coherent form as a graded cultural and socioracial continuum later on. But at this formative point Spanish, African, and Amerindian cultures interwove freely and chaotically while Spanish culture, especially Spanish language and religion, dominated everywhere and tried to penetrate everywhere so as to unify and possess everyone, as it were, from the inside.

The creole culture itself continued to be shaped by the social relations between the various groupings defined by the society. The ways in which that inherent heterogeneity was expressed and thus regularized was through social classifications formulated on the basis of inherited physical differences (such as skin color), ancestry, ethnicity, nativity, slave versus free status, and religion. This was a process of mutual definition in which the variation within the continuum was maintained by the ongoing cultural, genetic, and social mixture among the groups. It was not so much a thing as a process of continuous and continuing definition and redefinition through encounters. This situation continued to condition what happened in later periods and in the history of the African religions in Cuba. The processes through which the creole cultural continuum was defined continued; the structure of the social, cultural, and racial classifications evolved during this period remained essentially unchanged in later times, but the content of the cultural categories and their meanings did change and frequently became a point of conflict, contest, coercion, and manipulation later on.

The creole culture, then, was a syncretic cultural continuum participated in by most of the population regardless of ethnic or racial origin. Comprised of Spanish, Amerindian, African, and Islamic influences, it remained nevertheless oriented toward Spain and, as a result, was dominated proximally by the vision of Spanish culture current among the island's hegemonic elite. This elite in its turn saw the "ideal," the conquest culture promoted by the union of the Crown and the church, as its model and promoted it actively, selectively, and by example to the rest of the population.

Before 1774 Cuba was a settler colony of artisans, frontiersmen, petty bureaucrats, and small-scale farmers. Over the course of the entire Atlantic slave trade Cuba received between 702,000 and one million black slaves, with the greatest number coming in during the last thirty years (Curtin 1969:46, table 11; Thomas 1971:170, 183; Moreno Fraginals 1977:188–89). Cuba was a relative backwater of the Atlantic slave trade through the sixteenth, seventeenth, and most of the eighteenth centuries. Between 1511 and 1788 about 100,000 blacks found their way to Cuba (Aimes 1967:269;

Mauro 1960:113–14; Wright 1920:358). The island did not have many settlers of any kind through most of this period, and the slave population was, in the beginning, but a small part of the total number of people in Cuba.

The most lucrative and extensive exports were tobacco (a royal monopoly) and beeswax. The production of tobacco and beeswax required neither extensive land holdings nor much labor but were commercially rewarding and could be run as family businesses. Only a few families could engage in large-scale farming, and the dominant form was grazing. Seen as a rather aristocratic pursuit, cattle breeding was an occupation appropriate to a gentleman, and hides were also an important export (Knight 1977a:232; Thomas 1971:24).

Cuban economic life was relatively undifferentiated by modern standards. Farmers and merchants were indistinguishable. Agriculture and manufacturing did not become separated until after the abolition of slavery (Klein 1967:245; Atkins 1926:39). Trade was simply an appendage to agriculture, not a specialty. Trade, agriculture, and positions of importance in the royal bureaucracy, the military, and the town councils were so interwoven that a strong correlation between office holding, military service, and wealth before 1792 is evident among the 450 elite families reviewed by Knight. Trade produced quick wealth, and these people were favorably placed to exploit it. Minor official positions were bought and sold, and the buyers thought of such purchases as investments, speculation against the future economic gains of being the right person in the right place, all the more as Cuba's agricultural production slowly began to diversify.

Coffee soon became a new commodity, but it was sugar that dominated all. The area given over to sugar cultivation increased dramatically, the prototype of the Cuban sugar mill and the sugar plantation formed, and the demand for labor to work them became ever more insistent. The development of plantations to produce commodities for European consumption was a vital first step in the history of overseas capitalism (Mintz 1974:9). When sugar became the most economically rewarding tropical product to market internationally, it made the trade in enslaved Africans the single biggest moneymaker of the time. It is surely no misstatement to say that the majority of Cuban colonists came seeking wealth. But this does not mean that there were not forces preventing everyone from acquiring it. These forces were both internal and external.

In many respects the Cuban economy was barely on the fringes of capitalism. One aspect of Cuban social life in this period that clearly illustrates this point is the lack of a developed cash economy. Actual money was scarce, and in lieu of cash the colonists employed a complex system of barter. In feudal systems, with their localized, self-sufficient productive units, money had limited value. "Barter and direct reciprocation of services was the means of exchange" (Cox 1970:144). The Cuban case was different, a peculiar hybrid. Commodity exchanges were assigned values in terms of cash, but no money was involved in the exchanges (Knight 1977a:238). The island's inadequate banking and economic system stymied small producers and small landholders. They simply could not raise the substantial investment needed to operate a sugar plantation. When the sugar revolution went into full swing, the early inhabitants who had vast stretches of land were ideally placed to take advantage of the burgeoning plantation economy. Because of their family and political connections they were also in the position to promote laws that restricted the avenues to acquiring land. This reinforced their position even more.

The most serious external force inhibiting the acquisition of wealth in the colony was the colonial metropolis, Spain. Before the sugar boom Spain refused to give up its allegiance to mercantilist ideas which identified gold bullion and trade as the principal axes of its wealth and power among nations. As long as these conceptions held sway, Cuba certainly had little to offer and was hardly a prime target for capital and investment. An even more decisive brake on the accumulation of wealth was the Crown's rigid monopoly over the island's land. Before the nineteenth century land could be inherited but not sold. Even to sublet or divide land required permission from Spain and payment of a fee (Knight 1977a:239). The Crown reserved the hardwood forests (a natural competitor with sugar cane) for naval shipbuilding, and Spain monopolized not only the growing of tobacco but its manufacture as well. Some of the generous land grants given out by the Spanish government to the sixteenth century conquistadors and pioneers remained in the hands of their descendants three hundred years later, pointing up one important factor that impelled people with surplus capital to invest in land: security. To found a landed trust required not only strong personal and official connections but a sizable outlay of cash to guide the request through the various levels of palms which had to be greased on its way through the imperial bureaucracy. What was myopia for the metropolis was stagnation for the colony. Rather than being an example of colonial underdevelopment, Cuba at that time was an example of peripheral, lagging, or nascent capitalism.

The Catholic Religion

Unlike Africans, the Spanish were able to import not only their culture but also their society to Cuba, though it would undergo modifications in the Cuban context. Spanish cultural hegemony was the process by which Catholicism was called into the service of the state. From that vantage point the Catholic Church tried to envelop all and everything in a web of connections permeated with both blatant and subtle exhibitions of power. With antagonistic, oppressed, or marginal groups, its relationship through the state was founded on domination, repression, persuasion, and cultural dominance. With allied and kindred groups within the state, it tried to manifest leadership based on moral authority within a set of social alliances that included a common ideology and cultural basis in Spanish Roman Catholicism.

Spanish Catholic religious manifestations can be grouped under two headings. One is the basic cult, which consists of the seven sacraments of baptism, confirmation, matrimony, extreme unction, the eucharist, penance, and holy orders. The other is a cult of personages. These are the specialized cults of Jesus Christ, the Virgin Mary, and the saints. From the cult of personages arises a vast array of religious phenomena: legends and miracle stories elaborated into folk dramas, the yearly cycle of feast days, the festivals of patron saints. Attached to these personages is a great variety of beliefs, some of which encapsulate pre-Christian ideas and practices within the context of Spanish popular Catholicism. While the basic cult and its sacraments were definitely the domain of the priests and official Catholicism, the cult of personages (especially Mary and the saints) were open to folk interpretations. The consciousness of folk Catholics remained ambivalent. There were some experiences and meanings in their lives which could not be expressed in terms of the official teachings. Nonetheless, they were lived out and practiced on the basis of a residual form of culture. The residual nature of this folk religion put it at a distance from the ecclesiastical one, but under certain conditions this distance lessened to the point where the dominant form absorbed some of the residual ones. The church struggled against these folk interpretations but also sometimes accommodated them. At times it seems even to have embraced them. What was embodied as a uniform image in the ideology of the ruling classes at the apex of society was splintered and reflected back on itself at the various lower levels according to class, rural versus urban residence, and the availability of churches and clergymen.

The Catholicism imported to Cuba was Counter Reformation Catholicism. The Spanish missionary movement and the reaction against Protestantism had changed the character of the religion and, according to Ortiz, other factors also led to the "sinking of the Church to the level of masses" in the sixteenth and seventeenth centuries:

> the change from an intellectual to an emotional outlook, the decline of the spirit of criticism and the reaction against Protestantism led to excessive importance being attached to rites, images, devotions, relics, indulgences and of other attributes of an external, formal religion. (1971:211)

There is no doubt about the importance of rites, images, and devotions in Catholic Spain and Catholic Cuba. What Ortiz sees as a sinking to the level of the masses is from my view the church's embrace or tolerance of attitudes and practices previously confined to the folk. These might be expunged from official Catholicism for export, but they could not be erased from the minds of the carriers of folk Catholic traditions; over their minds the official church had no decisive control. Votive offerings of tin, silver, or wax shaped into limbs, arms, female breasts, eyes, legs, and heads were common sights on or near saint's images in Spain. The offerings were at once symbols and but one step in the acts of devotion and plea.

> A sufferer hangs the figure appropriately symbolic of his ailment on the image of his special devotion, at the same time lights a candle and offering a prayer, hopeful that his token of faith will bring relief. (Foster 1960:160)

Between these two descriptions we have the quintessential acts of folk Catholic devotions: prayer and the lighting of candles.

As potent intermediaries between humans and God, ones who would respond to pleas and offerings and imitation, saints eclipsed the other forms and objects of worship. Among folk Catholics it was the saints who received the greatest adoration. Saints were venerated at domestic altars as well as in church. The official church could no more completely control the worship of these saints among the folk than it could control the distribution of the saints' images upon which so much of folk Catholicism depended. Attendance at mass paralleled, or was replaced by the erection and tending of a home altar containing religious icons.

This more emotional, ritualistic, and icon-centered form of devotion was paralleled by a metamorphosis of sainthood, so much so that the increase in the number of saints and the importance attached to them by the sixteenth- and seventeenth-century church was (and is) viewed by some as a sinking of the church to the level of the masses. Surrounding hundreds of towns and villages in Spain, up on the hilltops, there proliferated numerous small chapels housing the images of virgins or saints which had miraculously appeared or been discovered there and become attached to those sites. As objects of homage, pilgrimage, and festival, these images became the patron saints of their communities and were said to possess extraordinary powers. In the sixteenth century the church of Spain was eagerly adding new saints to its altars and the climate was fertile for miracles.

> It is inconceivable the number of miracles worked everyday in Spain, most of them trivial or easily explained away. But to explain them away was to lay oneself open to reproaches . . . whenever a holy person made a name for himself he was credited with the most extraordinary graces: he could read thoughts, be in two places at the same time, work miracles. (Ortiz 1971:212)

Nothing could better underscore the difference between the ecclesiastical and folk understandings of sainthood. For the church, saints were human beings who led virtuous lives; they manifested in human form the spectacle of realized holiness. The folk, however, did not focus on the inner religiosity of the saints nor focus on them primarily as exemplary religious figures, models of what human beings should or could be. Instead they sought the external signs of the saints' ecclesiastical virtues, signs which could be manifested as forms of power and generosity that could made a difference in their own daily lives. For them the saints were human beings who had miraculous powers (Gudeman 1976:710).

This tension between the two Catholicisms was particularly important in the context of Spanish hegemony in the New World. Since the popular religious concept of miraculous sainthood was a major area of experience and consciousness from the past of both the white and black Spanish settlers, some version of it had to be incorporated if the ecclesiastical form was to make sense. Furthermore it was dangerous to allow too much of this popular religious practice and experience in the colonies if it resided outside the church and was not articulated to the ecclesiastical system in some way (see Williams 1980:40–41). The priests, bishops, and cardinals viewed this folk understanding of sainthood as misguided, but they could not put an end to it. Nor would they have done so even if they could have, for this understanding, misguided as it might be, still bound the folk to the church in a very powerful way. As much as they wanted to impose on the New World an official and purified dogma as opposed to the folk religion, they found they could not import one without the other. In the New World this folk religion was doubly residual. Although adapted somewhat by Cuban ecological conditions and the Spanish-dominated but syncretic Afro-Indian-Spanish culture of its environment, it was really emergent from a form of society which no longer existed. What were essentially feudal and medieval values were to suffer erosion under the effects of the industrial age, slavery, capitalism, and foreign contacts.

THE MARCH OF THE SAINTS

At one level Catholic hegemony was alienating and coercive. Whether through naked force (as in the case of the Africans and Amerindians) or through control of the definitions of reality and the ability to bestow or negate the significance of things, ideas, and events, it remained compulsive and separating. At another level, though, it bound together those who were, in reality, opposed. Despite their resistance, the powerful and the powerless, the master and the slave, the oppressors and the oppressed were tied together in a veil in which their relative positions were simple facts of life and in which, by a kind of spontaneous consent, people learned to want to do what they would have to do anyway. Thereby they avoided suffering the results of force. By these means hegemony radiated outward. Beginning at the point of appropriation of the land itself, it proceeded to the work site and the appropriation of the worker's labor and value. From there it extended beyond and further still into family life, into the sources of secular power, and into the abyss of misfortune and relief.

THE SAINT AS A CHARTER FOR CONQUEST

Richard Davey, traveling through Cuba in the 1890s, made a tour of Havana's churches. In the Church of the Merced he found a painting of a group of Indians being slaughtered by Spaniards. In the center of this painting was a wooden cross on the transverse arm of which sat the Virgin Mary holding the infant Jesus. Davey was good enough to translate into English the inscription immediately below this picture:

> The Admiral, Don Christopher Columbus, and the Spanish Army, being possessed of the "Cerro de la Vega," a place in the Spanish island, erected on it a cross, on whose right arm, the 2nd of May, 1492, in the night there appeared with her most precious Son, the Virgin, Our Lady of Mercy. The Indians, who occupied the island, as soon as they saw Her, drew their arrows and fired at Her, but as arrows could not pierce the sacred wood, the Spaniards took courage, and, falling upon said Indians, killed a great number of them. And the person who saw this wonderful prodigy was the V. R. F. Juan. (1898:135)

The miraculous apparition of the Virgin, transplanted from Spain to Cuba, was colored in the process by the colonial context. It had become linked to the conquest of the island, the superiority and supernatural sanction of the conquerors, and the slaughter of the Indians against whom the cross and the conquistadors remained invulnerable. The appearance of the Virgin had become a charter for conquest.

A CURIOUS RITUAL

It was common in the Cuba of this period for plantation owners to have their sugar estates "christened" with Catholic rites (see Abbot 1971:36–37). In effect, the sugar estate acquired a kind of personality and many of the estates were named after saints. Through this ritual the plantation obtained a heavenly patron who could come to its aid; and slavery and profit, if not actually sanctified, were certainly legitimized through being linked to the major sources of power and tradition in the society.

When the new sugar estate had been planted, the buildings necessary to house the slaves, overseers, machinery, draft animals, and so forth all completed, and the process of sugar production advanced to the point where the sugar cane was ready to be ground, the master of the estate arranged for the christening. He engaged a priest to officiate over the process. Like a newborn child the new estate had to have godparents, and these had to be selected for maximum benefit and help in the future. While visitors, overseers, and slaves looked on, the priest, the estate's master and mistress, and the godparents gathered before the grinding machine. After praying and sprinkling holy water on the machinery, the priest uttered the benediction most appropriate to the occasion: "In the name of God, go on and prosper." The team of oxen started up the grinder and the godfather put in the first stalk of cane to be ground. After this the African slaves continued the grinding. The planter and his family, friends, and relatives went away to rejoice and feed themselves. Meanwhile the slaves continued what the godfather had begun, grinding and grinding.

The christening of the sugar estates was a curious and potent example of the power of symbolism as well as the symbolism of power. It compressed into a few dense acts of religious ritual the whole complex of European capital, American land, and African labor under the hegemony of Spain and all that it depended upon.

THE UNION OF THE CROSS AND THE SWORD

Sunday was always a fete day in Havana, Santiago, and Matanzas, but the churches were mainly attended by women—women and soldiers. The soldiers put in their appearance at military masses. These took place Sunday mornings at eight in Matanzas, but the spectacle actually began earlier with the clamor of the church bells summoning the people and the arrival of the female aristocracy. They arrived in groups of twos or threes, some bringing along children and adolescents. The images of the various madonnas in the churches were frequently attired in the court dress of sixteenth-century Spain, complete with ruff and farthingale, and the elaborate dress of these women seemed to be modeled upon if not in competition with them: elegant brocade, silk, lace, a black lace mantilla partially veiling the powdered face, hoops, and flounces. A middle aisle served as the passageway to the center of the church, their reserved space. Here they looked around, chose their position and signaled the black or mulatto servant who had trailed in behind them like a scarcely visible shadow. The servants, too, might be finely attired, the females with bandanaed and turbaned heads and fine skirts, the men with waistcoats and boots. Having placed down prayer carpets and low chairs for the mistress and her party, the servant watched her drop to her knees and open her missal. The servant drew out and straightened the folds of the mistress's skirt so that no beauty or effect would be lost and knelt modestly behind her on a handkerchief. The mistress prayed the rosary interspersed with elaborate genuflections.

The entrance of the regiment was signaled with trumpet calls from outside. An entire regimental band marched in along with the soldiers and played a processional for them while they took their positions around the inside of the cathedral, officers in the chancel and in special pews set aside for high government functionaries and foreign consuls, an honor guard of eight soldiers on either side of the priest, the rest standing around the sides of the church. The regimental band accompanied the communal prayer recitations and songs. At the elevation of the host the field drummers sounded out a tattoo, the honor guard presented arms and all the soldiers unsheathed their swords. Further drumbeats announced the retiring of the swords and rifles. With the end of the band's music and the end of mass, the regiment marched out just as they had entered, with martial music and trumpet calls. They were the first to leave and stood around outside the cathedral waiting for the exit of the women. Inside, the servants took up the low chairs and folded the prayer carpets. The swishing of the flounces, fans, and mantillas hid the sounds of their steps as they solemnly exited the church a few feet behind their mistresses (Abbot 1971:67; Howe 1969:143, 191–92; Wallace 1898:25–26).

THE SAINT AS MIRACULOUS HEALER

The Spanish folk Catholic theme of the miraculously found image which thereafter becomes connected with a specific site and manifests wonder-working powers is replicated in the story of Cuba's patron saint, La Caridad del Cobre (the Virgin of Charity of Copper, later syncretized in Santeria with the Yoruba goddess Oshun). An image of this miraculous virgin was found floating in the water near the coast of El Cobre, a mining area rich in copper. The finders brought it ashore and housed it in a church, where they placed it upon the altar (Wright 1922). La Caridad, however, chose not to stay there and disappeared. The spot where they later found her was where they built the church that has sheltered the image ever since.

El Cobre was honeycombed with vivid contrasts. In El Cobre men who were lowered a thousand feet underground in rope drawn cages had been emerging grimy day in and blackened day out from mining copper ever since the sixteenth century. Yet high above the mines, upon a hill, above brick-paved terraces and wide flights of stairs, was a shrine where a diminutive wooden image was said to work miracles, to heal those who simply asked and believed. Pilgrims came on horseback and carriage, on foot from the countryside and other towns, even from overseas to this hill. Some ascended the whole length of the terraces and stairs on their knees, beginning their plea with an extra gesture of piety before they were even in sight of the saint's image (Wallace 1898:32).

The pilgrim's rite was a simple one. He or she knelt before the Virgin's image and prayed and invoked her blessing. Many pilgrims, armed with a large spoon, ladled out some of the consecrated oil from the lamps into a vial and carried it home with them; others, after a brief prayer, swallowed the oil right there, taking its virtue into their bodies.

The saint was such a little thing, maybe twelve or fifteen inches tall and made of wood. The statue was enclosed in glass and flanked the altar on its right. At its feet were jewels left by those the saint had helped. Above, suspended from the ceiling by massive chains of wrought silver imported from Spain, large pans filled with oil served as lamps. Wax tapers floated in the oil and were kept constantly aflame to illuminate the saint. Behind the sacristy, the padre tending the shrine would show visitors the concrete testimonials left to the saint's healing powers: the crutches thrown away by those who no longer needed them after encountering La Caridad, the costly jewels and stiff garments embroidered with gold left in gratitude (Wallace 1898:31).

The many women who came to the shrine of the Virgin of Charity of Cobre and left such treasures there as offerings of thanks for loved ones healed brought their African servants with them, for once again it was the slave's task to set down a prayer carpet for them to kneel on so their knees would not hurt nor their dresses be sullied. The servant then knelt behind the lady during mass and during her petitions to the priest and the saint. One can only wonder how these slaves understood what they saw, what they made of it. Surely they must have wondered about this small, dark wooden image which had floated in from the sea and then disappeared only to reappear on this very hill. What unknown power resided in the carved figure that allowed it to fulfill the hopes and sustain the faith of believers? Was there not in it, somewhere perhaps, the secret of the power of the whites?

The Sugar Boom and Expansion of Slavery

The period from about 1790 through 1870 forms a real watershed in the racial and economic history of Cuba. Cuba before this period was one thing, Cuba after this period was becoming something else. Large sums came to the island following the Haitian and American revolutions as refugees made their way to Cuba from Florida, Louisiana, St. Domingue, and the former British colonies. The more Cuba produced the more it consumed and the less could Spain be either the market for all of its goods or the arbiter of what Cubans should want to consume. Cuban trade became internationalized in a new way, with the United States being its largest trading partner. Like everything else in the colony between 1750 and 1850, the amount of wealth one had to possess to be considered a success became tremendously inflated. Land became more than the symbol of wealth; it became the prerequisite to attaining wealth. Accomplished by both legal and illegal means, the increasing restrictions on landholding created a class of landless Hispano-Cubans who were nevertheless still dependent on the plantation, sugar production, and slavery.

With the sugar boom of the late eighteenth century, Cuba's economy became further differentiated. Trade became a specialty detached from agriculture. Through it merchants joined the landed group. Like cracks in a formerly solid wall, new interests in purchasing, transportation, distribution, and supply opened up, and large numbers of Basque, Catalan, and Canary Island folk came from overseas to fill them (Klein 1967:142; Knight 1977a:250).

As the opportunities for attaining wealth diversified and the time needed to acquire wealth was telescoped, high social status and family connections became dispensable. What occurred was not the "supreme organizational triumph of capitalism" which Oliver Cox described in Europe (1970:147), i.e., the complete shattering of the feudal estates. In Cuba the old families and the old order began to lose their wholeness but did not shatter. The criteria of social status among the Europeans became diffuse as the system was infiltrated by the newly developing values and relations of production. The sugar revolution created a new milieu in Cuba which Madrid tried to direct. Tasks became more specialized. The economy differentiated. New cities were established. Through trade the colony became involved in a wider world of political, economic, and social contacts. Trade was the great dynamo generating wealth. By 1850 almost all wealth that went into the sugar plantations came from trade, much of it directly from the trade in African slaves (Knight 1970:105). In the nineteenth century the old families began to fall behind the new individuals and corporations in spite of their initial advantages. The new transformations in technology and capital ate away at the old oligarchy's influence and control. The sugar revolution, brought about by the skills of the oldest Cuban families, brought to the island new men, new economies, new money, and the beginnings of the industrial age—all connected to the different facets of the production of sugar by African slave labor. The island's international political and economic dependency was obscured by the drama of the pursuit of wealth. So was the polarization of ethnic groups and their antagonisms. And so was the process of social disintegration. Every segment of economy and society sought material goods and possessions. Slaves sought their freedom. Free people sought wealth and status. Those without wealth and status sold their labor or their intellectual skills to acquire wealth and status. Those already possessing these things used them to acquire more titles, more land, more machinery, and more slaves.

When the plantation sector of the Cuban society began to rapidly develop, leaving behind centuries of stagnation in response to the growing European and North American demand for sugar, tobacco, and coffee, the need for plantation and farm labor was serious and pressing. This ravenous hunger for labor power was satisfied by the importation of African slave labor. Importing large numbers of slaves dramatically shifted the demographic balance and initiated a process common to most of the Latin American colonies—one that was to have profound social and cultural consequences. Between 1790 and 1822, 240,000 Africans entered Cuba. The Cuban-born creole population was swamped in an avalanche of Africans. There were now ninety-six Africans on the island for every four creoles (Moreno Fraginals 1977:193). By 1861 the population of slaves replaced the nonwhite free population as the island's second-largest demographic component (Knight 1977a:234).

The process began with a high ratio of slave imports relative to the total island population, but the plantation economy's swing into full production led to the decimation of the imported slaves. The birth rate decreased and mortality leveled them. Only the number of slaves sufficient to fill the deficit was imported, and as the number of Cuban-born slaves increased, the demand for imports lessened correspondingly. If we exclude the loss to slavery of those who obtained their freedom, we can see that the slave population was naturally decreasing. The causes were many. Overwork; accidents involving machinery and boiling sugar on the sugar estates; epidemics of cholera, yellow fever, and smallpox; brutal punishments at the stocks, whippings, and outright murder; the high infant mortality rate coincident with the relative infertility of African-born slave women as compared to the Cuban-born ones, as well as the decreasing number of women of childbearing age imported as the slave trade wore on—all contributed to this early and characteristic decrease (Kiple 1976; Thomas 1971:175–76; Elben 1975:240). Between 8 percent and 10 percent of the slaves working sugar plantations had to be replaced every year. About one-third of all slaves worked on these plantations. On the coffee plantations losses were not as great, about 3.75 percent a year, but the toll in loss of life and in human misery was still awesome. Given the high replacement rate caused by the plantation work regimen, the living conditions, and the fact that the Cuban masters never established slave-breeding farms as their colleagues in Virginia did, the end of the slave trade was not only a legal but also a numerical precursor to the end of slavery itself.

Despite the losses, though, the total black population did increase. In fact, throughout the first half of the nineteenth century Cuba was a colony with a black majority. In 1840 it was 60 percent black. By the 1850s this majority was much slimmer, and by the end of the slave trade (1868) the Europeans and creoles had a clear lead due to immigration and natural increase (Kiple 1976).

The demographic character of the new arrivals differed from previous waves of forced African immigration. Contrary to Eblen's estimates, Moreno Fraginals found that the percentage of women imported as slaves increased steadily and dramatically throughout the nineteenth century (Eblen 1975:240; Moreno Fraginals 1977:192). The demographic structure of the pre-1790 population of plantation slaves was markedly abnormal. Plantation owners preferred young healthy adult males as slave laborers. As a result the plantations were prisonlike places without women, children, or old people (Moreno Fraginals 1977:192).

With the continuous rise in the price of slaves during the nineteenth century, planters began more and more to resort to the strategy of having their slave populations reproduce rather than replacing losses by further purchases of slaves. Two things were required for this strategy to be successful: more women had to be imported and the planter had to provide better medical facilities. The purposes of the improved medical facilities were to better conditions for birthing mothers and to prolong the life spans of the slave laborers. Slowly the demographic structure of slave communities began to resemble that of a normally reproducing population with members in all categories of age, with children, adults, women, and the elderly. Besides more adult women, more African girls and boys from eight to twelve years old were brought over from about 1845 through 1868. The death rate fell. It was difficult indeed for family relations to develop stably in the pre-1790 situation. In the nineteenth century it was much easier.

From about 1850 onward seven out of every fifteen slaves imported to Cuba were women (ibid.: 193). These Yoruba women would be encouraged to have children to replenish the slave masters' stocks of slaves, but some would use any of the number of native abortives that still constitute a part of the herbal pharmacology of Santeria. Others would have children, and the children of these slave mothers would live to know freedom. Old people who lived long enough to be unfit for the strenuous plantation work and children below age nine came to account for almost 20 percent of the slave population (195). Hence family relations could solidify more and, with the family, the transmission of religious traditions.

African slavery was doomed when it became clear that there was no longer any real and economical way to replace losses. As a result most black Cubans descend from slaves brought to Cuba in the nineteenth century, especially the last thirty years of the trade when some 250,000 were imported (Murray 1971). The last African slaves to reach Cuba came in 1865, though rumors persist that a few were shipped over and smuggled in as late as 1870. At that time about 75 percent of Cuba's black population had been born in Africa (Thomas 1971:170). By 1907 there were just under 8,000 blacks in Cuba who had been born in Africa (517). By this time they were elders, old former bozales whose memories of Africa were perhaps dim and perhaps hazy or inaccurate but nonetheless still real.

Lucumi Ethnicity

Originally there was no comprehensive term of reference for all of the heterogeneous Yoruba subgroups in Nigeria, and people designated themselves by the names of their subgroups (Bascom 1969b:5). The name Yoruba itself was imposed originally by the Hausa or Fulani and referred only to the people of Oyo. Later it was expanded to include all speakers of the Yoruba language. In Cuba people from all the Yoruba subdivisions were mixed together with people from all over West and Central Africa. These were classified into groups called *naciones* (nations), and each bore a distinctive name. Descendants of the Yorubas and some of their neighbors became the Lucumi nation. In the same way that nationalities qua ethnic labels in the United States were a secondary phenomenon precipitated by the experience of European-American immigrants, Lucumi is a secondary phenomenon in Cuba, a result of the inclusion of heterogeneous Yoruba subgroups within an exploitative system of urban and rural slavery alongside Africans from other areas. (For tribes as secondary phenomena, see Fried 1975; for nationality as ethnic identity also considered as secondary phenomena, see Hannerz 1974, Herberg 1956, Feminelli and Quadagno 1978, and Mullings 1978.) Just as Apulians, Sicilians, and Calabians all became Italians in the United States, Oyos, Egbas, Ijebus, and Ijeshas all became Lucumis in Cuba. Whether the ethnic label was borrowed from the slaves by the slave traders and then imposed on the Africans or whether the slave traders learned to use it to designate the African Yoruba in the same way the Yoruba gradually came to designate themselves is unclear, but the building up of Lucumi as a distinct cultural identity probably did not occur immediately. It must have taken several generations.

Without doubt Lucumi ethnic identity was closely linked with Yoruba culture and descent and forms one basis of Santeria. Some people refer to Santeria as "Lucumi religion" or "Lucumi" to this day. Lucumi religion is dominated by Yoruba traits, and Lucumi, the ritual language used in Santeria's prayers, chants, and songs, is dominated by Yoruba vocabulary and Yoruba phonetic and syntactic structures. Many of the Lucumi claim to be Yoruba descendants (Bascom 1950, 1952; Olmstead 1953). Nevertheless Lucumi religion has traits derived probably from Dahomey and Benin, and from the Hausa and Nupe as well. Some of this borrowing may have occurred in Africa as part of the ongoing evolution of the religions of different Yoruba subgroups in contact with other groups. It may well have occurred in Cuba also. The name Lucumi may have come to include people sold by the Yoruba, as some neighboring groups not included in the cluster of Yoruba subdivisions were also called Lucumi. The Arara (people of Allada) and the Ibo were frequently included within the Lucumi nation and must have contributed to the composition of Lucumi religion (Ortiz 1916:26, 38; Castellanos 1987:97). Still the core of Lucumi subculture and its ethos and organizing principles in Cuba retained a Yoruba focus.

While one may be willing to admit that the ethnic nation names slave traders and owners used to classify their slaves were often arbitrarily chosen and corresponded very uncertainly with the geographical realities of Africa at times, this does not erase the fact that there is another aspect to this issue, one which is internal to Cuban society and does say something about that society. Regardless of the geographical or ethnic relevance (or lack of it) of the names of the African nations, the classifications based on these names had a social reality within Cuba. These national designations became descriptors for groups of African peoples having distinct languages, cultural attributes, physical characteristics, and ways of behaving. Slave owners developed stereotypes concerning each of these categories which were important in their selection and purchasing of slaves. Hence, according to these stereotypes as recorded by various authors, Carabali were proud, Mandingas excellent workers, Gangars thieves and runaways, Fanti also runaways but revengeful as well, Ebros "less black than the others and of lighter wool," Congos short in stature, and Lucumi industrious workmen (Abbot 1971:14; Ortiz 1916:38; Rout 1976:32). Slaves, too, used these designations to classify themselves and to regulate relationships between subgroups of slaves within the same plantation. If this were not true, statements such as this one from Montejo, who was born a slave in 1860, would have been impossible:

> there was no love between the Congolese magic-men and the Congolese Christians, each of whom thought they were good and the others wicked. This still

goes on in Cuba. The Lucumi and the Congolese did not get on either. . . . The Lucumis didn't like cutting cane, and many of them ran away. They were the most rebellious and courageous slaves. Not so the Congolese; they were cowardly as a rule, but strong workers who worked hard without complaining. In the plantations there were Negroes from different countries, all different physically. The Congolese were black-skinned, though there were many of mixed blood with yellow skins and light hair. They were usually small. The Mandingas were reddish-skinned, tall and very strong. I swear by my mother they were a bunch of crooks, too! *They kept apart from the rest.* The Gangas were nice people, rather short and freckled. Many of them became runaways. The Carabalis were like the Musungo Congolese, uncivilized brutes. They only killed pigs on Sundays and at Easter and, being good businessmen, *they killed them to sell, not to eat themselves.* From this comes a saying "Clever Carabali, kills pig on Sunday." I got to know all these people better *after slavery was abolished.* (Montejo 1968:37–38; emphasis mine)

The accuracy or inaccuracy of these tribal-ethnic stereotypes does not change the fact that even at this late date in the history of slavery in Cuba these national names distinguished subgroupings within the slave population and were used by the slaves themselves to classify each other and to regulate social relationships. They also used these names to trace ancestry. Thus Montejo could claim "my father was a Lucumi from Oyo" (1968:17). (Many Cubans are still able to trace their ancestry in this fashion.) Furthermore these designations were often used as family names. Moreno Fraginals rightly points this out for the name Congo (1977:190); Bastide notes this instance as well (1971:8); and for an example we need only consult the classic autobiography of the Cuban ex-slave Montejo again, for his godfather bore this name (1968:17). Afro-Cubans established separate clubs, fraternities, and dance groups distinguished by these ethnic terms as well as by distinct types of drums, other musical instruments, rhythmic patterns, and religious observances (Ortiz 1921:23–24). We have to take these national names seriously and not only because they were part of a very systematically organized trade in which people were concerned to specify as precisely as possible what they were buying. We must take them seriously because they formed an element in the organization of social relations among African slaves and later among the same people when they were freed.

If we look at the ethnic origins of the imported slaves we see a significant fluctuation during the last period of the trade, say from 1850 until its end around 1870. In this last period the Lucumi nation dominates the imports in a sudden and gigantic increase. We can see this in Moreno Fraginals's data from Cuban plantation records (1977), which I adapt here in table 2. From 1760 to 1790 the Congo and Carabali nations dominate among Cuban slaves at a little above 30 and 25 percent respectively. In 1800–20 these two groups still represent the largest segments of the Cuban plantation slaves. Carabali replace Congo by a 3 percent lead, and the

TABLE 2. Origins of African Slaves on Cuban Sugar and
Coffee Plantations

Ethnic Grouping	Period (by Percent)*		
	1760–69	1800–20	1850–70
Congo	30.30	22.21	16.71
Carabali	25.31	25.53	17.37
Mandinga	18.00	19.18	¶
Lucumi	8.22	8.38	34.52
Mina	5.76	6.75	.93
Ganga	3.50	7.57	11.45
All others	13.91†	10.38‡	16.02

Source: Adapted from Moreno Fraginals 1977:190–91, tables 2, 3, and 4.
*Estimated number of slaves imported: 4.307 in 1760–69, 5,402 in 1800–20, and 9.177 in 1850–70.
†Includes 19 ethnic groupings.
‡Includes 38 ethnic groupings.
¶Includes Mandinga among 28 other ethnic groupings.

Mandinga gain proportionately. In both these periods the Lucumi hover just above 8 percent of the total slave population. In the succeeding period their share of the slave population multiplies fourfold. A substantial number of Yoruba, then, entered Cuba at an opportune time in an unfortunate situation. They formed a third of the slaves imported during the period when the care of slaves improved and when the demographic structure of slave communities approached nearer a normal distribution in terms of both the sex ratio and the distribution of people in age categories. More important, they entered as a substantial portion of the slaves imported during the final twenty years of the era of slavery.

Lucumi religious traditions over the whole course of the slave trade were like a flickering light, a lamp handed, trembling, from one generation to the next, brightening with each limited influx of new Yorubas, dimming with each decimated generation, only to flicker weakly or almost die out in the corrosive forge of subgroup competition among slaves, interethnic marriage and sexual liaisons, racial domination, and the grinding brutal regime of slave labor. At some point the Yoruba traditions may actually have died out completely only to be revived or sown anew by the next influx of Yoruba slaves. At the same time, though, people from the various Yoruba subgroups were becoming Lucumi and their religion was being fed by the input and practices of other neighboring and closely related African peoples. Free Yoruba faced many of the same problems as their enslaved brothers and sisters but felt more keenly the pull of Catholicism and the forces of racial and cultural assimilation present in the cities. As we will see, it was in the cities that a reintegration of African religious forms became possible. It is here that we begin to see the importance of a dialectical approach. For the forces affecting these Afro-Cuban religious and cultural systems were contradictory in nature. It is the ongoing interplay of continuity and discontinuity—the forces promoting the disintegration of African cultural forms, forces promoting the reintegration of these same forms and forces promoting their transformation—that gives African-American cultures their peculiarly evanescent and multidirectional character.

Syncretism of African and European Religions

In reference to Santeria we need to account for the survival of Yoruba religious forms in different contexts on one hand and some concerted effort at syncretizing these forms with Catholicism on the other. It is the necessity of establishing the relationship of these two conditions that forces us to reject rural slavery as the context in which Santeria most likely originated. While we believe that Yoruba slaves were able to preserve ancestral religious ideas and practices against great odds, it seems that opportunities for consistent exposure to Catholicism and the aspects of that religion that have found their way into Santeria were slight.

It is necessary to understand something about Yoruba family structure and its relation to the transmission and practice of orisha worship. The four important units of Yoruba family life all traced their ancestry through the male line back to a common ancestor. Members of this descent group all considered themselves blood relatives. Sibs were the widest group of kin, each sib claiming common descent from a specific male ancestor. A collection of extended families who traced descent through the male line back to a common ancestor was called an *omole*. At the core of each of these extended families was a man, all his relatives on his father's side, and the children of these male relatives. The immediate family composed of a man, his wife or wives, and their children was the smallest family unit.

There were three different routes for the transmission of orisha worship. A child could inherit an orisha from either its mother or father and continue their worship of it. In this case a triangular relationship existed between the child, the parent, and the orisha. Much depended on the parent's relationship to the orisha as well as the orisha's relationship to both parent and child. Although it was the parent's responsibility to train the child in the deity's rituals, the child did not have to continue to practice that worship. Depending on the way in which the parent had acquired the orisha and the fortunes of their relationship with each other, the parent might cease worshiping it, thus terminating the child's veneration of it as well. Cases of divorce or other loss of a parent might also terminate the child's relationship with an inherited orisha. In such cases there was no obligation for the child to continue the worship.

In return for a successful pregnancy or because of remarkable circumstances concerning the birth itself, a newborn child might be assigned to a particular orisha. This was a second mode of transmitting orisha worship. In this case a child had an obligation to worship the orisha, and it was the mother's responsibility to do the religious training. Once embarked on this worship the child tended to maintain it lifelong.

A third route for the transmission of orisha worship passed through the lands of sickness and bad luck. Sometimes, as part of the therapy for misfortune and illness, Yoruba healers required that the sufferer adopt an orisha and take up its worship or that an orisha whose worship had been neglected should receive some attention again.

The immediate family was crucial for the transmission of orisha worship and for training in mythology and ritual. Recreation and survival of the Yoruba immediate family was crucial for the recreation and survival of orisha worship in Cuba. Whether transmission occurred father-to-child or mother-to-child, training in religion began early, so that a large portion of the Yoruba boys and girl imported to Cuba in the 1840s had more than a surface knowledge of ritual gained from the playful imitation of their parents. Those who had been born dedicated to an orisha had sat at the feet of specialized cult priests, and others had received special coaching in religion from their fathers (Bascom 1944:23–24).

The predominance of male slaves certainly did not disappear right away. Because of this it might be thought that transmission of orisha worship from father to son had the best chance of surviving. This is true. But it was also true that the worship of an orisha received in this way was not obligatory and so constituted a weak mechanism for continuing the practice of that worship. As long as there remained a scarcity of Yoruba females, the practice of assigning orisha at birth could not ensure continuity of their worship either. In marriages and liaisons between Yoruba men and the women of other ethnic groups, the tradition was imperiled. Unless the wife was from a group with a similar tradition, such as the Dahomean or Bini groups, the tradition only survived if she adopted the customs of her husband. Failing this, the father would have to take on the responsibility of providing Yoruba religious instruction or find some Yoruba relative, elder, or neighbor to do it.

In the midst of the divisions and tensions within the communities of African slaves, the elders held an aloof yet vital place. Together with children too young to work, mothers giving birth, and workers temporarily ill, these old people formed the only idle components of the community of slaves. In their idleness they could preserve and transmit tradition, gathering together the shreds of disparate practices, using the memories of other elders to prompt and vivify their own recollections. The same Esteban Montejo who could pithily describe the animosities and ethnic distinctions among his fellow slaves could also say of these people that "the only ones who had no problems were the old men born in Africa. *They were special people and had to be treated differently because they knew all religious matters"* (1968:37; emphasis mine).

In seeking the social contexts of nineteenth-century Cuban society in which Santeria might have arisen, the most obvious place to look would seem to be the rural sugar plantations and the tobacco and cattle estates. The majority of African slaves spent their lives on these estates, and as the slave trade and the sugar frenzy wore on, increasing numbers of Africans found their way there. Moreover, it is a common expectation to find that folkloric and archaic traditions are better preserved in the countryside than in urban areas. In this we would be misled. The cities and towns of Havana and Matanzas provinces, rather than the countryside, are the strongholds of Santeria, and they have been so for some time (Sandoval 1979:142; Lachatanere 1938:xxx–xxxi). In much of Cuba where there were sizable numbers of both plantations and Africans, Santeria is un-known or little practiced.

Far from maintaining that there were no fragments or reminiscences of African religion in the countryside, I do just the opposite. I admit this, for the evidence is clear that this was so, and we have already seen how the ebb and flow of African immigration must have affected the preservation of these traditions. But what we seek is not only the framework in which African religious practices and ideas survived; we seek those contexts in which they became syncretized and assumed a definite form. These two things are not the same.

The Catholic Church was not able to implement on the plantations the kind of guided culture change, eventuating in syncretism, which it was able to produce elsewhere. Moreover there is little to indicate that the masses of African plantation slaves had any great craving for Christianity such that they would have created this syncretism themselves before emancipation. In rural Cuba there were frequently no schools, no formal associations be-yond the family or neighborhood. There were frequently no churches ei-ther (Lowry 1950:175; Crahan 1979:158). Cuba's churches were located mainly in urban areas, and persons living in the countryside often had to trudge long distances to attend mass, with the result that many Cubans who declared themselves Catholics might not have seen a priest since baptism.

Throughout the seventeenth and eighteenth centuries the church at-tempted to gain and then to keep a foothold in the countryside and es-pecially on the sugar estates. The churchmen attempted to insinuate themselves into the grinding machinery of sugar production by suggesting that by Christianizing the African slaves the padres might be able to keep more of them alive and working and less prone to commit the transgres-sions that so often eventuated in their harsh and brutal punishment (Hall 1971:44). This was necessary because the number of slaves rendered use-less for work following harsh punishments for disobedience, murder, and pilfering increased year by year. If the clerics could instill in the slaves greater humility, more conscience, and less ire against their overseers, they thought the planters would view religion as more in line with their own economic interests. Still, it was precisely these economic interests that limited time for religious instruction. Ortiz describes the leisure time activities of slaves as consisting of dances, of diversions coincident with holidays; and on Saturday nights drumming was prohibited only if it continued too long or too loudly (1916:228, 230–35). But his description surely belongs to an earlier period than the one we are considering, a period when there were few slaves, the sugar mills were small, and the work schedules more leisurely. With the sugar boom this pattern was largely shattered.

The change seems to have been rather abrupt. In 1789 the Cuban Fugitive Slave Law dictated that slaves should not work on the church's holidays; by 1817 the diocesan bishop had granted permission for slaves to work on Sundays and saints' days (Klein 1967:93; Moreno Fraginals 1976:52, 57). While the earlier small-scale planters may have viewed the slave diversions as harmless, the later large-scale planters who had continents to feed and sweeten with sugar viewed such diversions as quaint but unproductive. The picture of the nineteenth-century sugar mill and its work regimen presented by Moreno Fraginals seems almost the opposite of Ortiz's description of this earlier era. He describes a brutal and incessant regime of work without any respite except sleep, no days of rest, whether Sundays or saints' days, no hours of free time as such, and all available hours used for sugar production except for a fifteen-hour period during which a reduced work force cleaned machinery (Moreno Fraginals 1976:56, 1977:199–200). Workdays during harvest time were the longest, sixteen to eighteen hours. At nonpeak periods fourteen-hour to sixteen-hour workdays were normal on the plantations Moreno Fraginals studied (1977:200). Such regime left little time which clergymen might use to teach most slaves anything but the most rudimentary Catholicism, if that. Clerics who managed to squeeze themselves in between the cracks in this schedule found themselves with the unenviable task of trying, in the evening, to teach these workers, who had worked sixteen hours in the fields or in front of burning ovens and who desired not so much spiritual comfort as sleep, an alien religion in a language which many of them did not understand (Spanish) only to teach them prayers in another language they did not understand (Latin). It is no small wonder that for most slaves their contact with Catholicism consisted only of prayer instruction and that what was considered necessary was simply a pronunciation of the words and not an understanding of them (Moreno Fraginals 1976:53).

Even when the church was able to get a foothold, the opportunity was diverted or submerged in other interests. For example, the church might have gained ground in the countryside through its role in christening and burying slaves, since Cuban laws ordered that slaves be christened in church and buried in consecrated ground (Hall 1971:43; Moreno Fraginals 1976:52). In time the christening came to have little or no religious significance and became essentially a form of taxation by the church against slave owners (Hall 1971:43). Sugar plantation owners used the Real Cedula of 1795, which authorized the construction of cemeteries in Havana, as a screen behind which they could construct cemeteries of their own adjacent to their mills. The church protested but, in the end, lost (Moreno Fraginals 1976:55).

Before the 1830s it had been customary for each estate to retain a chaplain (Hall 1971:44). In this way the church hoped to spread itself more forcefully into the countryside, at least among the planters. Poor priests from Spain and the United States chaplained these estates and mills. Inevitably conflict arose between the church and these chaplains as they slipped further and further into the employ of the estates where they worked as opposed to the church organization itself (Moreno Fraginals 1976:52). By the late eighteenth century both the planters and the church had lost interest in these sugar chaplains; by the end of the century sugar mill owners had put an end to all religious services on the plantations beyond the yearly minimum required to save face; and by the 1830s the custom of sugar estate chapels and chaplains had faded into oblivion (Hall 1971:44).

The influence of the church in the countryside declined even from this weak level through the middle and late nineteenth century. The Good Government Laws of 1842 took responsibility for the religious instruction of slaves away from the clerics and gave it to the slave masters, thus assuring that slaves received little religious instruction and at the same time keeping the priests out of the planters' hair (Hall 1971:46). In 1847 Fiscal Oliveras responded to the 1842 laws by proposing that the clerics could improve the religious instruction of the slaves by improving the religious instruction of their masters. This only demonstrated how desperate church officials had become in trying to retain their rural mission and how tenuous was their relationship with the Cuban secular authorities. It also demonstrated their utter powerlessness before a government thoroughly saturated with corruption, slavery, and sugar estate interests (Hall 1971:46–47; Martinez-Alier 1974:47). The church's efforts to bring religion to the whites in the countryside were scarcely more effective than their efforts to bring it to the African slaves. In this same period the slave and free black populations had the same percentage of baptisms as the island's white population (Klein 1967:96–97). Most likely the opinions of the urban padres would have echoed those of the always perceptive Philalethes, who visited Cuba in 1856: "The country people of Cuba as well as the other inhabitants are not very religious. Most of then learn a few prayers by heart, which they repeat without understanding their import. This does not prevent, however, images of the Virgin and of saints being in every house" (1856:52). The relative fruitlessness of the church's efforts at Christianizing the African slaves was commented upon in the testimony of Regino Martin before an 1846 Havana committee charged with investigating the causes of the high rate of suicide among them. His testimony was curt and damning: "It is not necessary to have lived very long in the countryside to know that with few, but very honorable exceptions, the slaves have hardly more religion than the stupid idolatry which they brought from their country of birth" (quoted in Hall 1971:45).

Who were these "few but honorable exceptions"? They were probably domestic slaves, Christianized house servants with relatives in the fields who, under continuous exposure to the Hispano-Cubans, had come to differentiate themselves from the masses of slaves by adopting the religion of their masters and mistresses. The position of this group of slaves is complex and ambiguous. Most probably they were creole Africans rather than fresh imports, and they could speak Spanish. On one hand they served as messengers of the Catholic priests to the field slaves, trying to do some of the instruction the clerics disdained. This most often took place in sugar mill towns rather than on the plantations (Montejo 1968:36). On the other hand, while they still visited their relatives in the barracoons, it was clear that they lived in a world apart. They "made out they were Christian" not only to their masters but also to their fellow slaves (36).

It is evident that in a piecemeal and possibly unreflecting fashion, female slaves passed African religious and cultural lore on to some of the white children they cared for. Since it was the custom of aristocratic Cuban families and those who used them as a model to leave all domestic and child-rearing responsibilities to servants or slaves, members of the creole upper class were frequently reared by African or Afro-Cuban nursemaids who enculturated them with beliefs and attitudes derived from African religion and magic (Lowry 1950:175–80; Sandoval 1979:141).

There may well have been another equally important avenue of cultural interchange between the female domestic slave and her white mistress. It is easy enough to imagine the exchanges of information and instruction that must have taken place around food preparation, housekeeping tips, requirements, and advice. Furthermore both the black female servant and her rural plantation mistress were women pushed into constricted roles on the margins of a hierarchical and claustrophobic world dominated by white men. In some cases it is possible that an ambiguous and ambivalent kind of female solidarity developed between them in the twilight zone of intimate contact and yawning status differences that both joins and separates mistresses and servants. Might not the exchanges around food and housekeeping, which at once obeyed and crossed race, culture, and class lines, have been followed by exchanges of magical and religious lore, a process of exchange that went from servant to mistress as well as from mistress to servant and which both would keep secret from the master?

Just as house slaves served as messengers from the European priests to the field slaves, most probably they were the people who brought the African and Afro-Cuban healer to the "big house" when its inhabitants took sick. The lack of medical facilities of any kind in the rural areas left Spanish curanderos and African healers the only medical practitioners available for blacks and whites alike. Under the pressure of suffering or stress, the upper-class creoles made use of everything that was available, the Catholic priest, the Spanish curandero, and also the African healer (Sandoval 1979:141). All the elements of the potential syncretism of Santeria seem to be present: Christian influence, perhaps shallow but still consistent, and the African influence as well.

Still it is unlikely that there was a syncretic cult. It seems unlikely that Santeria evolved within the unstable crack in the system of rural slavery represented by house slaves. The house slaves were a small population and most likely were kept ethnically diverse for the same security reasons that the mass of field slaves were kept diverse. It is doubtful then that they would have evolved a cult so dominated by Yoruba traits as is Santeria. Nor is it likely that they evolved such a complex system of ritual and a hierarchy of priests directly under the eyes of their masters, who almost always equated African religions with witchcraft even, or perhaps especially, when it cured them. Perhaps these Christianized house slaves maintained some magical practices which they continued to perform alongside the Catholicism of their owners (as we have seen, the Catholicism of their owners was none too rigorous or pure), but these elements alone do not make a cult. Moreover, in order to assume a more definite form this same mixture of heterogeneous traits would require some other social framework in the postslavery era. It seems unlikely, then, that Santeria's ideological and ritual systems or its distinctive social organization evolved at this time among rural domestic slaves or field slaves.

But not all the Africans in the Cuban countryside were slaves. Many were former slaves, Africans who had escaped estates and plantations and taken refuge in the forests and mountains. As early as 1526 there were wandering bands of escaped slaves, *cimarrones* as the Cubans called them, secluded and hidden in their own communities (Klein 1967:69; Franco 1973:41). They gave aid to pirates, helped the French attack Havana in 1539, and for many years were the only emblem of resistance to the colonial system. Cimarron communities, *palenques*, existed well into the nineteenth century, and suppressing them was the major concern of the colonial government. Palenques were dangerous because they offered havens for runaways and served as bases from which revolts could be staged, and the cimarrones themselves frequently raided plantations, stealing, killing whites, and freeing slaves. Between 1795 and 1846 the Cuban Office for the Capture of Maroons reported the existence of thousands of runaway slaves and the capture of thousands of them, whom it placed in special prisons (Franco 1973:47).

The palenques were made up of scattered cabins with attached plots of cultivated land. Hidden in the surrounding wilderness, they depended for defense on pits full of forked hardwood poles sharpened to knife point and sunk in the ground. Though hidden and hunted, they were not isolated. Cimarrones from different palenques communicated with each other, with plantation slaves, and with whites (De La Riva 1973:53). Palenques were so well hidden that many expeditions went right past them, even though they were often located near enough to plantations for the cimarrones to carry on regular communication with enslaved Africans who helped them gain what they needed to defend themselves. The cimarrones supplemented the pistols and rifles they stole from plantations or raiding parties with those they received in trade with disreputable whites in the countryside (53, 57).

The majority of cimarrones were probably fresh imports from Africa, but creole Africans also took to the woods. They escaped alone, in small groups, and in large breakouts. It is possible that some of the groups were ethnically homogeneous, but it is difficult to tell. Cimarrones probably constituted a very mixed group.

Free blacks or mulattos living in the country were often the leasers of farms, and despite harassment by district judges and night patrols, they doggedly worked their farms with their wives and children (Philalethes 1856:33). Yet the cimarrones, though perhaps in contact with them, did not reside with them. Perhaps these free blacks could not offer them enough protection. It is possible that skilled rural slaves could have found freedom and anonymity in the Cuban cities among urban slaves and freemen. But the cimarrones did not do this either. They were people whose experiences, however diverse and complex, had driven them to reject not only the slavery system in the countryside but the option of attempting to make their way to the cities and fade into urban anonymity as well.

There would have been varying degrees of acculturation among the cimarrones, for house slaves as well as field slaves escaped; imported Africans and Cuban born slaves populated the palenques. What kind of religion the cimarrones practiced in the palenques remains mostly a mystery. De La Riva suggests an African base but uses a confusing and biased terminology to describe it:

> Men and women lived in absolute promiscuity and were dominated by their leaders (whom they called Captains) and by the sorcerer or *santero* who would at times function as witch doctor. (1973:52)

De La Riva does not say that the cimarrones themselves called these African-style priests or doctors santeros, and his use of the term may well be an anachronism. Even in some Cuban anthropological writings one finds *Santeria* used as a rubric under which all Afro-Cuban religious forms are confused. In particular it seems that for De La Riva *santero* denotes any African-styled Cuban priest, doctor, or sorcerer rather than one specifically practicing a form of Yoruba religion. The information on palenques is simply too fragmentary to demonstrate any substantial Yoruba influence.

Captures of cimarrones often netted religious or magical items of apparent African origin. Abbot describes the effects found in the hideout of a runaway slave: "a pouch manufactured in Guinea style with a lappet and a separate cap to shut over it for the more perfect security of the treasure therein . . . his name written by his master as a passport, a fetish, two keys, money carefully done up in a rag, a wax candle of his own manufacture" (1971:58). When a Cuban expedition finally captured and killed the cimarron Mariano Mandingo they confiscated "fourteen spears, four machetes, four large baskets with magical paraphernalia" (De La Riva 1973:52).

It is difficult to know what to make of all this. There were palenques in Havana and Matanzas provinces, but the more permanent ones were on the other side of the island, four of which survived through the 1860s. El Cobre had been a palenque for many years and was still one in the 1850s when Philalethes visited Cuba (Philalethes 1856:38). All told El Cobre was a palenque for fifty years, and El Cobre was not the only palenque to grow into a town after the end of slavery and lose all resemblance to its former desperate and fugitive existence. El Cobre remains a center of Santeria in Cuba, and Jovellanos, where William Bascom conducted fieldwork on Santeria in 1952, was once a palenque named Bamba (De La Riva 1973:52; Franco 1973:47–48). Without more research it would be difficult to prove that there is any connection between the Santeria practiced in either El Cobre or Jovellanos and the palenques that used to exist there. A more direct connection is needed to prove this. Also it is doubtful that the palenques were any more homogeneous culturally than the plantations that the cimarrones fled. For a context in which Santeria might have developed we will have to look elsewhere.

Historian Herbert Klein estimates that in mid-19th-century Cuba between 20 and 50 percent of all African slaves worked in towns or cities in nonrural occupations (1967:158). There they worked as artisans, tradesmen, domestics, factory workers, and day laborers. Shipbuilding, cigar making, and construction of military fortifications were other urban occupations using slave labor (Thomas 1971:169; Klein 1967:159). Urban slaves and freedmen as well were prominent figures in Havana, Guantanamo, Santiago, and other towns. Those slaves who possessed a skill formed an important element of the urban work force, and unskilled slaves formed the major portion of the unskilled labor force in towns (Klein 1967:163–64).

Urban slavery was a less restrictive institution than slavery on the plantations. Many urban slave owners invested training and education in their slaves so that they would be more productive in their owners' businesses, and some slave owners rented out their skilled slaves as professional cooks, musicians, etc. in order to gain additional income (Klein 1967:158, 163). In this kind of arrangement the slave would hand over his earnings to his owner, but he might not be living with the owner and the owner would not have direct control over all the slave's activities (73). Some slaves used this uncontrolled time to employ themselves, and by the mid–nineteenth century slaves controlled a sizable number of bars and taverns in Havana (74). For urban slaves the city provided contacts with freemen, contacts with other urban slaves, taverns and clubs for recreation, and plenty of opportunities for escape and for plotting revolts. It also offered an abundance of places to hide, since the slave could melt into one of the numerous classes of other blacks residing there—free blacks, slaves working and living away from their masters, slaves who had purchased their freedom, and Africans freed by the British patrol boats that were trying to suppress the slave trade (Kiple 1946:42–43; Klein 1967:161).

Free blacks in the towns worked in many of the same occupations as the slaves, though many more were artisans and shopkeepers or owned small businesses. Some also owned houses, and it was not uncommon for free blacks to be literate (Philalethes 1856:33).

Most of these freemen were probably creole blacks, but a sizable number of Africans arrived in Cuba after being captured at sea before they could be delivered to Cuban slave owners. The British landed them in Cuba and set them free. It is not known how many of them became free blacks, how many were reenslaved, or how many died soon after arrival, but Kiple's census lists indicate that the number of Africans entering Cuba in this way increased considerably between 1846 and 1860. In 1846 there were 1,052 Africans who had arrived in Cuba as free people; by 1860 there were 19,000 (Kiple 1976:42–43; also see Corwin 1967:40–43). These Africans would have arrived in Cuba's major port cities and swelled the number of blacks there.

Before 1854, when manumission by self-purchase became a matter of record, the number of people who bought themselves out of slavery is considered to have been insignificant (Kiple 1976:42–43; Turnball 1840:147–48). The mulatto offspring of white masters and African slave women composed a large percentage of Cuba's free black population, and a comparison of the figures for mulatto freemen and mulatto slaves suggests that the majority of masters freed their offspring from these unions (Thomas 1971:173). Cuba's free population, therefore, was a heterogeneous one not only ethnically but also physically and in terms of how and for how long they had been free.

Despite their diverse origins all were subject to the generalized discrimination against people of African descent. Far from equalizing the differences among them, racial discrimination seems to have exacerbated these differences, producing marked cleavages in the ranks of the free black population. Free blacks distinguished at least nine types of free blacks in terms of their generational distance from slave status and amount of European versus African ancestry (Martinez-Alier 1974:98). Free blacks further distinguished among themselves in terms of whether they had been born in Cuba or in Africa. Martinez-Alier commented on these cleavages in the African population in terms of how they related to La Escalera, a famous but ambiguously documented conspiracy among sectors of the free and slave populations to end racial domination by seizing the island in an armed revolt.

Among the colored people a very general aspiration was to become as light and
to get as far away from slavery as possible. Instead of developing a consciousness
of their own worth they made their own the white discriminating ideology imposed on them from above. The same disdain with which they were regarded by
most whites they often applied to their peers. It is true there were occasional
outbursts of rebellion, such as the famous conspiracy of the *escalera*. And the
whites made much of the menace to the social order constituted by the colored
population. It is significant that those who participated in this conspiracy were
the most educated and socially advanced of the colored people, who were
bound to feel most strongly the injustice of the system. And at the other extreme, it was slaves who proved most rebellious, killing overseers, escaping or as
a last resort committing suicide. The middle sector of the colored community,
however, those who had managed to make some status gains but had not yet
come up against the upper limits of mobility, probably constituted the most
status-conscious and conformist group. They not only accepted passively the
constraints imposed by the social order but lent it their active consent.
(1974:96).

In her study of marriage, class, and color in nineteenth-century Cuba
from which this excerpt was taken, Vera Martinez-Alier documents in great
detail the self-denigration so rampant in the middle and upper sectors of
the free black population. Denial of the African past, efforts by light-
skinned members to pass as white, the breaking of kinship ties with darker-
skinned relatives, opposition of white parents to their children marrying
people of color, opposition of mulatto parents to their children marrying
people darker than themselves, legalistic machinations by which one could
buy white status or overcome the imposed burden of color through a fee
and a piece of paper—all articulate a dizzying merry-go-round of imposed
inferiority and self-hatred (71, 91–99).

There were only a few spheres of life in the cities in which people of
African descent and people of European descent met at a level approach-
ing equality. One such sphere was the services of the Catholic Church,
where free blacks had equal privileges with whites. There was no segrega-
tion in seating; they could kneel next to whites and advance to the altar the
same as anyone else (Abbot 1971:67). The church was the major guarantor
of the urban slave's free time and provided, through its educational institutions, a means of upward mobility for those free Afro-Cubans it chose to
help (Sandoval 1979:141).

The other major arena where there was a refuge for Afro-Cubans from
the atmosphere of racism was in their own clubs and fraternal organizations. Thomas reports that by the nineteenth century the number of African clubs and bars had increased and that in the 1820s a secret society of
Havana slaves had de facto control over the oldest quarter of the city
(1971:180). It is these clubs that were important centers for the preservation of African religion in Cuba's cities; they were also the targets of church
efforts at guided culture change.

In the mid–eighteenth century Havana's Bishop Pedro Agustín Morel de Santa Cruz started a campaign to bring Catholicism into the clubs where Afro-Cubans gathered to drink and dance. He found that there were twenty-one of these in Havana, each with a house of its own open to Afro-Cubans of both sexes. In his own words he "attempted the gentle method of going by turns to each of the cabildos, to administer the sacrament of confirmation, and praying the Holy Rosary with those of that organization, before the Image of Our Lady which I carried with me. Concluding this act I left the image in their houses charging them to continue with their worship and devotion" (quoted in Klein 1971:100).Bishop Morel de Santa Cruz then appointed a specific clergyman to go to each of the clubs on Sundays and holy days to teach Christian doctrine. Each clergyman appointed a particular virgin to be worshiped in each club under his charge and directed that worship. Morel de Santa Cruz even suggested that clerics learn the African languages so that they might be more effective in transmitting church teachings, but this suggestion was never officially implemented (Klein 1971:100).

Morel de Santa Cruz's efforts were but one in a long chain of attempts to recreate in Cuba the Spanish institution of the *cabildo*, or *cofradia*. These were religious brotherhoods whose major religious functions were the indoctrination of members in the principles of Catholicism, the veneration of specific saints, and taking part in the festivities of the church's holy days by appearing, bearing their saint's images, in public processions. Cabildos and confradias had social functions as well. They were mutual aid societies which provided help to members when they were ill or, in case of death, funeral services. In Spain cabildos and cofradias had been grouped in terms of occupations, by ethnic designations and by symbolic colors (Foster 1960:184). By the fifteenth century blacks in Spain had become members of these Catholic fraternities—free blacks as well as slaves. Whites of Iberian stock would often be members of those same fraternities, but there were also wholly black or wholly mulatto brotherhoods (Russell-Wood 1974:546; Pike 1967:357). All of these groups took part in citywide religious festivals, in processions marked by elaborate regalia and costumes. It was through such brotherhoods and their relationship to the parish churches that much in the way of mutual aid and religious instruction went out to the public at large in Spain. Among the common features of the cofradias were emphasis on Christian morality; corporate responsibility for the welfare of the members of the fraternity and their families by providing them with clothes, medicine, charity, and a decent burial; plus an obligation to help the sick and impoverished of the church parish (Russell-Wood 1974:567–68). The Cuban Catholic Church fostered the organization of these societies for evangelization and mutual aid. In Cuba they were organized along ethnic lines, at least the specifically African ones were.

The Catholic-sponsored cabildos represented the Cuban urban version of the kind of guided culture change that had succeeded so well in Mexico but had proved a dismal failure in the Cuban countryside. Under the direction of a diocesan priest the cabildo allowed for the accommodation of African customs to the church's worship. Through this guided syncretism the priests hoped that the Africans would be swept up into the mainstream of Cuban Christianity, in time forsaking African customs. In the meantime, the church allowed cabildo members to inject an African flavor into the European Christian rites. The cabildo's ecclesiastical functions in Cuba remained the same as they had been in Spain, in particular producing the *comparsas* (carnival processions) and marching in the parades which celebrated the festivals of their saint or occupation. The cabildos also served as centers of recreation, devotions, and social life generally. It was the cabildos rather than the parish churches which were the principal organizations for the religious life of urban Afro-Cubans up until the twentieth century. Where impoverished versions of the cabildo existed in the countryside they might have constituted the only non-familial sodalities. Wealthy people of color sometimes endowed cabildos, and with the aid of the church and fellow cabildo members, a slave was often able to purchase freedom (Ortiz 1921:14–15).

According to Ortiz, whose 1921 article remains the most important report on these organizations, the earliest of these cabildos was Nostra Señora de los Remedios, founded in 1598 in Havana by free Africans of the Zape nation. This cabildo was actually inside a church. One by one the church and the free African population jointly established other cabildos. Not much is known now about the internal organization of the cabildos beyond the fact that membership was by election and that the cabildos each elected a person called *el rey* (the king) or *capataz* (boss or overseer) who mediated between the cabildo and both the church and the police (Ortiz 1921:20). Ultimately it was the rey or capataz who was held responsible by the church or police for any problems occurring at the cabildo. By the nineteenth century at least fourteen African nations had their own cabildos.

A major regular recreational activity of the cabildos was staging dances. These were African dances performed in the style of the nation after which the cabildo was named. The cabildo dances bore the names of the drums which played for the dancing, and the drums themselves were considered ethnically significant symbols of the different nations. Connected to the distinctiveness of the different drum types were the distinctive songs, music, language, and drum rhythms of each nation. Well aware of the possibilities of interchange and the transfer of rhythmic patterns from one drummer to another across cabildo and ethnic lines, cabildos generally prohibited the playing of drum rhythms other than those of their own nation at their dances (26). The most important dances occurred on the Catholic religious holidays, but the dances performed remained African in origin and style. It would be very surprising, indeed, given the intimate relationship which exists between music, dance, and religion in African cultures, if these dances did not turn into religious ceremonies at times, complete with spirit possession. All of the elements were there, and most of the time these dances would not have been supervised by the church or the police.

The history of the cabildos from the late eighteenth century on through the nineteenth century is one of increasingly restrictive laws and increasing interference of church and state in their affairs until, finally, the cabildos were driven underground just before the turn of the century.

The 1792 Good Government Law prohibited cabildos from staging their dances on days other than Sundays and feast days and limited them to the hours preceding or following the times at which Catholic priests offered mass (18). Later laws, in 1835 and 1843, reinforced the earlier law but were even more restrictive. This legislation is significant in that by describing the practices it intends to prohibit it gives us a clue to what may actually have been occurring in the cabildos. The 1792 law forbade "negros de Guinea" from raising altars to the Catholic saints for the purposes of dances performed "after the manner of their land" and imposed a fine and possible confiscation of the altars as punishments for repeated offenses. This same law also forbade the cabildos to hold funeral rites for their members, for at these rites they danced before the dead and wept before them "as they did in their own lands." The law therefore enjoined them to pass on the corpses to funeral parlors rather than perform their own rites (19). Furthermore the 1792 law forbade the cabildos to participate in the street festivals if they bore any ethnically distinctive insignia of their nation. If they carried about African images or brought their African drums out into the streets, they risked eight days of hard labor in public works. Besides regulating the participation of the cabildos in public festivals, beginning in 1792 there was an increase in legislation governing the internal functioning of the cabildos. Article 36 of the 1792 Good Government Law forbade the cabildos to sell alcohol or allow it to be consumed at their affairs (20).

Later laws, following the trend originating in Havana, were even more restrictive. An 1835 law promulgated from Matanzas Province allowed the cabildos to have dances only on festival days and pushed the celebrations away from the main processions and out to the cities' periphery. Repeated infringements of the ruling netted the capataz a fine and loss of his position within the cabildo (20). The Good Government Law of 1842 once again attempted to restrain the participation of the Afrco-Cuban cabildos in the church's festival days by banning them from all except the annual Epiphany celebration, the Día de los Reyes, which was the most important and popular of them all, not the least because one of the Three Magi was represented as a black. Even the participation of the cabildos in this festival operated under limits. Only the Abakwa sect was permitted to appear in distinctive regalia. They sponsored a group of masqueraders appearing as spirits. These spirits became identified in Cuba as *diablitos*, "little devils." In practice the law fell into disuse and all the Afro-Cuban fraternities entered into the processions anyway, performing in the manner described by Wurdemann in 1844, complete with distinctive costumes, masks, and music.

> The next day being el dia de los Reyes, twelfthday, almost unlimited liberty was given to the negroes. Each tribe, having selected its king and queen, paraded the streets with a flag, having its name, and the words *viva Isabella,* with the arms of Spain, painted on it. Their majesties were dressed in the extreme of fashion, and were very ceremoniously waited on by the ladies and gentlemen of the court, one of the ladies holding an umbrella over the head of the queen. They bore their honors with that dignity which the negro loves so much to assume, which they moreover, preserved in the presence of the whites. . . . But the chief object in the group was an athletic negro with a fantastic straw helmet, an immensely thick girdle of stripes of palm-leaves around his waist, and other uncouth articles of dress. Whenever they stopped, their banjoes struck up one of their monotonous tunes, and this frightful figure would commence a devil's dance, which was the signal for all his court to join in a general fandango, a description of which my pen refuseth to give. . . . Only three tribes paraded the streets of Guinea [the small town where the author was residing] but Havana is on this day in a perfect hubub, and the confusion that seems to reign among its colored population is undescribable. On all the plantations the negroes, also, pass the day in dancing to the music of their rude instruments; and the women, especially, are decked out in all the finery of tinsel and gaudy clothes. Songs are often combined with the dance, and in their native dialects they ridicule their owners before their faces, enjoying with much glee their happy ignorance of the burden of their songs. Their African drums are then heard far and near, and their sonorous sound, now falling, now rising on the air, seem like the summons to a general insurrection. (Wurdeman 1844:83–84)

Ortiz lists eighteen of the Afro-Cuban cabildos and attempts to trace their history. It is clear that there is no continuous history or connection between the cabildos he names and those of earlier eras. Even the ones that were founded early, such as the Arara Magino, apparently lay dead for more than a century before being revived (Ortiz 1921:25–27). Of particular interest is the existence of a specifically Lucumi cabildo, El Cabildo Africano Lucumi, whose patron saint was Santa Barbara. This cabildo existed as early as 1839, but even at that date it was the result of the reestablishment and reorganization of a still earlier cabildo. El Cabildo African Lucumi expelled members for any taint of vice; it prohibited non-Lucumi drum rhythms at its dances; and each year on December 4th, Santa Barbara's day, the cabildo sponsored a solemn mass for its deceased members; the following day it held a small procession of its own (26).

One or more Lucumi cabildos, however broken or discontinuous their historical connections with each other or with preceding Lucumi cabildos, would fulfill the requirements we have been seeking for a social framework in which the unique mixture of folk Catholicism and Yoruba religion called Santeria probably evolved. The cabildos were centers where the practice of

Yoruba religion could have continued with a minimum of interference. The people who frequented them would have had, at least in the early period, direct connections with Yoruba culture from birth. Many of them would have been freemen, urban slaves, or Africans freed by the British. The legal status of the organization would have sanctioned their blend of Catholicism and Yoruban rite during the period when the Catholic Church was actively pursuing a policy of guided syncretism, a policy which was interfered with increasingly by the state. The church's efforts would account for both the existence of the syncretism and the limits of it.

Transformation of the Old Religion

As we have seen, many peoples came to Cuba, but the island was under the dominance of Europeans. Spain's position within the structure of an expanding world capitalism encouraged the growth of a society crystallized into a structure of colonial, class, ethnic, and racial domination. Imposition of the saints as representations of spiritual and social powers, and acceptance of Catholic terms and Catholic imagery as the idiom in which distinctions could be made that applied to all the groups, united them and were elements assuring the cultural hegemony of the kingdom of Spain over the colony. The cultural continuum that resulted was the product of a ballet of interaction, detachment, and self-definition. This was the context in which these varied peoples had to define themselves and their relationships to each other. Conceptions of African ethnicity, reformed but still closely related to distinctive beliefs, behavior, and descent, were important in relations between Africans whether slave or free. Lucumi ethnicity evolved within the context of the creole culture and was affected by cultural assimilation, the threat of the disintegration of old cultural ties, and the physical decimation of whole generations of Africans from the Bight of Benin. This is the matrix out of which Early Santeria grew. We now need to look at what the Old Religion had become in the period between 1790 and 1860.

Yoruba religion was preserved in the urban cabildos, possibly in the maroon communities, and among rural slaves, but the guided syncretism the church hoped to foster was most evident in the urban cabildos. In slave quarters in the countryside, where the priest rarely tread, there was a more diffuse Catholic influence emanating from the creole culture as much or more than from the church or priests.

Out in the countryside the children of the orisha worshiped under the eyes of their overseers and masters and also in secret. Some of this worship was unobtrusive. Slaves could make libations to the ancestors and the orisha at any time in the barracoons or out in the open air. "The Lucumi like rising early in the morning and looking up at the sky and saying prayers and sprinkling water on the ground," writes Esteban Montejo. "The Lucumi were at it when you least expected it" (1968:34–35). Divination played a role in settling disputes among the slaves, and the African women who collected herbs and made brews and infusions were the mainstay of plantation medicine (38). Trees, hills, and fields could serve as shrines. A shrine existed wherever a collection of appropriate objects could be brought together. All that was necessary was to invoke the orisha and offer a sacrifice of some kind to "feed" it. Some elders created images of the deities in cement and wood and turned the insides of the barracoons into ersatz temples through inscribing the walls with a secret religious iconography (36).

In the urban areas worship took place in church cabildos, in the independent cabildos (i.e., those not physically located in church buildings), and in the homes of devotees. At the autonomous cabildos and in the homes of free blacks it was possible to have permanent shrines and altars, even if they had to be hidden. The cabildo and the home took the place of the temple and became known alternately as the *ile ocha* (Yoruba, house of the orisha) or *casa templo* (house temple). When permitted, the great religious processions, the comparsas, were the major public venues for Lucumi worshipers, but temporary wayside shrines could be put up in parks and near large trees, and the cathedrals also figures in the practice of Lucumi religion.

Except possibly for the palenques, the countryside was barren of communal orisha worship, communal ancestor rites, and an organized priesthood. Lone devotees and priests or priestesses from the Nigerian cult groups continued their devotions but without any desire to proselytize and often in great secrecy. Even being the son of a Lucumi did not automatically grant access to the knowledge which the elders kept. "These blacks [the old Lucumis] made a secret of everything. They have changed now, but in those days the hardest thing you could do was to try to win the confidence of one of them" (Montejo 1968:36). The urban cabildo, though, provided the place for the reconstitution of the African priesthood and for communal worship. Here drumming, song, and dance came together in the drama of the orisha made visible in the bodies of devotees. Whether communal ancestor veneration played a prominent role in cabildo rites is not known. Perhaps the Egungun Society took part in the comparsas at one time; it has not survived in Cuba to the present day. Veneration of the ancestors continued at small shrines in devotees' homes. Inside the cabildo, ancestor veneration came to refer to the lines of ancestral priests and priestesses and blood kinship became ritual kinship after the manner of the Catholic institution of *compadrazgo*. The sons and daughters of the orisha became the *ajihados* and *ajihadas* (godchildren) of the priests. All the godchildren constituted a religious family of brothers and sisters. There was a fusion of the Nigerian and Catholic institutions such that it is not possible to separate them and tell where one starts and the other stops (Bastide 1971:159).

While visiting the Cabildo Lucumi of Havana in 1851, Frederika Bremer met Africans who had been princes and chiefs in their homelands.

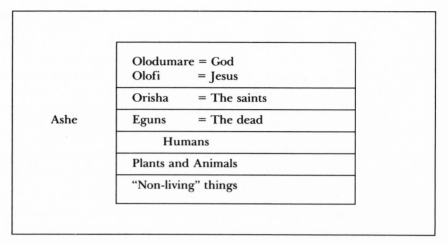

FIGURE 2. Hierarchy of beings in Early Santeria (1760s–1860s).

Despite the respect they received, these men were not necessarily major figures in the cabildo, for the reconstituted religious groups were now separated from any concrete institutional connection to their ancient kingships (Aimes 1905:22). Many cabildos maintained it in the form of the official position called el rey. The king was elected and could not pass on his position to his descendants. The symbolism, if not the reality, of kingship continued in el rey's use of a highly decorated throne and regalia. Metaphors of kingship, including the throne and elaborate regalia, remain in the rituals and chants of initiation into the priesthood (Brandon 1983:395, 402, 405).

Three important changes took place in the cosmology and pantheon during the passage from Yoruba to Lucumi religion: syncretism between the orisha and the saints, integration of the separate Nigerian cults into a single religious structure, and the demise of the cults associated with the earth (see figure 2).

In both the countryside and the city the orisha came to be called *santos* (saints), and each orisha came to be identified with a particular saint (see table 3). Which orisha were known and the saint with which they were identified varied some between locales. An orisha corresponding to one saint in Havana might correspond to a different saint in the countryside. The same was true within the rural areas themselves (Brandon 1983:174–80.) Yoruba deities who were widely worshiped in Yoruba, Benin, and Dahomey are prominent in the pantheon of Lucumi religion and those connected with Oyo especially so.

Whereas the orisha had formerly been worshiped by separate families and priesthoods, in the Cuban cabildos all the priesthoods and families

TABLE 3. Correspondences between Orisha and Saints

Orisha	Saint	Attributes
Olofi	Christ	One of the three aspects of Olodumare (God)
Obatala	Virgin of Mercy	Father of the orisha, guardian of morality, order and tradition; gives peace and tranquillity
Shango	Barbara	God of thunder, lightning, and fire; the wrath of Olodumare; rules the passions
Oya	Virgin of La Candelaria	Guardian of the cemetery, justice, and hurricanes; concerned with death and the business world
Oshun	Virgin of Caridad del Cobre	Patroness of love, money, and yellow metals; rules sex and marriage
Yemaya	Virgin of Regla	Mother of the saints/orisha, goddess of the sea and mother of the world; rules maternity
Eleggua	Holy Child of Atoche	Messenger for all the orisha, keeper of doors and crossroads; rules communication, chance, and hazard
Babaluaiye	Lazarus	Patron of the sick, father of the world because of his power over illness (especially smallpox)
Ogun	Peter	God of iron, warfare, and sacrifice; rules employment
Ibeji	Cosma and Damian	Twin deities; bring good fortune and protection against sorcery
Orunmila	Francis of Assisi	Owner of Ifa divination, guardian of the knowledge of past and future

gathered together under one roof. To deal with organizing access to the priesthood, they drew on the old principles of hierarchy and ranking. The orisha and their priesthoods were placed into a hierarchy topped by the *babalawo*, the high priest of Ifa, the divination deity. The grades of initiation inside the religion were correlated with the attainment of the secrets of specific deities and possession of their witnessing objects (Brandon 1983:355–435; Sanchez 1978).

The cults of the earth disappeared. For the most part, neither in the cities nor in the countryside did land belong to blacks. The slaves farmed, but the land produced for the whites. Urban slaves and freemen no longer farmed. Those free blacks and mulattoes who owned land in the western sugar zones or outside of them seem not to have kept or supported these traditions. In Lucumi religion the earth retained its symbolic role as the abode of the ancestors, but in the absence of a permanent link to individual or communal ownership of land the two cult groups specifically associated with the earth, the Onile and the Ogboni both died.

I believe that the relationship of the orisha and the ancestors to human beings was not separate from the relations which the devotees of Lucumi religion had with other groups in Cuba. If the orisha remained ancestors for some devotees and not for others, if ancestor veneration became confined to the home rather than communal, and if the orisha were inherited by some and not others, this is because of the pulverizing of African lineages and families, which was a result of Cuban slavery. Slavery, though, was not the only reason. Interethnic marriage among Africans weakened the link between Yoruba ancestry and Lucumi religion. Mating between Lucumis, white creoles, and Indians also imperiled this connection unless descendants chose to identify specifically with their Lucumi ancestry. Nonetheless it was possible that people might become Yoruba by initiation. This path would have been open to the scions of interacial and interethnic unions with Lucumis regardless of their physical appearance. Lucumi devotees knew that other African nations had their own religions and their own cabildos devoted to different deities, different ancestors, different powers, and different practices. In the mist of all the African cabildos, the relationship of the orisha to their devotees took on an ethnic-racial character which it had not had in Africa because of the nature of the Lucumis' interactions with other groups in the society—whites, Indians, other African nations, and later the Chinese—and the ways they defined themselves and each other.

IV

Cuba: Santeria (1870–1959)

A nwa awa o ri
A nwa awa o ri
Awa o sun awa o ma
Awa o ma ye ya o
Ara orun ta iye

We are searching for him, we can't see him
We are searching for him, we can't see him
We do not sleep, we do not know
We do not know where he turned to
The people of heaven sell memories
        A Lucumi song for the ancestors

An Economic Transition

The economic isolation forced upon Haiti after its revolution left Cuba
with a virtual monopoly on the production of sugar for the world market.
Cuba's position went unchallenged until the 1870s, when competition
from Europe, which produced sugar from beets rather than cane, threatened its dominance. Sugar prices dropped through the 1890s; after that
they swung up and down precipitously. Large, efficient, aggressive sugar
producers survived, but the small farms went under. Out of this shake-out
a new system arose: an industrial complex of mills called *centrales,* renter-
planters (*colonos*) who ran the centrales, and a low-paid pool of seasonal labor that worked the cane.

American businessmen capitalized the big land purchases, the railways,
the engines and machinery, and the water supply lines needed to run the
new centrales. The demise of the small sugar farms and the abolition of
slavery supplied the rest. A few ex-slaves who became colonos rented land
to till and planted cane for sale to the mills, but the majority of colonos
were whites and mulatto farmers and it was only the larger white colonos
that made much money. Most former rural slaves became seasonal wage
laborers alongside Chinese contract laborers, Amerindians imported from
the Yucatan Peninsula, and black immigrants from Haiti and the British
West Indies.

By the 1920s the effects of this combination of capital, land, and labor
were becoming clear. As more land was turned over to sugar, less was
available for subsistence and Cuba was forced to import more and
more of its food from abroad. The United States became Cuba's main

market for sugar, its main source of manufactured goods and capital. Any fluctuation in the U.S. price or demand for sugar sent convulsions through the island.

The large planters, financial speculators, and merchants made monstrous fortunes from this arrangement. Palatial mansions suddenly sprang out of the ground. The doors of exclusive country clubs that swung one way to keep out the mass of Cubans swung the other way to let in American gangsters, elaborate floor shows with chorus girls, and a Cuban economic elite glittering with new money. At the same time the increasing mechanization of the centrales and the wild seasonal swings in the demand for labor ensured that the majority of workers, and especially the rural blacks, were unemployed half the year.

These economic changes were echoed in the relations between races. The number of African slaves imported during the eighteenth and nineteenth century sugar boom drastically darkened the racial composition of the island's population. The eastern areas of the island, which were not given over to sugar cane, retained much of the socioracial structure of the pre-1760 period, but in the west, where the sugar zones were located, the racial continuum began to polarize. The intermediate range of coloreds was a small part of the continuum there, and it was the extremes that stood out and grew more numerous: the whites and "light coloreds" as owners and employees of the large sugar estates on one hand and the "dark coloreds" and the mass of black slaves on the other. By the end of the nineteenth century Havana and the western sugar areas had acquired a reputation for racism. The introduction of peoples from Yucatan and China between 1853 and 1873 and the black immigration from the British West Indies and Haiti, which the government encouraged between 1913 and and 1928, complicated the issue, but the main problem remained the place of Cuba's own large, impoverished, and culturally distinct black population. A pattern of increasingly harsh and partly public racial discrimination became evident. Efforts to "Cubanize" the work force by sending the immigrant workers back where they came from were linked with efforts to attract European immigration and lighten the complexion of the island both culturally and physically (Hoetink 1985:67).

The condition of the Afro-Cuban population took a turn for the worse after the wars for independence. The gains that had been made during the wars evaporated immediately afterward. Afro-Cubans were underrepresented in government and public administration, and they were boxed out of the electorate. High illiteracy rates meant that only a small fraction of Afro-Cuban males met the requirements for exercising the right to vote. Opportunities in government employment, the hope of many an educated black or mulatto, simply never appeared (Perez 1988:212). Establishment of the Cuban Republic did not ameliorate the destitution in which the majority of the Afro-Cubans continued to live. The advent of a North American dominance replacing the dominance of Spain in 1898 may have actually made things worse, since the American occupation troops infected native Cubans with a racial virus even more virulent than the homegrown variety. Discontent with what blacks gained from their participation in the Ten Years War (1868–78) and the War for Independence (1895–98) fueled attempts to organize black political parties, black participation in labor unrest, and a Negro revolt in May 1912 that cost thousands of lives.

These economic trends form the backdrop against which we can observe the fissioning of the Cuban middle class and the distinct ideologies which it promoted during the latter half of the nineteenth century and the early part of the twentieth.

The War for Independence was the death knell of the colonial planter class's economic dominance of Cuban society. This group had been the creole bourgeoisie of the colonial period, and the power of sugar had given them a great deal of influence with the colonial government, but they had never been that government. When the United States effectively usurped both political and economic dominance of the island, it separated a formerly dominant social class from state power (Perez 1988:192). The creole petit bourgeoisie now found itself in competition with their old elite. These foreign-born Spaniards who had been governing on behalf of Spain were no longer the dominant political class; nonetheless they held on to the economic position and cultural positions which they had reserved for themselves during the colonial period when they had state power. In the early years of the republic they retained important positions in retail commerce, industry, and the Catholic Church. In many Latin American countries independence led to a drop in the number of peninsulares; Cuba went in the opposite direction. Old families stayed and new ones immigrated from Spain at the invitation of governments concerned with tilting the island's population back toward a white majority (Perez 1988:202).

The middle class, which had earlier divided over the issue of independence, now debated whether Cuba had won its political independence from Spain only to lose control of its economic resources to the United States. Politics became a jockeying for power among the various factions of the creole bourgeoisie (the separatist coalition, the new entrepreneurs, the intellectuals and social reformers). The army and the mobilized proletariat waited in the wings plotting their turn at the table. Whoever achieved state power on the island found themselves beholden to and dominated by outside political and economic interests, especially those of the United States. Political leadership was always transient and impermanent, frequently corrupt, and often violent and repressive. The 1930s under the leadership of Machado seem to have been particularly repressive. The political violence, newspaper censorship, political jailings, torture, assassinations, executions, and extensive police surveillance were the legacy of the 1930s and Machado to future decades. By the 1940s and through the 1959 revolution, Cuba Libre was a long gone, and various forms of domestic and international gangsterism had settled in for the long term.

The various factions of the Cuban middle class took ambivalent, vacillating, and contradictory stances toward the issue of African culture and Cuban identity. In the fluid political and economic context of the postindependence era, three contrasting attitudes toward the African religions emerged: an anti-Africanist tendency, a syncretist tendency promoting the blending of spiritism and the African religions, and an avant-garde tendency among some Cuban intellectuals that promoted the African religions as sources of artistic inspiration and national culture. These middle-class ideologies had varying impacts on the Afro-Cuban religions.

The Suppression of the Cabildos

After the 1860s relations between the cabildos and the government continued to deteriorate. The waning of the Catholic Church's power, the end of the slave trade, the ravages of two Cuban wars for independence, and the end of slavery all contributed to the deterioration. The colonial government came to see the cabildos as possible sources of insurrection and intervened more and more in their internal affairs. Furthermore the cabildos themselves were changing in response to the abolition of the slave trade in Cuba (1868). Abolition meant that there would no longer be sizable imports from the ethnic nations around which the cabildos had been organized. Eventually they would become obsolete or would have to change and admit people who, despite being Cuban-born, might still be able to trace some ancestry back to the cabildo's nation. In Cuba, because of the extensive intermarriage, such cabildos would gradually cease to be racial enclaves, if they ever really functioned in a racially exclusive fashion.

By 1877 the state had imposed laws saying that meetings to elect a capataz or meetings concerning the administration of funds had to be presided over by a representative of the state or police officer, a *celador*, or watchman. Starting in 1882 the Cuban governor general required that cabildos renew their licenses every year (Ortiz 1921:22). This was an indirect recognition of the changes that were taking place in the cabildos. They were ceasing to be organized solely as ethnically exclusive mutual aid societies. Rather, the African *de nación* and the African *de criollo* now mixed in the cabildos. The governor general saw the cabildos as losing their original purposes, losing their original ethnic and religious character, and becoming more like simple social clubs. When they finally assumed this character they would be regulated in the same way as any other social club which had no connection with the church. The state viewed their functions as primarily recreational rather than religious (22).

The final blow to the old-style cabildo came in 1884 when the Good Government Law forbade all meetings of African cabildos and forbade them from appearing in the streets the night before or on the Día de los Reyes. After 1884 Epiphany was much quieter and a unique Cuban spectacle passed into history. In April 1888 the governor general served a disposition forbidding the authorization of any cabildos organized along the old lines. All newly organized cabildos had to abide by the common law and without the protection of a special religious status, the same as bars, social clubs, and taverns (22, 23).

Several of these cabildos were organized in the 1880s and 1890s. These late legal cabildos may have predominated in the practice of African religions as before but they did so secretly and remained alive mainly for this purpose and to manage whatever effectiveness they still retained as mutual aid organizations. Arara Magino cabildo was revived under the new laws in 1890 only to die again and be reorganized once more two years later (25–27). El Cabildo Africano Lucumi was reorganized as a mutual aid society in 1891 and was concerned with aiding its members in cases of sickness and death. As mentioned before, this cabildo existed in 1839 as the result of the reestablishment of an earlier institution. At some point El Cabildo Africano Lucumi died again but was resurrected once more in 1902. It continued its Santa Barbara's day mass and its procession (26). In this way El Cabildo Africano Lucumi tried to maintain its link with the old style cabildos despite the lack of an official church connection.

Such organizations were urgently needed in Cuba in the last two decades of the nineteenth century. Slavery ended comparatively late in Cuba, being phased out in stages until around 1888. In the period after the end of slavery Afro-Cubans fresh from the countryside probably came to the cities and sought out Africans from their own nations. Those who could trace their descent even to specific African nations would have done the same, for ethnic affiliation had some importance in both the city and the countryside. Fragments and revivals of African tradition that had managed to solidify in the countryside in the final years of the slave trade when sizable numbers of Yorubas were imported were probably gathered together in the cities where it was possible to find a reconstituted priesthood in the cabildos.

Membership was probably opened gradually to non-Yorubas who spoke the Yoruba language such as some peoples from the modern Republic of Benin (formerly Dahomey), then to people who could trace Lucumi descent. With the cessation of the trade in slaves, membership became open to non-Lucumis; these people became Lucumi not by birth or descent but by initiation. In time the secret religious practices ceased to be solely the property of Afro-Cubans. They were passed on to peoples with mixed ancestry. All along the line there would have been whites who had been assisted by African healers, who sought out good luck or counsel from Yoruba diviners. These would have been the upper-class creoles raised by African house servants, the poor white peasants who worked in the fields beside former slaves in the days after emancipation, whites who inhabited the same underground into which the cabildos had been forced and where Ortiz found them when he began his studies in the first decade of this century. In at least one city, Regla, there was a strong tradition of Santeria practiced primarily by the Hispano-Cubans who constituted the majority of Regla's population (Lachatanere 1942:33).

Cabildos from different nations were independent of each other, and cabildos from the same nation in different cities were independent of each other. Each cabildo in the same city was autonomous and had a separate history and line of tradition which was itself discontinuous. From the cities, where the traditions were best preserved and where the syncretism with Catholicism had assumed a coherent form, Santeria probably made its way back out into the countryside with each returning group of Afro-Cubans who found the cities uncongenial.

As momentous as it was, the abolition of slavery in Cuba did not happen all at once and it did not change everything in the lives of Afro-Cubans. Indeed the condition of the masses of Afro-Cubans remained almost as bad as it had always been, while illegal but nonetheless widespread racial discrimination thwarted the ambitions of the formerly elite class of free blacks. In addition to the cabildos, Cuban blacks created a variety of political parties and other organizations to advance their cause from the turn of the century onward.

In 1892 an Afro-Cuban Protestant minister named William George Emmanuel founded an organization called the Union of Africa and Her Descendants. The organization's goal was to create a union of all the Africans in Cuba for the purpose of establishing schools and health services. In 1893 the union adopted an African flag copied from that of the Congo and in 1894 it named Emmanuel as "sole representative of the African race before the Government" (Ortiz 1921:28). In 1894 Emmanuel proposed the reestablishment of the scattered African cabildos. What he campaigned for was a union of the African cabildos to form a powerful coalition that would monopolize representation of Afro-Cubans before the government (28). The union changed its name to Aurora of Hope in 1895 and extended its jurisdiction to encompass the whole island. San Rey Magus Melchior (the black among the Three Magi) became the organization's patron, and the Aurora supported the idea of steamboat traffic between Cuba and Africa. Emmanuel convened a council of the representatives of the cabildos of ten different African nations, not including the Lucumi. When the council met in 1896 it expelled Emmanuel from his own organization despite lively protest. The Aurora of Hope did not cease to exist, however. Representatives of Congolese, Mandinga, Carabali, and Mina cabildos agreed on a new charter for the organization, but it subsequently faded from sight and out of history (28).

In 1910, sensing the seeds of a black revolt and fearing a white backlash, Morua Delgado, the only Afro-Cuban to hold the office of president of the senate, promoted and put into law an amendment forbidding the organization of political parties on a racial basis. It is possible that succeeding republican administrations also came to see the cabildos as possible sources of insurrection and because of this intervened more and more in their internal affairs. When the Cuban sociologist Fernando Ortiz met Emmanuel, also in 1910, he found him a bitter and disappointed man. Emmanuel had not abandoned his goal of representing the Africans of Cuba and their civilization before the government, but he no longer saw the cabildos as a useful means of doing it. Instead, being an attorney as well as a minister, he looked forward to receiving certificates of dissolution from them (28).

Neither the abolition of slavery nor the victorious War of Independence made much difference in the treatment of the Afro-Cuban religions. From 1902 through the 1920s the wave of nationalism which one would expect in a newly liberated country assumed a peculiar form in Cuba. The celebration of indigenous traditions was replaced by a campaign of Europeanization which denigrated everything revealing the African presence. This campaign to de-Africanize Cuban culture also drew the support of a minority of Cuban blacks, the *negros finos* (refined blacks), a culturally assimilated, upwardly mobile elite that hoped to become members of the new ruling class (Nodal 1983:160).

One part of the campaign focused on the persecution of the African cabildos and the confiscation of religious paraphernalia, especially the ritual drums which were such potent symbols of African culture. Laws forbade the use of these drums, and confiscated drums were destroyed. African religionists tried any number of strategies to get around these laws, including changing the structure and construction of their religious drums. They added metal keys and wooden strips to them and changed their shapes so that they looked more like "white drums," i.e., more creole and less African.

Persecution of the Afro-Cuban cabildos pushed them underground; they became fugitive again. The positive moral influence the cabildos once represented—their public dances, recreational activities, funeral masses, and mutual aid work—had all been sacrificed to no good end. What public respect the cabildos had once possessed was now lost. Furthermore, persecution of the cabildos stigmatized them without providing anything to take their place in the religious life of Afro-Cubans. The cabildos took on the characteristics of secret societies coated with a thin veneer of Catholicism sufficient to conform to the codes of the secular authorities and sufficient to shield the African rites they still practiced (Ortiz 1921:30). Their connections to the Catholic Church became even more tenuous than they had been in the past. Instead members of the cabildos were forced into a subterranean world where they now mixed with exploitative sorcerers, occultists, and adepts of the new religion of Espiritismo.

Espiritismo

Espiritismo is a variant of the spiritism founded in France by Hippolyte Rivail (1804–69), an engineer who wrote under the pseudonym of Allan Kardec. Kardec's spiritism was part of a wider European and North American spiritualist movement of the second half of the nineteenth century. His particular form of spiritualism was unique because of its combination of scientism and progressivist ideology with Christian moral teachings and personal mysticism. He claimed that his books were dictated to him by spirits who had reinterpreted the New Testament, yet he wanted to subject the spiritual world to human observation and to found on those observations a positive science.

Amalia Soler (1835–1912) actively promoted the spiritist movement in Spain. Its literature appeared in Latin America by the 1850s, and in the 1870s it was a veritable rage throughout the Spanish and French Caribbean and Central and South America, where it took the form of many small groups of mediums and clients (Bastide 1871:107; Macklin 1974; and Pressel 1973).

Spiritist literature first arrived in Cuba and Puerto Rico in the company of other illegal books around 1856 (Bermudez 1967:5, 14n.6; Perez y Mena 1977:129). The belief that people could communicate with spirits of the dead flew directly in the face of teachings of the Catholic Church, and the idea that people could communicate directly with God or the saints without a priest was clearly heretical. Still when Kardecism became popular in Puerto Rico the upper classes adopted it first, creating numerous periodicals devoted to discussing and promoting Espiritismo (Morales-Dorta 1976:15). In Cuba, where a Spanish-born upper class dominated the Catholic Church, middle-class Cubans were the first to become involved. Many of these people were antagonistic toward the Catholic hierarchy they could never penetrate. Others were *independistas* and saw the church as an arm of the Spanish monarchy which was draining the island. Other forward-looking elements of the population—people with an interest in science, political democracy, and new ideas—felt very uncomfortable with the rigid and conservative church. For these people Kardecism provided an ideological alternative to institutional Catholicism. Its progressivist, scientistic orientation appealed to them; so did its explicit and implicit criticisms of institutionalized Christianity.

The Espiritismo of the creole middle class focused on communication with the spirits of the dead and on the "scientific" and philosophical aspects of Kardec's work. They thought of Espiritismo as an expression of science and not as a religious manifestation. Nonetheless the multitude of spirits with whom they communicated were invisible supernatural beings and spiritism was a general explanation about the nature of the world and the place of human beings within it. And while these middle-class Cubans did not think of themselves as ritualists, their actual practice was for groups of believers to gather in each other's homes, seat themselves around a table, and having made specified invocations, fall into trance (Bermudez 1967:5). Their insistence that their way of communicating with spirits was pure, orderly, and scientific and that their practices excluded all methods not explicitly set forth in Kardec's writings led to their being dubbed *científicos* and their style of practice *Espiritismo de mesa* (Bram 1958:344; Morales-Dorta 1976:15; Sandoval 1979:141, 150).

Espiritismo spread from the creole middle class to the other urban classes and then radiated out into the countryside. As the diffusion process went forward Espiritismo acquired class-related differences in emphasis and cultural content.

Many Cubans sought solutions for their sickness and material problems in religion. Among the lower middle and lower classes Espiritismo was directed at healing, the here and now, and problems of living (Garrison 1977; Rogler and Hollingshead 1961; Koss 1975; Harwood 1977). This variety was called *Espiritismo de caridad,* of charity (Bermudez 1967:5). The advent of Espiritismo cast new light on the causes of suffering and relief from suffering. Espiritismo was modern, experimental, and scientific. Furthermore, it was both verifiable and efficacious; verifiable because the believer could see and talk to the spirit through its medium, efficacious because the spirit medium provided immediate solutions for people in distress. Catholicism provided neither. In Catholicism one prayed for help before a saint that never spoke, and even believers who brought with them a strong faith left the saints without advice or prescriptions. At the same time this crack in the wall of the church's hegemony also called up a whole regiment of ancient ghosts, the repressed denizens of Europe's prescientific past: vestiges of Spain's pre-Christian religions remained among folk Catholics; the suppressed practices of Christian mystics and students of the occult resurfaced and coalesced under the banner of Espiritismo de caridad; and medieval demonology provided Cuban spiritism with its beliefs in witchcraft and the sorcerer's art (Ortiz 1973).

Chameleonlike, Espiritismo also took on the colors of its creole environment. Espiritismo grew by accumulating elements of Spanish and Cuban herbalism, Native American healing practices, and the merest scent of African magic. In Cuba Kardec's spirit guides frequently embodied the popular stereotypic images of Cuban ethnic, racial, and professional groups. Not only did Cuban espiritistas in their mediumistic trance manifest spirit guides that resembled themselves, both physically and in temperament, but both black and white mediums manifested spirit guides who were *Africanos de nación*—Lucumi, Mandinga, Mina, and Congolese tribesmen who had suffered and died in slavery (Cabrera 1971:64–65). None of this was in Kardec.

When it reached the lower class and out into the rural areas, Espiritismo became mixed with the prevalent folk Catholicism. Cubans called themselves Catholic whether they went to a church or not and whether or not they also practiced Espiritismo. Some of those who attended church also practiced Espiritismo at home with their friends and relatives. Other folk Catholics who rarely saw a priest became devoted to what was in essence an uninstitutionalized saint cult using techniques and concepts derived from Espiritismo.

Between 1868 and 1895 the colonial government and the Catholic Church closed ranks to battle against all the possible supporters of independence from Spain. They suppressed liberal ideas along with political separatists. Political parties, worker's organizations, and ethnic associations all had to resist to survive. So did the growing spiritist movement. At the same time that the Afro-Cuban cabildos were the targets of increasingly restrictive legislation, Espiritismo was spreading in the cities and countryside. It was inevitable that the two would meet within the occult underground that permeated Cuban society like a system of subterranean waterways.

In some ways the healing-oriented Espiritismo probably appeared to Early Santeria practitioners as a more congenial form of Christianity, a truer Christian teaching than that of the Catholics, just as it claimed. Certainly some aspects of Espiritismo were familiar. There were the familiar Christian concepts and symbols and, like both Santeria and Catholicism, Espiritismo had saints. Espiritismo and Santeria both addressed themselves to the immediate issues of their devotees' lives. Both religions provided alternative perspectives on the world, alternative values, and a basis for personal identity. Both were opposed by the Catholic Church for this. Repression provoked resistance, but the arena in which that resistance took place guaranteed that some of what was being resisted would be absorbed. The two religions had resisted assimilation into the hegemony of the state and its church but were affected by it just the same, because more diffuse forms of Catholicism permeated Cuban culture outside the official institutions.

The printed works of Kardec and Soler marked Espiritismo as a white literate tradition like Catholicism and unlike Santeria. In other ways Espiritismo was both similar and different from Santeria. Espiritistas made fine distinctions within the world of the dead which Santeria did not make and generalized those which it did. Espiritismo threatened to creep into every crevice vacated by the ancestral dead, but it did not give lineal ancestors an exalted and powerful place. Even though Espiritismo had saints, they were different. In Espiritismo the saints were pure and remote and not at the ready call of the medium; instead, mediums relied on a variety of lesser and more accessible spirits. As a result the spirit guides and angel guardians of Espiritismo were lumped together with the saints or orisha; in turn the saints or orisha assumed new roles as protectors, spirit guides, and guardian angels.

Although both santeras and espiritistas believed in reincarnation, Espiritismo taught that reincarnation was progressive: through death incarnate souls gradually ascended the grades of a spiritual hierarchy and eventually, after the tests of many lifetimes, became saints. The traditional Yoruba concept of reincarnation, if it was still extant in Lucumi religion, was nonprogressive. It was concerned with returning from death to Earth in one's family line rather than with rising in the hierarchy of an invisible spiritual world after death. Nonetheless the spiritist concept seems to have been adopted by some santeras.

Though more intimate in many ways than the relationship santeros now had with the Catholic Church, in this regard Espiritismo was not any different in kind. Orisha devotees continued to participate in the baptismal and funeral rites of the Catholics. These rites could be utilized without being absorbed directly into Early Santeria's ritual system. Regardless of how the santeros might interpret them, these rituals were conducted by the Catholic priest and performed in church, the Catholic priest's ritual space. The santeros could symbolically annex that space for their own purposes and for the power, prestige, or legitimacy that lay within it, but they could not control what went on there. Likewise the spiritist seances and most spiritist healing practices were not absorbed directly into Santeria either.

It is not surprising that the spiritist style of mediumship was not absorbed directly into Santeria. Insofar as spiritist mediumship was ceremonial spirit possession, Espiritismo had nothing new to offer, but there were other issues at stake. The way mediumship works in Espiritismo puts the spiritist medium in direct competition with the diviner who has spent so much money, time, and work training in his or her profession. The Santeria divination devices themselves are symbolic of membership in the religion and also of a specific African ethnic heritage. The spiritist medium does not use such devices but replaces them with other symbols. As I said before, in Espiritismo the saints are pure and remote spiritual beings and are not at the ready call of the medium. The result is that the medium usually serves as the vehicle for lower classes of spirits, while in Santeria the saints speak through the divination devices and the santero has access to them any time they are needed. Another aspect of Espiritismo which did, however, have some impact on Santeria ritual was healing work.

Isolated techniques, objects, and gestures were brought over into Santeria and remain in the practice of some contemporary santeros. These did not replace the Santeria rites but augmented them. If what santeros now say and do is a clue to what went on in the past, santeros evidently came to view the espiritistas as healers who were specialists in helping people whose problems were brought about by *causas*. Causas are a category of lowly evolved, intranquil spirits which are important in Espiritismo's explanations of disease and suffering but had not been a part of Lucumi religion. Santeros who accepted the existence of causas could annex the healing abilities of espiritistas by referring clients to them, thus making use of their rites without having to participate in them. The espiritista remained for them a specialist in causas while the santero remained a specialist in the worship of the saints or orisha. Mediumship and training in Espiritismo then came to be seen as a developmental step toward the semiadvanced levels of Santeria practice. In other words, once Santeria itself had taken some of the ideological and ritual elements of Espiritismo into its own framework, santeros regarded Espiritismo as a lower level of Santeria-type practice.

One further mechanism for controlling the relationship between the two religions was the physical or temporal separation of their rites. Rituals from the two religious systems either take place in separate spaces or in the same space at different times, with the difference in context indicated by the presence of the appropriate symbolic objects. Even the santero who was also an espiritista separated the times, locations, and symbols of the two religions.

Afro-Cubanism

The survival of African culture, the early and continuing work of Fernando Ortiz, and an energetic group of writers, painters, and musicians gave the Cuban intellectual scene a peculiar dynamism in the 1920s. The movement of Afro-Cubanism, an important ideological trend of the period, was one product of this dynamism. Afro-Cubanism can be seen as a response to the political, social, and cultural problems of the Cuban Republic and as a response to international influence of the European artistic and intellectual avant-garde of the time. As a result we find the movement concerned both with questions of race, social inequality, economics, and Cuban national identity and with a kind of aesthetic primitivism and recourse to the irrational with an implied critique of Western civilization derived from Spengler in philosophy, Stravinsky in music, Picasso in painting, and Lorca in poetry (Echevarria 1977:43, 52; Janney 1981:20, 24–25).

Other sources of that dynamism coming from abroad were artistic trends in France, Germany, and the United States that reflected a reevaluation of African and African-American culture. The lectures and writings of Leo Frobenius on African culture, the promotion and appropriation by the European avant-garde of African sculpture and dance, of ragtime and jazz, and the poetry and prose of the Harlem Renaissance turned previous artistic attitudes upside down (Willet 1978; Frobenius 1913; Helbing 1972). The primitive became the advanced. Peoples without culture suddenly possessed it in extreme modernist forms. Black heads, formerly seen as the abode of a dull and empty void, became filled with magic, an irrational, intuitive élan vital with which avant-garde artists and intellectuals hoped to vivify or destroy the decaying structures of Europe.

At the same time as Afro-Cubanism allowed the avant-garde intellectuals of Cuba's middle class to establish a common ground with currents from Europe, it also provided them with a sense of uniqueness within the modernist movement. Unlike the Europeans, Cuban artists did not have to look abroad for the magical presence both of them sought; Africa existed right on the island. If modernism delighted in the primitive, the irrational, and the exotic, in dreams and hallucinatory rites, then the Cuban writer and artist had a prime source for all this. The magical, primal presence they sought they found in a fiercely concentrated and in a relatively uncontaminated state in the religion and culture of Afro-Cubans. Moreover, this presence of the magical was not new but had been there all the time, ignored and suppressed by whites in the service of a European world on the wane.

One of the fathers of Afro-Cubanism was the lawyer turned social scientist Don Fernando Ortiz. The hallowed image he later attained as an intellectual and cultural figure, particularly his relationship to the Afro-Cubanist school, has tended to detract attention from the ideology and attitudes that informed his early work, i.e., the body of writings that ignited Afro-Cubanism in the first place (Becerra and Comas 1957; Le Riverend 1973; Guillen 1969). It is significant that Ortiz's entrée to Afro-Cuban religions was through its most feared and reviled element: sorcerers. In the beginning his interest in Afro-Cuban religions was neither aesthetic nor cultural but criminological. He was interested in African culture as criminal activity. This is clear in his first and in some ways his most influential and classic book, *Hampa afro-cubana: Los negros brujos,* which appeared in 1906. The book's full title translates as "Afro-Cuban underworld: black sorcerers, notes for a study of criminal ethnology." Despite its mixture of fictional and journalistic techniques and the wealth of archival material and popular social mythology on which it draws, *Los negros brujos* is essentially a treatise on criminology, complete with a set of police mug shots at the end. It is a study of witchcraft and sorcery among Cuban blacks which was aimed at producing a coherent and accurate description of the sorcerers and their beliefs and practices in order to eliminate them more quickly and efficiently. This issue assumed great moral urgency at the time, since many whites were converting to Afro-Cuban religions. Ortiz's effort was a socially and morally committed one. He hoped to provide information that would help save society from the degradation he thought would inevitably result as whites came under the power of black sorcerers and joined them in the activities for which they were best known to the police, the press, and the general public: ritualized murders, necrophilia, and a long roster of lurid and bizarre sexual practices.

The incendiary influence of Ortiz's writings on the Cuban literary, musical, and artistic avant-garde of the time cannot be overestimated. The value of his early work to Afro-Cubanism was that it provided a first systematic account of Afro-Cuban culture, especially Afro-Cuban religious beliefs, myths, and rites. *Los negros brujos* was projected to be the first in a series of works examining what was, from the viewpoint of a white, middle-class, foreign-educated intellectual who had had practically no contact with blacks, a submerged and unknown world. This promise was richly fulfilled. Even so, in his early period Ortiz found the presence of the African element to be a regressive force. There is a strong biological determinist underpinning to his early works, and in *Los negros brujos* his

solutions to one aspect of Cuba's social and cultural problem were ethnic
selection of the superior (white) over the inferior (black) race and the civ-
ilizing of the primitive mentalities of the blacks through cultural assimilation (Ortiz 1973a:395).

While Ortiz's early works provided fuel for Afro-Cubanism rather than
being a spearhead for the movement, he was actually converted to it after
it took shape. He retained the respect and admiration (not without reser-
vations) of the major figures in the movement, the generation of artists
that included poet Nicolas Guillen, novelist Alejo Carpentier, composer
Amadeo Roldan, and painter Wilfredo Lam. Their regard for him even
increased as his voluminous works on Afro-Cuban history, society, and culture appeared. His writing came even to span the Afro-Cubanist movement itself through his monographs on its painting, poetry, and music.

As his writing and thought evolved—some of his ideas changed to the
point where he abandoned race as a concept—Ortiz's basic ideology remained that of a liberal bourgeois reformist: positivistic, rationalistic, seeing the inevitable, gradual progess of Cuban history and society leading to
the obliteration of African culture on the island (Echevarria 1977:46–49;
Mullen 1987:117–19). On this he differed with the more radical Afro-
Cubanists. Afro-Cubanism proposed for the island a creole identity, a com-
posite multicultural, multiracial identity in which the African was central.
Afro-Cubanism opposed, therefore, both the anti-Africanist spirit of the
conservatives who, as we have seen, hoped to wipe out African culture and
religion by force and the liberal tendency, represented especially by the
early work of Ortiz, which sought to uplift and assimilate them out of existence (Carpentier 1946:236; Janney 1981:18.).

Afro-Cubanism became a dominant force on the literary scene around
1920 and soon showed up in the visual arts and concert music. Its period of
greatest activity was between 1926 and 1938. Journals were established and
a tremendous amount of creative and scholarly activity came out of the
movement. Much of this work depended on participation and firsthand
observation of the folk culture and religious life of Afro-Cubans and
brought many whites and mulattoes into contact with Santeria who might
never have sought it out otherwise (see Carpentier 1933 and Calvo 1932 as
examples). While the persisting historical rumor that Ortiz himself may
have become a convert to one of the Afro-Cuban religions in these years
has been denied by Nicolas Guillen, an at least tangential involvement with
the Afro-Cuban religions became fashionable during the period and some
other Cuban artists, intellectuals, and entertainers may very well have converted and practiced (Guillen 1969:6).

Afro-Cubanism was a complex artistic and intellectual response to the
crosscurrents of Cuban social and cultural life. What began as a movement
with more than its share of *épater le bourgeoisie* overtones gradually began to
concern itself with the social and political issues of the Afro-Cuban population as well as reevaluating the religious and cultural contributions of

Afro-Cubans. In some circles the movement came to be seen as politically as well as artistically radical, and at several points some of the leaders were imprisoned or forced into exile. By 1940 Afro-Cubanism no longer existed as a distinct and isolated movement; its main contributions had been absorbed into a place in the firmament of Cuban intellectual life.

It is difficult to evaluate the effect this movement had on the actual treatment, membership, and status of the Afro-Cuban religions during the 1920s and 1930s. Whatever the effects, they were probably restricted primarily to the intellectual centers in the cities. There the new vogue engendered a tolerance, and even an admiration, for Santeria which had not previously existed. It made involvement with the religion, if not entirely respectable, at least modish, exciting, and acceptable in some sectors of the middle class. The conversion of older and younger artists and intellectuals to the movement forced a shift in the perception of Afro-Cuban religion among some members of the middle class (black, white, and mulatto alike). Because of Afro-Cubanism it became possible to view Santeria as folklore rather than witchcraft and crime. The movement awakened interest in the Afro-Cuban as a cultural creator in religion as elsewhere and in the present as well as the past. It also proposed Afro-Cuban religion and Afro-Cuban culture more generally as inalienable parts of what it meant to be Cuban.

Although Afro-Cubanism extended a degree of legitimacy to Santeria and the other Afro-Cuban religions, the profound reevaluation of African culture this group of white and mulatto intellectuals brought about was by no means the dominant current in Cuban thought in the 1920s and 1930s. Afro-Cubanist ideas competed with anti-African and liberal reform tendencies throughout the period. Furthermore the majority of Cubans did not derive their image of Santeria from state officials, social reformers, or intellectuals but from the mass media and stereotypes embedded in popular culture.

When Harold Courlander made a trip to Cuba in 1941 to record Afro-Cuban liturgical music, an informant apprised him of the popular attitude toward Afro-Cuban religions by showing him newspaper clippings. Courlander commented:

Newspapers are hungry for this sort of thing. They present their material in the most factual news style, but the basic misunderstanding and misrepresentation is astonishing.

To most white Cubans the word "cult" is synonymous with "savagery" and "crime." Their knowledge of cults comes entirely from news columns and gossip. Journalistic reports tell of ritual murders by the Kimbisa people in various parts of the island, of all the horrible remnants of cult feasts found by the police, and the disappearance of children ("obviously" stolen for cult use) usually white. The chief delight seems to be recounting the objects seized by the police in raids, as though each one of them were prima facie evidence of debauchery and degradation . . . "objects dedicated to fetishism, images of Chango, snail shells, glass beads. . . ." (1944: 462–63)

Despite such a negative public image, devotees continued to worship even if in secret and santeros continued to attract a diverse clientele. Poor and rich came, white and black. Politicians often came to santeros for predictions and to pay for festivals to ensure that the African gods would help them get elected. Politicians found that sponsoring religious events of this kind was good propaganda even if the events were hidden from the eyes of most respectable Cubans (Lachatanere 1942:36). Several Cuban presidents actively courted the black secret societies to gain votes and support (Dominguez 1978:49).

Treatment of the Afro-Cuban religions continued to oscillate between periods of relative tolerance and periods of repression, just as it had before. Santero Nicolas Angarica, who lived through several of these periods of persecution, wrote with great bitterness of the mistreatment of people of African descent and its effects on the religion of Santeria.

> We are turned back in a dizzying way in our religion in Cuba. One of the basic points on which it rests or assents is to listen to, obey and respect the elders, it being understood that the eldest in consecration [to the orisha] by his condition as such, has seen, labored and learned the most; therefore he must have more experience in the matter than younger people. In reality this is the logic, but unfortunately in our religion in Cuba . . . here there is not one Lucumi who teaches anyone, not even his own son. They set aside the things of the religion because they fear what might happen: the continuous mistreatment aimed at them on the part of the Spanish authorities (and to which they submitted). With the advent of the Republic they were equally mistreated by their own countrymen who, forgetting that these Africans and their descendants poured out their blood for the liberty of this bit of earth, made false accusations against them and in many cases imprisoned them unjustly so that some influential personage could be pulled out of jail only afterwards to hold him against his will at the favor of politicians.
>
> Present day priests and priestesses cannot have forgotten the persecutions and absurd accusations that we have been made to suffer in a fully free Cuba. Even recent events such as occurred in the year 1944, when there was the case of Juan Jimaguas in the Perico; the author of this book himself has been the victim of an ignominious accusation. There were the trampling . . . of those little old people, their ochas [orisha shrines or altars] hurled out into the street, many so embarrassed, so shamed that they sickened and died. These outrages and abuses that the Africans and their closest descendants suffered infused such fear and heaviness into their souls that they chose not to teach the religion to their own sons. (Angarica n.d.:81)

The postindependence persecutions threatened to break the transmission of religious traditions from one generation to the next, but this was not the limit of their effects. He continues:

> For all these reasons brother Iguoros, we find that, as a rule, the majority of contemporary elders suffer from a defensive superiority complex about their

years of consecration and yet are ignorant of many of the basic points of our consecration. I will enumerate here a case of ignorance or bad faith on the part of an elder that was encountered at a ceremony where the officiating Orihate was as a disciple of mine. This was a Nangare and there was the singing, as is natural, mentioning all of the dead elders of the family. Calling, getting his attention was a woman, an elder, with forty or forty-five years of consecration saying to him "In the Nangare it is not necessary to invoke the Dead." My disciple informed me, with great sadness on his part, that he had affirmed, and I had to agree to this damning affirmation with as much pain, that this woman, in spite of having forty or fifty years of consecration, she did not know or was not acquainted with the origin of the Nangare. The Nangare, in distinct tribes of Yoruba territory as in Arataco, Egguado, Takua, Chango, etc. had a particular application: in these places it is employed uniquely and exclusively to refresh the Egun [the ancestors]. . . . All this was made in those territories or tribes because of the constant warfare the Yoruba sustained with other regions and with the purpose of pacifying the ancestral dead. It is for this purpose that they are mentioned in the song: to all the ancestral dead, relatives, acquaintances and the rest. (81–82)

The dizzying, upside down atmosphere Angarica faced in Cuba in the 1940s was one in which fathers no longer taught their sons, elders were ignorant of fundamentals known to the young, and the dead were in danger of truly passing out of existence through the ignorance and forgetfulness of their descendants.

The Ambivalence of Repression and Resistance

The main societal dynamic affecting the history of the Afro-Cuban religions in the postslavery period was the oscillation of the society's attitude between the poles of tolerance and repression. In summarizing the ground I have covered in this chapter, I will have to examine this ambivalence more closely. Why was there this back and forth swing? Why the ambivalence? Besides the economic and political factors I described earlier in this chapter, the answers seem to lie in part in a peculiar logic of power which is as curious and irrational as it is simple and persistent.

As a group the colonizer or dominant class tried to repress or destroy the colonized and their culture. A variety of motives intervene: racial, political, cultural, economic, psychological. One of the most important motives was to stem the movement for independence from Spain, a movement which, like the American Civil War, was linked to the abolition of slavery and the fate of Cuba's African population. Between 1868 and 1895 the colonial government and the Catholic Church closed ranks to battle against all the possible supporters of independence from Spain. They suppressed liberal ideas along with political separatists. Political parties, worker's organizations, and ethnic associations all had to resist to survive. The colonial government came to see the African cabildos as possible sources of insurrection and intervened more and more in their internal affairs.

As we have seen, when independence and the abolition of slavery did arrive in Cuba one of the results was a new heightened level of racism in which public racial discrimination was paired with efforts to attract European immigrants from abroad. The goal was to lighten the complexion of the island physically as well as culturally (Hoetink 1985:67).

The colonizer endowed the colonized with demonic and extraordinary powers. Projections of this kind arise in hierarchical regimes based on dominance with surprising frequency. Men impute a mystery to women, the civilized endows the primitive with a raw and eruptive power, the Christian perceives pagans to be in league with Satan or to be masters of demons if not demons themselves. The Europeans' own experiences and ideas concerning witchcraft surely affected their perceptions of African religions. In Catholicism the idea of magic includes the notion of false religion. This put the Afro-Cuban faiths out of the realm of religion and into the domains of magic and witchcraft at which the African priesthoods were presumed to be adepts (Mauss 1972:30). Yet some white Cubans did make use of African practitioners. This was true both before and after slavery but was probably even more widespread in the postslavery era. Indeed it seems that in the period covered by this chapter some whites from virtually all the classes, including the upper class, put their faith in black healers and sorcerers even as they called them brujos (witches) (Ortiz 1973:286–88). The repressors used the magical power of the repressed, in part a power with which the repressors themselves had endowed them. Ortiz traces the dominant class's faith in the magic of the Afro-Cuban underclass to a "not very solid" culture among the rulers of Cuban society but one also has to wonder about the role that the black healers played in this. It is peculiar and ironic for the ruled to sustain their rulers not only materially with their labor but also magically through their religious practices. An economy of money and magic arose between the two groups which, while acted out as a subaltern politics of magic, was still subordinated to a society where the rulers and ruled had very different places.

The dominant group was not only a group with group interests but also individuals with individual interests and selfish, entirely personal ambitions. Opposing the destructive tendencies of the colonial apparatus as a whole, there is a countervailing tendency which opposes individual's interests to those of the dominant group.

Hence members of the ruling class—as individuals—tried to make use of the alleged extraordinary powers of the ruled but within their own ruling group to advance individualistic ambitions. Politicians, frustrated lovers, vengeful business partners, defendants in lawsuits, the bewitched and sick—it was common for whites of all classes to avail themselves of black healers and sorcerers. The this-worldly and pragmatic outlook of the African religion was important. For whites who supplemented their Catholic adherence with African magical powers, the saints and the orisha were all powers that existed for use in the problems of this life and this world.

The endowing of the enslaved and the colonized with demonic and extraordinary powers does not exist solely as a facet of racism. It is a vital
element in aesthetic modernism as well. From its beginnings modernism
drew on a cult of the primitive and the exotic as sources of energy and inspiration. It needs to be asked whether, in essence, this is any different
from the upper class female who went to a santero for a love philter. In the
spirit of early modernism the European avant-garde tried to reform reality
by severing its own relationship to the past. The several faces of modernism
delighted in three refuges from the past: the gleaming, rationalized world
of modern technology (Futurism); exotic states of consciousness that could
be found within the self, such as insanity, hallucinations, and dreams (Ex-
pressionism, Surrealism); and non-Western, premodern societies where exotic states of consciousness were thought to be a normal part of waking life
(Primitivism). What the artists of Afro-Cubanism sought was the source of
an ejaculatory discharge of explosive force, a violent outbreak of feeling
that would blast away the moribund edifices of their own half-European
heritage. They declared that they had found it in the person of the Afro-
Cuban and in the lore of the Afro-Cuban religions. Just as influential politicians sometimes protected santeras whose owners helped them conquer
a heart or win an election, the success of Afro-Cubanism made it possible
for Cuban artists and intellectuals to present Santeria as folklore rather
than witchcraft and crime, and thereby build artistic reputations. Other
factors become evident as we follow out the ambiguous logic of repression
and resistance still further to its next step.

*The conquered acquired the accoutrements of the conqueror's power to protect
their own powers from detection.* After the turn of the twentieth century Cuban
blacks created a variety of political parties and other organizations to advance their cause. All this organizational and political activity yielded very
mixed results. The same period that saw Afro-Cubans elected to significant
seats in government also witnessed the 1910 ban on all political parties organized on a racial basis, the brutal crackdown on the Negro Revolt of
1912, and the continuing suppression of the Afro-Cuban cabildos.

For some believers today the equation of the saints and the orisha is not
real but is an historical residue, a practice standing over from when the Africans used the Catholic saints to mask the worship of their own deities.
This may also have been the case for some believers during the Santeria
period. For them syncretism was a strategy of subterfuge. It was assimilation in the service of preserving the tradition. The believer gave some to
keep some. This is analogous to what happened to the ritual drums during
the anti-Africanist campaigns in the early days of the republic. When the
anti-Africanist campaign focused on the African cabildos and the confiscation of religious drums, believers in the Afro-Cuban religions changed
the structure and construction of the drums. They added European features to them, metal keys and wooden strips, so that they looked more creole, less African, and could escape seizure (Nodal 1983). Once again, in the

process of resistance, the believer gave some to keep some. This apparently contradictory movement is accompanied by another which parallels that of the colonizer and which, while setting up the subaltern politics of magic mentioned earlier, can be either benign or predatory.

The conquered tried to acquire the accoutrements of the conqueror's power for individualistic advancement within their own group as well as within the wider society. Not all magic succeeds, and in practicing magic the Afro-Cuban inevitably experienced failures. Rather than skepticism, these failures may well have led to more complex efforts. In this case the individual seized upon key symbols of the powers of the dominant society and treated them as powerful symbols through which social realities can be manipulated by means of magical or religious rites. Viewed from below and in relation to social and magical power, to include the saints in the pantheon of the blacks was not necessarily submission to a higher power (even though it took place in the context of dominance of Catholic ideology and religious hierarchy) but was instead the acquisition of the saint's power. Thus these Africans did not convert to the saints but converted the saints to themselves; in this way the Africans came to possess the saint, in order to work their will through its means. As was the case with some whites, the saints of Catholicism and Espiritismo, along with the orisha, were all powers that existed for use in the problems of this life and this world. This takes us to the final step in the powerfully simple but peculiar logic we have been tracing.

The conquered, the enslaved, and the colonized acquired the symbolic accoutrements of the colonizer's or dominant class's power as one means of representing, to and for themselves, the situation they found themselves in and as a means of setting up a context in which they could make symbolic attempts to gain some control over that situation. The notion of a dominant ideology and a subordinate one is inadequate to describe the complex interplay that went on. Colonial Cuba had rested on a network of underground canals admitting the sorcery of three continents. After independence from Spain, the end of slavery, and the suppression of the African cabildos, the underworld of the culture of conquest folded into the culture of the conquered. This infolding was an active process and a jab at the eyes of church and state power. Catholicism, Espiritismo, and the Afro-Cuban religions were not mutually exclusive or self-contained; they contested with one another while often drawing on a shared pool of concepts and symbols (Hall 1985:104). Even so, Santeria and Espiritismo addressed themselves to the immediate issues of their devotees' worldly lives as well as promoting alternative views of the world and alternative bases for personal identity; that is why the church and the republic tried to stamp them out. State and church repression provoked resistance, but the arena in which that resistance took place guaranteed that some of what was being resisted would be absorbed. Santeria and Espiritismo resisted assimilation into the hegemony of the state and the church but were affected by them just the same because more diffuse forms of Catholicism permeated Cuban culture outside of the official institutions.

The earlier religious traditions that remained and diffused among the Cuban population, whether they were from Catholicism, Lucumi religion, or Espiritismo, were not simply testimony to the tenacity of tradition. Instead they were mythic images that reflected and condensed the appropriation of the history of conquest and made it available to the experience of contemporary believers. That history formed analogies and structural correspondences with the hopes and tribulations of the present. The variety of practices and mixed forms arising within Lucumi religion and forming the Santeria of this period represented the appropriation and incorporation of history into the present in a tradition which was imperiled both from within and from without.

Cuban Postscript

It is difficult to get a picture of the state of Santeria in either the city or the countryside on the eve of the Cuban Revolution of 1959. It may well have been in decline in the cities of western Cuba as a result of persecutions and disruptions in the preceding years. A study done in 1959 in La Guinea, an isolated and conservative all-black community in Las Villas Province, revealed a significant influence of Santeria as well as of the Bantu religion Palo. But Palo had been losing believers there since the 1930s, and Santeria had declined in importance, too, because the local religious leader had died and there was no one to replace him (Herrera 1972:145, 147–50). If La Guinea is in any way indicative of what was happening in the countryside, then both of these Afro-Cuban religions were on the wane before the revolution.

Santeria probably continued to serve the functions it always had: it satisfied the inner religious needs of a significant segment of the Cuban population, mainly people of African descent but also poor whites in the countryside and probably a wider spectrum of whites in the cities (Butterworth 1980:87). The African religion helped people cope with the problems of illness and the practical difficulties of everyday life. Within it believers created and maintained important social networks which were useful in themselves and a means for such upward mobility as Cuba's underdeveloped economy allowed for those who were a notch above blackness and poverty. Those who did not find enough fulfillment and recognition in work, play, or family could find it in the high prestige that believers gave to their priests and priestesses.

A wide range of variation in ritual and degree of Catholic versus African influence continued to exist both before and after 1959. At one end of the continuum were Santeria houses, the majority of whose rites imitated Catholic ceremonies complete with our fathers, hail marys, candles, incense, and the appropriate ritual gestures and material symbols. At the other end were houses where these Catholic elements never appeared. In these houses neither chromolithographs nor statues of the saints adorned the altars. Symbolic colors and stones represented the saints or orisha and the emphasis was on ceremonial spirit possession (MacGaffey and Barnett 1962:249–50; Thomas 1971:520; Butterworth 1980:88). Furthermore, among those who could still actually trace Yoruba descent, Santeria retained the specifically ethnic and kinship dimensions which, at an earlier period, had applied to all members. For some the worship of specific orisha still descended down family lines and the orisha was not only a deity but an ancestor as well (Thomas 1971:520).

Santeros fought on both sides during the struggle to overthrow the Batista government. Although some santeros fled the revolution, many could not and many did not. During the years of struggle the revolutionary guerrillas were not moved by antireligious feelings but were convinced that contradictions did not have to exist between the social revolution they hoped to win and the religious beliefs of the Cuban people (see *Granma* 1977, for example). The conflict between the revolution and religion was mainly a political conflict between the revolutionaries and the social class that tried to use the Catholic Church as a weapon to oppose the revolution. In the countryside attendance at Afro-Cuban religious activities was independent of all the cleavages that divided the communities and generally formed one of the few arenas for social participation beyond the family. Santeria and the other Afro-Cuban religions were a kind of social capital on which the revolution could build. Many women who had been heads of Afro-Cuban religious groups later emerged as leaders within the Cuban Women's Federation. In both the countryside and the cities the revolution was able to absorb leaders from the Afro-Cuban religions into some of its own political organizations (Dominguez 1978:484, 491).

Although the Castro government declared that there was no contradiction between the aims of religion and the aims of socialism, relations between religious groups and the socialist state oscillated between tolerance and repression. The Afro-Cuban religions rarely surfaced in discussions of the official policies toward religion. These policies were phrased in terms of church-state relations concerning the Catholic Church and, to a lesser extent, the Protestant sects. Since many santeros consider themselves Catholics, they were affected by official policies aimed at the Catholic Church and by policies aimed at religious groups in general.

The Catholic Church (including the Vatican) originally supported the revolution, but within a year of Castro's ascension to power the increasing suppression of religious freedom became a serious issue for the Vatican and for Cuban prelates. When the prelates organized protests, the government accused them of criminal and antirevolutionary campaigning and warned them to stay out of politics (Butterworth 1980:85). The revelation that two Catholic priests had participated as chaplains in the abortive 1961 Bay of Pigs invasion led to the arrest of priests on the island and the closing of churches. The government nationalized private education, thus eliminating the Catholic schools, and it confiscated church and Catholic school property, banned religious processions, and threatened to deport priests involved in political activity. Church-state relations began to improve around 1965, and Catholic churches were allowed to reopen but could not proselytize. Meanwhile Cuban youth continued to be taught an ideology which was at once nonreligious and atheistic. While the Cuban Communist party proclaimed "the right of believers to practice their religion with due respect for the law, the health of citizens and the norms of socialist morality" and subordinated the struggle for "a scientific concept, free of prejudice and superstition" to the struggle for social reconstruction, it neither encouraged nor supported any religious groups nor asked any favors of them (the quotations are from Communist Party of Cuba, Resolution of the First Communist Party of Cuba on Religion, 1975, 35, and Declaration of the First National Congress on Education and Culture, 1971).

The Castro government gave the Afro-Cuban religions public recognition as an element of the national cultural heritage. This recognition was not without its ambiguities and resulted in two paradoxes. The first was the paradox between the doctrine of a scientific, rational socialism and the respect for traditional Cuban folk beliefs and practices which is part of the liberal humanistic legacy of Afro-Cubanism. The second paradox was between public recognition and secrecy. Despite official recognition as an aspect of Cuban national identity, Santeria continued to be clandestine. Public recognition by the revolutionary government did not lead to a decrease in secrecy on the part of believers. The secrecy remained partly because it had become traditional and partly because people still feared the disapproval of the government.

Afro-Cuban religions received some tolerance and solicitude when the dance and music which are part and parcel of an entire religious complex were presented as "people's folklore." In the context of contemporary Cuban society, such folkloric performances of religious music and dance served not to promote religious practices but to desacralize them. In this guise the Afro-Cuban religions were represented by government-sponsored dance and theater companies which traveled throughout Cuba and to foreign countries. Outside of this zone of tolerance there existed a wider zone of ambiguity and conflict which conditioned the status of the Afro-Cuban religions. When folklore steps off the stage and erupts into the arena of everyday life, reactions can be quite different.

After the 1961 ban on religious processions was finally lifted, the annual pilgrimage to San Lazaro (Babaluaiye) at Santiago in Oriente Province could resume. On November 16 of every year a multitude of black Santeria devotees made pilgrimage to this shrine. According to Octavio Cortazar, who made a documentary film about this event, many of the pilgrims were descendants of Yoruba slaves. It would take the whole day for most of them to get there. They transported themselves by crawling on their stomachs or by crawling backward in a sitting position. Many women carried sick children on their backs, and cripples and the injured arrived dragging weights from their limbs. Cortazar interviewed Catholic priests, psychiatrists, workers, students, a leading santero, and the pilgrims themselves. What could be the meaning of such a pilgrimage in the midst of a socialist revolution, on the part of people who would otherwise consider themselves Marxist-Leninists? Cortazar's own comments probably mirror a major attitude of Cuban intellectuals of the period: "I was shocked when I saw them. The contradiction, the superstition. I cannot speak for the new generation and say they will not be religious. I cannot say that they will not believe in God. But I do know that with literacy, in the new Cuba this pilgrimage will not exist."

No religious group in Castro's Cuba suffered sanctions because of its beliefs, but some did suffer because of their actions if these were considered to be in political, ideological, or economic conflict with socialist reconstruction. This affected Santeria and the Afro-Cuban religions in a number of ways. In the early 1960s the Cuban National Institute of Ethnology and Folklore undertook investigations into African religious sects (*America Latina*, April–June 1964, Rio de Janiero; quoted in Moore 1970:71). Their studies were not purely anthropological in intent; they were also political. There were armed guerrilla bands of Afro-Cuban religious devotees who resisted and rebelled against the government and came into direct conflict with the revolution. Eldridge Cleaver witnessed the shooting of such a band during his troubled sojourn in Cuba in 1969 and gave a tantalizingly brief, muddled, and incomplete description of the band's symbols and beliefs (Gates 1976:201–2).

Aside from dealing with direct political opposition from antirevolutionary santeros, there is evidence that the Cuban government interfered in the religious practices of Santeria for ideological and economic reasons (MacGaffey and Barnett 1962:205; Crahan 1979:166, 181; Dominguez 1978). Some Afro-Cuban religious groups were subject to persecution because their African-based cosmologies did not distinguish between the sacred and the secular, an attitude incompatible with the ideology of the revolution. The tension from this went both ways. Some Afro-Cubans saw the Cuban National Folklore Ensemble as an attempt to destroy the Afro-Cuban religions (Moore 1970:71 n. 2). In the folkloric productions the Afro-Cuban religions were tamed and the worlds which the religions create in the lives and imaginations of their devotees were reduced to a much more partial one, a secular one defined as an entertainment. In an oft-cited series of articles criticizing the persistence of racism in postrevolutionary Cuba, Carlos Moore accused the Castro government of putting restrictions on the practice of Afro-Cuban religions. Members of the various Afro-Cuban religions were arrested on the pretext that they had organized their ceremonies on days other than those appointed by the government and that their practices were incompatible with socialist society (Moore 1970:61). Rationing and the elimination of private businesses made it difficult for believers to make the proper offerings and sacrifices to the orisha.

I have been told that when Santeria devotees performed obligatory sacrifices, which were increasingly under surveillance, all the meat not immediately offered to the African gods was confiscated by the government. To acquire the proper items became a difficult, expensive, and time-consuming operation. Despite the fact that ceremonies often had to be delayed or postponed and despite the difficulties santeros often had in bringing together everything needed for the ceremonies, they were able to obtain what they needed through networks of economic exchanges with relatives, other devotees, friends, neighbors, and people in the countryside. Because of their continuing secrecy, their ramified networks, and their mutual aid functions, the Afro-Cuban religions constituted an informal underground economy not under the control of the government and thus came into conflict with the revolution.

While some santeros were opposed to the revolutionary government, others were not or saw no relation between adherence to Santeria and either opposition or support of the government. Others regarded the separation of religion and politics as desirable and adopted the government's views on this while remaining believers and religious people. Lazaro Benedi, a santero and palero, was a prominent diviner before the revolution. In an interview with Oscar Lewis Lazaro, Benedi revealed an ambivalence toward the place of the African religions in the new socialist society, though he remained committed to both.

The fact that I am religious has not done me the slightest harm with the Revolution or in any other way. After all if the revolution didn't recognize the effectiveness of santeria, it would have suspended all religious festivities long ago. On the contrary, it leaves us totally free to belong to any religion as long as it doesn't interfere with politics.

I went to the museum of the African religion established by Fidel [at Guanabacoa] and was impressed. I'd never imagined a museum wholly dedicated to religion! I still think that the African religion will disappear completely, but I heard Fidel say that he wished they would build a temple to that religion, just as the masons and the Catholics have their temples.

I've had many arguments with Catholics and believers in the African religion, and have never been able to come to an agreement with any of them. There are those who say that the African religion is a myth, a dream, a web of deceit. But I, and all believers, have faith because we've had proof. . . . Each person must figure out whether he can reconcile his politics and his religion. . . . We cannot allow the confusion of politics and religion. . . . A man creates his own faith as he goes along. I believe in the African religion, but I've had faith in other things too. I believe the Revolution triumphed because of all the people who believed in Marti's ideas. When I find myself in difficult situations I concentrate on my faith, saying, "I do what I'm doing to save part of mankind and I trust this will help me" (Lewis, Lewis, and Rigdon 1977:130–31).

V.

Santeria in the United States (1959–1982)

With the advent of the Cuban Revolution a sizable number of Cubans sought refuge in the United States or Latin American countries. From 1959 through 1962 the exodus was composed largely of middle- and upper-class Cubans hostile to Castro. By 1968, 55,354 Cubans resided in the United States (Fagen 1968:54). Cubans continued to enter the States without hindrance from immigration quotas until 1973. By then the socioeconomic status of the immigrants had dropped and the lower middle and urban working classes predominated. By 1979 Dade County, Florida, alone had 430,000 Cubans who had arrived there since 1959 (Sandoval 1979:142.) The May 1980 release of prisoners to the United States from Mariel brought in 120,000 more Cubans. Cubans appeared in increasing numbers in New York City, Union City, New Jersey, and Washington, D.C. Some were Santeria devotees in Cuba, but more seem to have become involved after leaving the island. Santeria now almost certainly has more devotees in the United States than it had in Cuba at the time of the revolution.

The racial composition of the exiles and refugees is not representative of the population of Cuba. In 1970, the last year for which racial data were available on Cuban Americans, the group was 96 percent white, 3.1 percent black, and 0.9 percent other (Boswell and Curtis 1984: 102–3; U.S. Census, Subject report b (2) IC 1970). Seventeen years earlier, Cuba's island population was 27 percent mulatto, nine times that of the later Cuban-American population (Aguirre 1976:104; Boswell and Curtis 1984:103). The majority of nonwhite Cubans live in the northeastern states, especially the New York–New Jersey area where my research was conducted. However, most Cubans residing in the United States are considered white, and this is true of the senior Santeria priesthood as well (Aguirre 1976:115.) As we have seen, over the course of their development the secret African religious practices ceased to be solely the exclusive property of people of African descent; they were also passed on to people of mixed ancestry. In at least one Cuban city, Regla, a strong tradition of Santeria was practiced primarily by the Hispano-Cubans who constituted the majority of Regla's population (Lachatanere 1942:33).

Spirits in Exile

Despite the relative success of their adaptation to U.S. society, members of the first generation of exiled Cubans experienced a great deal of stress from a number of sources. The elderly in particular exhibited the harassed double consciousness of the exile. Behind was the past, loss, separation, nostalgia for the old ways, and sometimes death; ahead was the future with its uncertainties, fears, and imagined perils. In the present, though, were all the problems of adjusting to a society of strangers with a different language and customs. Furthermore, Cuban émigrés entered the United States during a period in which it was experiencing one of the most profound social, cultural, and political upheavals in its history. What would have been a trying experience in any case was made even more problematic by the struggles and movements for social and cultural change of the 1960s and 1970s. Psychedelics, flower power, the civil rights and black power movements, women's liberation, and the national crisis of conscience over the Vietnam War leading to a series of economic recessions created a dense and confusing context in which to adjust amid the profusion of positions and responses. The Cubans seemed to be trying to get a foothold in a society poised on the brink of chaos and confusion. This was reflected in the relations between parents and children, especially in the differing rates of adaptation to the new culture which are evident between generations (Rumbaut and Rumbaut 1976:397). Experiencing the same kinds of stress, the younger generation may react quite differently because of its greater cognizance of U.S. culture, particularly U.S. youth culture.

Typical psychiatric symptoms of Cuban expatriates relate quite directly to this situation. Depression, intense overwhelming anxiety, and inability to surmount the complex emotional problems presented by the anomie of exile were frequent in the expression of these psychiatric patients (Ascarte 1970, quoted in Rumbaut and Rumbaut 1976:396). Fertility was very low for Cuban Americans as compared with other U.S. ethnic groups, and the population seemed to be aging with declining fertility (Boswell and Curtis 1984:101, 108; Jaffe, Cullen, and Boswell 1980:51–62). In a group where so much of a woman's identity depends on marrying, having children, and working at home, the inability to have children provokes a constant psychological and cultural strain.

The role of culture, particularly magic and religion, complicates the picture Cuban Americans present in their encounters with mainstream physicians. Psychiatrists have remarked on the predominance of religious-mystical phenomena in the manifestations of emotional disorder among Cubans (Rubinstein 1976:76–77; Bustamante 1968:115–16). When Santeria emerges as an element of the cultural overlay underlying this process, the physician may be presented with what appears to be a frank delusional system but is in reality a deeply held religious belief spreading beyond its normal context and domain (Bustamante 1968). Hence there are real dangers of misdiagnosis for Cuban patients with American doctors.

It is not surprising that some Cuban Americans should go to santeros for help. In the santero they find a healer who speaks their language, shares their basic culture and world view, is able to describe and explain the problems they have, and can set in motion a course of action to deal with them. The adaptive nature of Santeria as a system of health care, particularly for mental health, has been seen as a factor promoting its persistence and growth here (Sandoval 1979).

In New York and New Jersey immigrants from Cuba and Puerto Rico have been extremely uncomfortable in the Irish- and Italian-dominated Catholic churches. Discrimination, poverty, the language barrier, and the paucity of real efforts by the church to reach out and embrace them led many Cubans and Puerto Ricans to view the church as rigid, unresponsive, and unable to help them in their daily ordeals. Many of these people leave Catholicism entirely and become Pentecostals or irreligious. Others go into some noninstitutionalized religious group with persisting Catholic connections such as Espiritismo or Santeria, sometimes both.

Lourdes Arguelles has noted the existence of anti-Castro groups in Florida that are grounded in Santeria. These are military, paramilitary, and political organizations involving older Cuban exiles and some younger Cuban males.

> They have some following among the younger Cubans who they train in covert operations and paramilitary techniques. Connections with organized crime are close and date back to pre-revolutionary Cuba. The subcultural milieu of their terrorist groups, which are divided into military and political units, is dominated by "Santeria," the Afro-Cuban syncretist tradition of superstition and ritual. . . . Participation in these groups is closely associated with low income and status and/or social discrepancy. (1982:299).

As far as I am able to tell, there were Santeria priests living in New York before the Cuban Revolution. My informants all agreed that the first Santeria priest of Ifa to reside in the United States was Francisco (Pancho) Mora. Mora came to the United States in 1946 and resided in New York until his death in 1986. In 1954 he initiated the first santera in Puerto Rico. He is credited with holding the first American Santeria drum-dance in 1964, and he initiated priests as far away as Venezuela, Argentina, Columbia, and Mexico. At one point he tried to found a mutual aid society for incoming santeros, but his plans to form a legal federation and to acquire a building in which to conduct rites never came to fruition.

Mercedes Noble has been credited with initiating the first priestess in North America, Julia Franco, in 1962. Noble was born in Cuba of parents from the United States and initiated as a priestess of Santeria there in 1958. In New York she headed a multiethnic Santeria house composed of Americans, Cubans, and Puerto Ricans. Leonore Dolme, a Cuban santera who came to the United States right after the revolution, seems to have initiated the first black American priestess on United States soil in Queens, New York, in 1961. This was Margie Baynes Quiniones, now deceased. Dolme no longer lived in New York at the time of my research. Her house, like Noble's was multiethnic, composed of Cubans, black Americans, and Puerto Ricans.

In addition to those inducted into Santeria on the mainland, a trickle of U.S. converts obtained their initiations in Cuba. The first native black American to be initiated into the Santeria priesthood appears to have been Oba Osejiman Adefunmi I, born Walter King. He went to Cuba in 1959 to be initiated into the priesthood in Matanzas Province just before the revolution. Upon his return he set up a public temple for the religion, the Shango Temple, and incorporated it as the African Theological Archministry. When he moved the temple to Harlem in 1960, it was renamed the Yoruba Temple. The Puerto Rican priestess Assunta Seranno, recently deceased, initiated priests in the Yoruba Temple when Adefunmi functioned under a ban that forbade him to do so. Seranno became a santera in Puerto Rico in 1960 and initiated Judith Gleason, who appears to have been one of the earliest, if not the earliest, Anglo-American priestesses initiated in the United States.

New Forms in New York

Two new formations of Santeria evolved in relationship to Phase III Santeria, the persisting form in the United States. I have encountered both of them myself, but in the accounts which follow I will also make use of the accounts of other researchers. The perspective here gives evidence of ongoing processes of change and structuration. What has been, and is, occurring in these formations points up how Santeria takes on the coloration of subcategories of ethnic groups which, in the context of ethnic, ideological, and economic competition, make decisions affecting the content of their religious ideology and practice. It should be noted that in both formations the exchange has taken place during the emergence of new ethnic identities.

In the mid-1960s anthropologists began to identify a new religious and folk medical form, Santerismo, which was emerging in the Bronx borough of New York City. This emerging form, which I have dubbed Phase IV Branch 1, is essentially a variant of Espiritismo which shows influences of Santeria. Although it has been found for the most part in the Puerto Rican spiritist *centros,* there is no reason to assume that its practice is restricted to Puerto Ricans. Most spiritist centros in New York are multiethnic in leadership, and the clientele and developing mediums frequently circulate among a wide number of centros run by mediums from different Hispanic ethnic groups. But because this practice has been so closely identified with Puerto Ricans by its students and appears to have a special meaning and relevance in relation to Puerto Rican religion and identity in New York, I will consider it especially in relation to them. The term *Santerismo* is an elision of the words *Santeria* and *Espiritismo* and refers to the emerging variant of Puerto Rican Espiritismo which has resulted from the incorporation of elements of Santeria into its ideological and ritual structures.

It appears that earlier students of Puerto Rican Espiritismo may have inadvertently come across instances of this emergent form but were unable to distinguish it from older spiritist practices. (This seems to have been the case with Leutz 1976 and Salgado 1974). In a paper published in 1974 Steiner identified instances of what we now know as Santerismo. He evidently recognized it as being something but did not see it as a coherent form or trend. Instead he viewed it as simply an idiosyncratic instance of the unruly "ecumenism" of spiritist cults (471).

Between 1966 and 1967 Garrison found, among the fourteen spiritist centros she studied in the Bronx, two which had introduced elements of Santeria into their practice (1977). One of them was headed by a woman who had been initiated into the Santeria priesthood in Cuba years before. Despite the fact that this priestess endeavored to keep the two practices apart and made clear intellectual distinctions between what was Espiritismo and what was Santeria, in her actual work within the context of her Espiritismo *reuniones* Santeria elements appeared. One result of this was that Garrison's work was the first to clearly distinguish the two religions and hence note the syncretism that was occurring. Harwood (1977) found that four of the six Bronx centros he studied between 1967 and 1969 were of this same type and practiced what he called the Santeria variant of Espiritismo. Harwood even went to the point of mistakenly identifying this variant of Espiritismo with Santeria itself. Harwood also thought that Santeria existed indigenously in Puerto Rico and that the syncretism observed in New York was the result of the erosion of status differences that had existed on the island and which had kept the two practices apart there (52). Given his mistaken identification of Santerismo with Santeria and the fact that there is no evidence of a tradition of Yoruba-Catholic practice akin to Santeria ever existing in Puerto Rico, little credence can be given to these statements. Santerismo evidently is arising from the interaction of Puerto Rican spiritists with practitioners of Afro-Cuban Santeria in the United States.

The major inroads of Santeria into Puerto Rican Espiritismo seem to be in the form of ideological referents. The espiritista distinguishes between *guías* (spirit guides who readily manifest in mediumistic trance, frequently presenting themselves as ethnic stereotypes and belonging to the class of "good" spirits) and saints, who are "pure" spirits, more remote and less accessible than spirit guides. Some people have saints as protectors and ritually treat these saints in the Catholic mode with prayer, candles, and requests. They do not expect the saints to communicate with them or to reveal themselves in any way. Still others, however, have identified the saints with the Yoruba deities and see them in trance as if they were spirit guides. In this sense the saint or orisha undergoes a double degradation. As a saint he or she becomes degraded to the status of a readily accessible lesser spirit within the spiritist hierarchy. As the orisha he or she becomes subject to the same stereotyping process as has led to the formation of the other ethnic spirit guides present in Espiritismo: in Garrison's words, "the Madama (a Black motherly type who was a curandera, or herbalist, and often a slave, in her material life), the Congo (a strong African), the Indio (a virile independent type), the Hindu (a wise philosophical spirit), the Gitano(a) (gypsy)." The orisha, then, take their place alongside this parade of older contributors to Espiritismo's pantheon, and this points to an ongoing process of accretion and consolidation within spiritist ideology. These ethnic stereotype spirit guides may be ideological representations referring to earlier syncretisms of healing cult practices from a variety of sources (Garrison 1977:83, 89). However, once this happens the orisha are no longer what they were within the context of Santeria and their status within Espiritismo also becomes inherently ambiguous. Harwood has described the spirit hierarchy within Santerismo (see figure 3).

The major way in which the orisha are represented in Santerismo is in chants, prayers, and chromolithographs to the Seven African Powers. This septet of orisha is not reported as a group in the classic Cuban Santeria monographs of Cabrera and Ortiz nor in the research of others who studied Cuban and Puerto Rican communities in New York and Miami in the mid to late 1960s and early 1970s (Cabrera 1971; Ortiz 1973a; Garrison 1977; Halifax and Weidman 1973; Sandoval 1977, 1979). But both Gonzalez-Whippler (1973) and Perez y Mena (1977) have identified them among Puerto Ricans in New York.

> The septet of African Powers controls every aspect of life with Chango (Santa Barbara) representing sensual pleasure; Eleggua (Holy Guardian Angel) opportunity; Obatala (Our Lady of Mercy—Las Mercedes) peace and harmony among people; Oshun (Our Lady of Caridad de Cobre), marriage; Oggun (Saint Peter), war and work for the unemployed; Orunla (Saint Francis of Assisi), gives power by opening the doors to the past and the future; and lastly, Yemaya (Our Virgin of Regla) fertility and maternity. (Perez y Mena 1977:133)

These correspondences are not entirely uniform. Harwood has identified syncretized forms not reported by other researchers. Other correspondences besides these have been reported for New York. Borello and Mathias (1977) and Harwood (1977) both report Saint Anthony of Padua as syncretized with Eleggua, and Borello and Mathias report Saint Martin de Porres, a black saint, as syncretized with one of the orisha but do not identify which. I have seen one representation of the Seven African Powers in which the Ibeji were included. In another very popular representation of the Seven African Powers the orisha names appear above typical orthodox renderings of the images of the corresponding Catholic saints. In the cen-

God
Pure spirits
Eternal entities of space (*angels, seraphim, and others*)
Saints/orisha
Heroes and leaders
Spirits of ordinary people
Intranquil spirits
Incarnate spirits

FIGURE 3. Santerismo spirit hierarchy (Harwood 1977:40).

ter appears the crucified Christ captioned as Olofi. Above Olofi's head appears a Virgin Mary which is uncaptioned.

The Seven African Powers are represented in chromolithographs, on glass votive candles, and in commercially printed prayers by their Catholic manifestations as saints. These syncretized orisha are brought over as a group and set into the ideological system of Espiritismo. The liturgical songs of the orisha appear in the centros on phonograph records, and the ritual elements that appear are often no more extensive than the giving of bead necklaces (collares) in the color patterns of the individual Seven Powers. The form of the collares has also been taken over, and new color patterns have been invented to represent other entities in Santerismo. I have seen these being sold in *botánicas* as "collares de espiritismo." The remaining orisha known to Santeria remain outside the new form's pantheon and have no representations of any kind.

Unlike Santeria, Santerismo is conducted in public centros where its leaders provide reuniones and consultations after the manner of other spiritists. The collares, the Seven African Powers, and the playing of recordings of orisha songs are important elements in their reuniones and make them distinctive, but none of the researchers reports the ritual dancing which is such an important part of many Santeria events and ceremonies. While some cult leaders adopt the trappings of Santeria's fictive kinship system and call themselves *madrina* or *padrino*, their relationships with their clientele retain the transitory, episodic nature typical of the espiritista and her client. The congregations of these mediums are constantly in flux, and the lifelong bond between the madrina and ayijado found in Santeria does not exist. Neither does the conception of the congregation as a religious family with obligations toward each other as well as toward the leader. Some leaders of these groups actually identify their practice to the public as Santeria. Other mediums have adopted some of the simple lower-level rituals of Santeria and call themselves santeros or santeras even though they have no affiliation with a Santeria cult house. Others are mediums who have several initiations in Santeria but are not fully initiated into the priesthood. While it is often said that priests who perform both Santeria and Espiritismo should practice them in different places, it is clear that many do not. Their economic condition and resources often simply will now allow for it.

Santeria priests are ambivalent about the practice of Espiritismo in that some think that it is bad for the santeros' heads for them to also work the dead; others believe that the santeros must mature in the Espiritismo before they can develop fully in Santeria. The relationship of Santeria to Espiritismo therefore remains ambivalent: it is either bad for the santeros' relationship with their orisha, good as a subordinate less powerful practice, or useful as a complementary system specialized for specific purposes.

> Santero(a)s insist that clients must be freed of all these malevolent spirit influences before they can undergo any of the major initiation rituals of Santeria. In Santeria the working of the dead is seen as a means of symptom alleviation, while the rites of the orisha are devoted to gaining health, personal and interpersonal power, and success. Thus, for the purposes of curing specific complaints Santero(a)s may also practice "the work of the dead" or they may refer clients to Espiritistas to have their malevolent spirits "lifted." (Garrison 1977:95)

This development has given birth to a number of distinctions which adepts now use to differentiate the practices. Older versions of Espiritismo, called "mesa blanca," are clearly differentiated from the incipient Santerismo. This distinction, while not new, takes on added salience with the emergence of Santerismo. Espiritismo as a whole, however, is also differentiated from all other occult practices, the others (including Santeria) being grouped together as Espiritualismo (i.e., spiritualism as opposed to spiritism.) Proponents of Santerismo, however, insist that they are spiritists. They also insist that santeros are, too. Puerto Rican Santerismo mediums have taken over the Cuban distinction between "the work of the saints" and "the work of the dead" which had evolved in the context of Santeria's encounter with Espiritismo in Cuba. That distinction did not exist in Puerto Rico (Brown and Garrison 1981:6). The "white table" espiritistas do not work the saints and, in their role as Santeria priests, santeros do not work the dead. Santerismo practitioners claim to do both.

The emerging practice is judged harshly by both espiritistas and santeros. Espiritistas see the major motive for people going into this practice as being the ability to charge fees. Espiritistas do not do this, but santeros do. By assimilating themselves to a position of santero or santera, the Santerismo mediums can take over one of the attributes of Santeria's specialized priesthood, the ability to demand and the right to receive fees for ritual services. This leads the espiritistas, even those who do not harbor a hostility to Santeria, to see the Santerismo mediums as exploitative. Many white table espiritistas, however, are hostile to Santeria and regard it as a form of black magic. Such people would regard Santerismo with horror even if the issue of economic exploitation was not involved. Many santeros, on the other hand, also condemn the Santerismo mediums for their treatment of the saints as low level spirit guides and see them as charlatans who claim powers in relation to the orisha which they cannot possess because they have not undergone the proper initiations and do not use Santeria's divination techniques. These distinctions, which are so clear to the adepts, are a source of confusion to the general run of clients seeking help. The clients often have difficulty telling one type of practitioner from another.

Much of this seems to be about three things: the evaluation of blackness in relation to Puerto Rican ethnic identity, the effect of spiritism on blackness as an element of ethnic identity, and interethnic competition between Puerto Ricans and Cubans. Roger Bastide, in a discussion of the role of Kardecan spiritism in Afro-Brazilian religion, once remarked that in the use of spiritism by these groups "it is clear that what we have here is a re-interpretation of the African ancestor cult and the cult of the dead through Kardec's spiritualism [sic]" (1971:168). The effect of this reinterpretation, though, is not necessarily a strengthening of the African practices. In relation to the rest of the system it may well become a means of negating the residual African culture in societies where there were significant numbers of enslaved Africans. Bastide sees this also and in another context remarks that

> spiritism represents a means of ascent to the man whose hopes and aspirations are blocked by the dual barrier of color and social class. It is the only means through which children of darkness, imprisoned in their skin, can dream of transforming themselves, in their future existence, into children of light. (1978:338)

Hence the effect of Puerto Rican Espiritismo on the evaluation of blackness is ambiguous both on the island and in New York. The clash between the realm of the sacred and the powers of secularization and capitalism which occurred in Cuba had their counterparts in Puerto Rico. But nothing comparable to Santeria existed there. Instead, what occurred was an erosion of black heritage, an erosion so corrosive that many of the practices derived from Puerto Rico's blacks are now no longer identified with them (Perez y Mena 1982:44). While belief in spirits and even communication with them was a common thing in Puerto Rico and some form of African ancestor veneration probably existed on the island at some point, when Espiritismo became important there its effect in relation to blackness was also paradoxical. At the same time that Espiritismo provided a means by which the upper classes, not wanting to identify themselves with the Africans, could still do what the Africans and lower classes did, i.e., communicate with spirits albeit "scientifically," it also provided a legitimization of the ancestor veneration already flourishing there (Perez y Mena 1982:36).

The paradox is further extended by the observation that the resurgence of spiritism in Puerto Rico over the past thirty years can be connected with unsettled conditions on the island, with confusions of identity, disruption of traditional norms, anomie. This collective insecurity feeds into the desire for power, understanding, and relief. But it also feeds into projections of fear, and that collective fear has often been directed by "white" Puerto Rican spiritists at black Puerto Rican spiritists without an understanding of the African origins of the practices of both groups (Seda Bonilla 1969:112–13, 152).

Espiritismo, which has a lower-class black image on the island of Puerto Rico and is associated with areas reputed to have a high concentration of people of African descent, is redefined by Puerto Ricans who migrate to New York. There it is ceases to be represented as confined to one segment of the population or restricted to only a few areas of the island. In the new context practitioners begin to view Espiritismo as a strong symbol of a specifically Puerto Rican identity (Brown and Garrison 1981:21; Morales-Dorta 1975; Harwood 1977.) Practice of Espiritismo becomes a symbol of the homeland, almost a national or ethnic symbol representing an identity that contrasts with general American norms and values. The eruption of blackness, in the form of the Seven African Powers present in Santerismo, therefore represents an affirmation of Africa as an aspect of Puerto Rican ethnic identity. Once the Seven African Powers become encapsulated and redefined with the context of Santerismo's ideology and embedded in its symbolism, they cease to be Cuban. They have been appropriated ideologically, and in terms of ethnicity they have become Puerto Rican. This is possible for Puerto Ricans on the mainland, and is found there, because of the forging of new self-definitions that the Puerto Rican undertakes as the result of the total migrant situation, including contacts with Cuban santeros. The acceptance of the orisha, the botánicas, and a positive approach to the African heritage as a means of symptom alleviation allows the migrant to accept as positive an element which was negative on the island (Perez y Mena 1982:50).

All this, however, is on the level of ideology. Whether the practitioner calls the practice Santeria or something else, neither rejection nor acceptance of this label prevents the incorporation of elements of Santeria ritual.

The bringing over of the Santeria ritual paraphernalia also brings over an aspect of the santero role which justifies payment. In Santeria the saints always work for a fee, and this concept is incorporated into Santerismo along with the ritual materials. As Perez y Mena has observed, the effect of this is the professionalization of the spiritist and the desire to imitate some aspects of the social organization of Santeria (1982:374–75). The Santerismo spiritist puts himself or herself into competition with the santero by trying to build a socioeconomic organization comparable to the cult house and by arming himself or herself with a version of the santero's powers, rituals, and paraphernalia in order to compete for clients. At the same time the Santerismo spiritist continues to place his or her beliefs, practices, and terminology within the ideology of Espiritismo. For those leaders who view Santeria as sorcery or black magic, this allows them to discourage clients from going to the Cuban santeros. For those who do not hold this belief, it allows them to mark themselves off from the santeros in terms of the spiritist's acknowledged supremacy in the work of the dead.

The second new formation of Santeria, Orisha-Voodoo, which I have dubbed Phase IV Branch 2, needs to be looked at from a dual frame of reference and within a dual ideological context. To understand it fully one needs to look at it in relationship to the black nationalist movements of the 1960s and to persisting Santeria. As an arm of the black nationalist movement, Orisha-Voodoo differed from other black nationalist groups in that its ethos and cultural ideal derived from Yoruba religion. From the point of view of Santeria, Early Orisha-Voodoo represented a semi-independent offshoot which had dispensed with the worship of the Catholic saints or any connection with the Catholic Church. It was composed of U.S.-born blacks who departed from Santeria tradition in their orientation toward Africa rather than Cuba as their homeland and in a number of other ways, such as their promotion of traditional Yoruba social practices, including polygamy, and their revival of the cult of the ancestors.

The movement was begun by Oba Ofuntola Osejiman Adelabu Adefunmi I in 1959. Adefunmi was born as Walter King in Detroit in 1928. He was baptized a Christian at age twelve but withdrew from the Baptist Church at sixteen. By that time he had already begun studying about Africa and African dance and ballet. Undoubtedly his father, a former member of the Moorish Science Temple and a participant in Marcus Garvey's Universal Negro Improvement Association in the 1920s, had a profound influence on him as a young man. His first exposure to African religion was when he joined the Katherine Dunham Dance Troupe in 1948. He left the troupe in 1950, settling in New York, working as an artists' model there, and making trips to Egypt, Europe, and the Caribbean. It was in New York in 1954 that he joined the African nationalist movement and began to found nationalist political organizations based on the practice of African religion. This was a period marked by much study of anthropological and political literature, attempts at liaisons with Haitian Vodun practitio-

ners and the remains of the old Harlem Garveyite movement, and cultivation of personal relationships with Africans and people knowledgeable
about African culture. In 1959 he went to Matanzas, Cuba, and was initiated into the Santeria priesthood as an Obatala priest, making him the first
Afro-American to do so. Once back in New York he founded the Shango
Temple with Chris Oliana, a Cuban who had gone with King to Cuba and
had received initiation into the priesthood at that time. King and Oliana
parted ways before the year was over and the Shango Temple dissolved. In
1960 King incorporated his organization as the African Theological Archministry, moved it to East Harlem, and renamed it the Yoruba Temple. By
this time he was using his African name, Oseijiman Adefunmi.

In its early days the Yoruba Temple was extremely race conscious. Adefunmi taught a mixture of political nationalism and African culture. Later
he began to emphasize the need for cultural redemption and encouraged
members of the temple to find personal and racial identity through studying African dance, music, and art as well as wearing African dress and
learning the Yoruba language. He stressed that black nationalism did not
have to be destructive and eschewed all forms of racism. For example,
whites were allowed to attend all but the most secret of the temple's ceremonies. "There is no room for racism in our religion," he said. "If the religion is valid for blacks, it applies to whites as well. We teach that when an
Afro-American has self-respect, he has no need to fear or hate the white
man" (quoted in Clapp 1966:5).

This did not mean that he did not see a fundamental opposition between African and Western cultures. He did: "The purpose of Western culture is to perfect the physical world. Africans want to perfect the spiritual
environment. Our achievement is 'human technology.' Here in America we
have been briefly conquered by European culture, but we are Africans
nonetheless." He and his followers found the resolution of this conflict in
the practice of Orisha-Voodoo. This involved utilizing the orisha idiom as
an array of personality types for blacks to use in the search for a personal
and cultural identity.

> Adefunmi said that Orisha-Voodoo involved a worship of one's own personality,
> with the recognition that one must limit the forces controlling the personality.
> The religion was frankly idolatrous, but idolatry made good psychological sense
> because it gave worshippers a set of ideal types they could use to understand
> themselves. Africans had been robbed of such ideal types when they were
> brought to America. "People can find their identity through their own partic-
> ular god," he said. "The religion has resulted in the rehabilitation of a lot of
> mixed up people." (Clapp 1966:16)

Alongside this emphasis on cultural, spiritual, and psychological issues,
Adefunmi remained active politically. The basic beliefs of his organization,
including the belief that black Americans constituted a cultural and historical "nation within a nation," served as his idiom of affiliation within the

broader black nationalist movement (Cohn 1973:6–7). As a result Adefunmi was able to develop lasting and cooperative relationships with the
Nation of Islam and the Republic of New Africa, of which he was at one
time minister of culture. He drew on these links in forming the African
National Independence Partition Party in 1961. This party aimed at securing an African state in America by 1972. The Yoruba Temple's special
place within the movement, though, was secured by its insistence that the
only solution to the creation of a viable African nationality in the United
States was the creation of a distinct culture through the practice of Orisha-
Voodoo, the ancestral religion, and training in African culture as a form of
"nationality education." By ever-deepening involvement in Orisha-Voodoo
and the permeation of more and more areas of their lives with African culture, values, and social forms, blacks would be able to "get back" to their
true selves. They could be reclaimed from their current condition as the
"walking dead," the "culture starved," a people suffering from "cultural
amnesia," "begging and whining for deliverance from an alien god" (Cohn
1973:30).

Adefunmi strove to place the Yoruba Temple and Orisha-Voodoo ideology into a broad international, diasporic context. He presented Orisha-
Voodoo as the core of the religious beliefs and practices of millions of
people throughout West Africa, the Caribbean, and South and Central
America. Regardless of the names of particular cults in particular places or
the varying degrees of Christian influence, he believed the core of the religions of Santeria, Vodun, Candomble, Macumba, etc. was Orisha-Voodoo,
purest at its place of origin in Nigeria. Orisha-Voodoo had been forced to
adapt to the conditions of different localities and circumstances throughout its existence, and the Yoruba Temple's work was simply another variation on this theme. Its ideological and ritual adaptations were especially
legitimate because they represented a return to pristine Yoruba values and
social forms. Given the common cultural heritage of all these groups
(Santeria, Vodun, etc.) it should be possible for them to unite on the bases
of their shared African religious forms and their shared experience of
white Christian domination.

Setting Orisha-Voodoo in this broad international context served several purposes. First, it legitimized Adefunmi's position as a priest by giving
him an ideological affiliation with Santeria. It also legitimized his use of
Cuban and Puerto Rican priests in his followers' eyes and in the eyes of the
Santeria priesthood as well. Second, it placed his relationship with the Cuban Santeria establishment in a framework in which he could explain his
actions not in terms of faithfulness to the values of Santeria per se but in
terms of the African origin and values that gave both Santeria and Orisha-
Voodoo their core heritage. Finally, after setting the Yoruba Temple, the
Haitian Vodun, and the Cuban and Puerto Rican Santeria priests in this
common internationalist framework, he could invoke the core African her-

itage of each group as a basis on which they could organize politically under the banner of black cultural nationalism.

In the hierarchy of the Santeria priesthood Adefunmi belonged to the lowest rank, the olorisha, or owner of the gods. Furthermore, he had been told that he was destined to become a babalawo, an Ifa diviner. That made it impossible for him to initiate people into the Santeria priesthood. He relied on Assunta Serrano, a Puerto Rican woman who had been initiated into the priesthood in Puerto Rico, to do this. Serrano was an espiritista medium as well and held spiritist sessions at the temple for its members. Adefunmi was also forced to rely on the presence of Cuban and Puerto Rican santeros to legitimize the temple's initiations. The presence of a Cuban babalawo at the initiation of a new priest was absolutely mandatory if the initiate was to be recognized within the Santeria community. While attaching himself to Cuban and Puerto Rican priests to study rituals with them in both New York and Puerto Rico, he also continued reading anthropological works and other sources of information on Yoruba and West African religion.

Adefunmi's relationships with the established Cuban priesthood became strained as time went on, but especially so after the founding of the African Nationalist Partition Party. The Cubans were not eager to introduce Santeria to black Americans on a large scale. In Cuba everything about the religion was secret, and the Cuban priests did not share Adefunmi's desire to proselytize among blacks. Furthermore there seem to have been some elements of racism and ethnic prejudice in their attitudes. They felt blacks were not ready for the religion and would denigrate it or, worse still, attract the attention of the police (Hunt 1979:27). There were other differences, too. Some members of the established priesthood did not view Santeria as being African in origin at all but saw it as having always been a Cuban occult practice. "There was some resentment among certain white Cubans when informed that the Religion was of African origin. They had come to regard it as a Cuban form of freemasonry!" (Adefunmi 1981:4).

In spite of their reliance on the Cuban priests, Orisha-Voodooists (Yorubas) did many things that opposed their practices. Adefunmi had built a public temple. This outraged the Cubans. Santeria's long history of persecution in Cuba had made secrecy not only an external adaptation to attack but almost an independent cultural element in its own right which defined Santeria as occult. In the new American context Santeria was not a suppressed religious sect but a secret society. It was not so much that Adefunmi endangered himself or other santeros. What he had done was break a socioethnic, rather than a religious, taboo. A similar instance of taboo breaking was his dispensation of Yoruba names. In Santeria, knowledge of an initiate's Yoruba or Lucumi name was the mark of being an insider and the names were used only among priests. Adefunmi gave out Yoruba names freely to women who came to the temple seeking names for their children and even to temple members who had not yet been initiated into the priesthood. Moreover he encouraged blacks to use these names publicly and to substitute them for their English or "slave" names. Open weekly *bembes* and performances on television and film were all part of his campaign to aggressively publicize the religion. Under his leadership members of the Yoruba Temple performed at the African Pavilion of the New York World's Fair in 1965. All this was consistent with his avowed intentions and cultural nationalist orientation, and throughout this period he was able to attract attention and new members to the movement.

But the public character of his activities ran entirely counter to what the Cuban and Puerto Rican santeros were doing. Their reactions were telling and fixed on key symbols. Adefunmi's violation of the secrecy taboo eventuated in death threats. Priests threatened to kill him by magical means. Santeros condemned and prohibited African attire, a prime symbol of Africanness in Orisha-Voodoo and the black nationalist movement in general. Most important of all was the Orisha-Voodooist's refusal to use saints' images in their shrines and on their altars. The replacement of these Catholic symbols with carvings copied from photographs in books of African art containing the actual Yoruba images was more than the Cubans could stand. For them it was clear that there could be no Santeria without the santos. Replacing the santo's representation with some unrecognizable alien figure taken from a book was a violation of what they considered the core of their religion—devotion to and aid from the Catholic saints. It was also tantamount to saying that the religion was not Cuban. For Adefunmi the removal of the saints' images was simply the most obvious expression of his explicit intention, that is, to purify Santeria of all non-African influences and return the remaining Yoruba-Dahomean elements to the form in which they had been practiced in West Africa.

Not all of the bad feeling existing between the Cubans and Adefunmi was being sent out by the Cubans. Adefunmi himself became more militant and under the influence of others in the African Nationalist Independence Partition Party was becoming more racist in his attitudes (Hunt 1979:28). This was not helpful in his dealings with the established Cuban priests, because by U.S. definitions the majority of these priests and all the babalawos were white. More black Americans were becoming involved in Santeria, both inside the temple and outside as the black power and black pride and black nationalist thrust swelled. Increasingly the Cubans directed black aspirants away from Adefunmi, calling him racist and incompetent, and initiated the blacks themselves.

These animosities did not deter Osejiman Adefunmi from attempting to carry out his original aim of unifying the different African-based religious groups around some version of a black nationalist perspective. In November 1965 Adefunmi met with a group of Cuban and Puerto Rican santeros to discuss a real unification of the American and Caribbean groups. Juan Rene Bettancourt, former president of the Federated Asso-

ciations of Black People of Cuba under Fidel Castro, mediated this conference (Clapp 1966:23). Nothing came of this attempt at conciliation,
however. The Cuban and Puerto Rican priests wanted nothing to do with
Adefunmi's black nationalist politics. They did not identify their interests
with those of African Americans. Adefunmi's acerbic and exasperated response to this was to tell the Cuban and Puerto Rican priests that they were
still "just a bunch of Christians" (Clapp 1966:23). This marked his final decisive break with the Cuban Santeria establishment. Though he no longer
could expect much from the established priests, there were Afro-Cubans
who were secretly sympathetic to the aims of the Yoruba Temple and continued to pass on vital ritual and other information to Adefunmi and others in the movement (Adefunmi 1981:4).

In 1965, after a series of severe personal and organizational crises, Adefunmi was forced to close the temple. He soon brought in a Puerto Rican
diviner to purify and revive the temple so that it might reopen. The diviner
was not successful, and the temple closed again until early 1966. The reading of the year for 1966 revealed the proper sacrifices, cleansings, and
herbal baths to revive the temple, and Adefunmi carried out the work himself rather than relying on the Cubans or Puerto Ricans. The success of this
work gave him great satisfaction and began his gradual divorce and independence from Santeria (Clapp 1966:40). He was already talking about
founding a Yoruba village in South Carolina, but this idea was not put into
motion until 1970. By then he had closed the Yoruba Temple and left New
York. In April 1970 he initiated three Afro-Americans without either the
presence or the advice of any of the Cuban babalawos or santeros. In August he initiated a second group of priests with the assistance of a Nigerian
priest and a former temple member who had been initiated by the Cubans
(Cohn 1973; Hunt 1979:39–41). To my knowledge none of these people
are acknowledged by the Cubans as legitimate priests. Hunt wrote that
Omowale, Adefunmi's first initiate into the Orisha-Voodoo priesthood, "argued that the Cubans had decided for themselves how they wanted to re-
organize the religion and so, too, had the Brazilians. Therefore it was time
for Black Americans to decide what the religion and culture meant to them
and how they were going to preserve it" (1979:39–40).

In Santeria's Phase IV, Early Orisha-Voodoo was clearly a case of cultural interpretation followed by divergence. This phase of its history
conforms to a situation A.F.C. Wallace described as a typical process and
situation for the origin of a revitalization movement: the triangular
alliance-and-identity dilemma (1966:112). In this dilemma one group (A)
finds itself surrounded by two other threatening or competing groups (B
and C). One of them (B) it admires and wishes to identify with in some respects, while the other (C) is defined as an enemy. If group A wishes not
only to identify with group B but also to form a political alliance with it and
is rejected, the result is a dilemma. As long as group A is unwilling to redefine the enemy (C) as an ally, the only solution remaining is a revitaliza-

tion movement within group A itself. This redefines the whole situation and gives group A a new identity, one so strong that it feels that it can go it alone without an alliance or an identification with either of the other two groups. Except for the fact that Orisha-Voodoo was already in the initial stages of a revitalization movement when this sequence of events occurred, this process describes almost exactly the dilemma of Early Orisha-Voodoo. White culture and increasingly whites themselves were defined as the enemy of Orisha-Voodoo and the black nationalists with whom Adefunmi was allied. He had sought out Santeria practitioners as allies against the enemy, admired the storehouse of Africanisms in their religion, and identified with them to the extent of joining their priesthood and becoming one of them as had other members of Orisha-Voodoo. But however deeply felt the alliance and identification were for Adefunmi and other Orisha-Voodooists, they were still tactical. For in their minds initiation into Santeria took place in the context of an ongoing political and cultural struggle against the hegemony of white culture over blacks. The strategic project still remained the repudiation of white culture as a means to the cultural and political liberation of blacks. When they sought alliance with the santeros to struggle together against the enemy white culture, they were rejected. Orisha-Voodoo then redefined the situation so that it did not have to be dependent upon Santeria for its priesthood. From the point at which it determined that it had the right to recreate Santeria and Yoruba religion in its own terms and the strength to consciously create a more satisfying culture, Orisha-Voodoo could initiate its own priesthood, assert itself as a force in its own right, and pursue its own direction, independently, without any alliance with either white culture or Santeria.

PLATE 10. Don Fernando Ortiz presents Santeria bata drummers to Cuban intellectuals from a concert stage. Havana, 1930s. Photographer unknown. Herskovits Papers courtesy of the Schomburg Center for Research in Black Culture.

PLATE 11. Large Afro-Cuban Santeria altar in the house of a santero. Matanzas, Cuba, 1930s. Note the differing elevations of the altar objects: distinctive Santeria objects (including containers for the orisha's relics and the decorative symbols associated with each of the orisha) are on the floor and the first level of elevation, while Christian items (including a glass votive candle, portraits of Catholic saints, and a pennant) are elevated above, on the table and walls. Photographer Manuel Puerto Villar. Herskovits Papers courtesy of the Schomburg Center for Research in Black Culture.

PLATE 12. Throne for Yemaya at La Casa de Los Hijos de San Lazaro, Guanabacoa, Havana Province. Photograph courtesy of the photographer, David H. Brown. (c) David H. Brown 1989.

PLATE 13. Chromolithograph of the Seven African Powers picturing Elegua, Ogun, Orula, Obatala, Yemaya, Ochun, and Chango, as well as Olofi. This print was made in Mexico but is very common in Hispanic communities in the United States and can be found on glass votive candles and handbills as well as posters like this one. The Seven African Powers are depicted using Catholic imagery but are nonetheless referred to by Lucumi names. The structure of the whole scene is of a set of medallions linked by a chain to form a protective necklace garlanded with a cutlass, a spear, a hook, a hammer, an axe, and arrows—weaponry associated with Ogun, the orisha of iron and warfare. Collection of the author.

PLATE 14. The author (second from left) at a spiritist session in the Bronx, New York, 1981. Photograph by Ana Hernandez. Courtesy of the Inner-City Support Systems Project. The woman in the center is a Puerto Rican spiritist medium who was also initiated as a Santeria priestess in Cuba in the 1950s. In the course of this session the woman on the far right was possessed by the Orisha Yemaya. The dark-skinned woman on the author's right makes quick movements with her arms while she is going into spirit possession. Author's collection.

PLATE 15. Santeria drum-dance, or bembe, for Yemaya (La Virgen de Regla) and Ochun (La Caridad del Cobre) in the Bronx, New York, 1980. Photograph by the author.

PLATE 16. Oba Osejiman Adefunmi I, founder of Orisha-Voodoo, the African Theological Archministry, and Oyotunji African Village, South Carolina; Ifa diviner and king of the Yorubas in America, around 1980. Photographer unknown. Author's collection.

PLATE 17. The Oshun shrine at Oyotunji Village, South Carolina, 1981. Photograph by the author.

PLATE 18. The Ogun shrine at Oyotunji Village, South Carolina, 1981. Photograph by the author.

VI.

Continuity and Change

I used to be different but now I'm the same.
Werner Erhard

In studying the contributions of Africa to the cultures and societies of the New World it has been common to speak in terms of African survivals, or retentions, on one hand as opposed to adaptation on the other to account for the persisting cultural distinctiveness of Afro-American culture. One can see the whole Frazier-Herskovits debate as hinging on the opposition of these two concepts. This debate was never resolved. There was no winner. It is entirely possible that such a debate can never be resolved; perhaps it can only be dissolved by asking different questions. If we ask new questions, maybe we will begin to get new answers.

To speak of Africanisms solely in terms of survivals is, in a quite literal sense, to speak of them as a kind of superstition. Superstitions are isolated traits or cultural forms left "standing over" after their original institutional supports have dropped away. The whole system of ideas and values that gave them coherence has collapsed around them like ruins worn to dust, rendered invisible, and, finally, lost to time. The survival seems denuded or without function, a frozen remnant; but true survival demands not petrification but plasticity, and what really survives is not a dead thing but is either living, being born, or dying.

Adaptation, on the other hand, is not necessarily a rupture with the past but an accommodation, a test and a testimony of fidelity to African tradition, concept, and style within the context of change. A tradition that doesn't accommodate itself to changed circumstances in ways that will allow it to persist will be unable to reproduce itself and will be extinguished. If the ancestral institutional forms have been cut off, that does not mean that new ones have not been found, filled with African content or molded in line with African patterns of social interaction, world view, or aesthetics.

The choice between survival and adaptation as approaches to the persisting distinctiveness of Afro-American cultures under the most alienating, oppressive, and corrosive conditions imaginable is a false one. Survival and adaptation are neither complementary nor inherently opposed. Even if the two approaches could be merged, the result would still smack of incompleteness, because attention to the internal dynamics of the cultures involved would be absent.

In searching out the contributions of Africa to the New World, the tendency to concentrate on individual traits which are traceable to African origins (words, performance techniques, aspects of family life, etc.) often leads to ambiguous or tendentious results. In many cases such a strategy proves impossible given the present state of knowledge, the specific interests of past investigators, and the momentous changes occurring in Africa itself. Even when found, and even when traced back to specific African ethnic groups, such individual items do not constitute the only, or perhaps even the most important, contributions. Indeed such items, even when they occur in abundance, are equivalent to a list of words from a poorly known language. Their continued existence is important but as a simple list the words are the surface of the phenomenon. Perhaps the individual words and their origins are not nearly as important as the patterns and structures that organize them. J. Dillard, from the point of view of the student of creole linguistics, has insisted on this point for language and it may well be true for other domains as well:

> If a lot of British occult beliefs—even an overwhelming majority of the items—are shaped in an "African" pattern, then "Africanism" is a very prominent factor in such beliefs. In fact, it could properly be said to dominate that belief system. (1973:9–10)

Once the idea that such organizational principles exist is seriously entertained a further possibility comes into view: not only might such principles of organization be preserved in New World contexts; they might also be generative and shape adaptations and new cultural production whether using African, European, or distinctively Afro-American materials. We would have new productions and adaptations according to preserved principles buried beneath the surface of disparate African and non-African traits. If this is so we can retain much that has been learned, but we should also begin to reorient our approaches to complement survivals with structures, adaptations with processes, and retentions with principles of creativity.

The dialectic between continuity and change is what the two sections of this chapter are about. The first is concerned with Santeria tradition and the mechanisms of collective memory; the second is concerned with syncretism and focuses on selected aspects of Santeria as examples of this type of religious and cultural change. I will put forward my own perspective on syncretism in Santeria, one which differs from the perspectives of other scholars who have written about African-American religions.

Problems of Collective Memory

In 1980 black psychologist Wade Nobles asked the basic questions with which we are concerned here. In determining whether and to what extent the African orientation has persisted, he wrote that we need to ask how it could have been maintained and what mechanisms and circumstances allowed it to be maintained. He went on to describe a number of necessary conditions for that maintenance.

> An orientation stemming from a particular indigenous African philosophy could only be maintained when its carriers were isolated (and/or insulated) from alien cultural interactions and if their behavioral expressions did not openly conflict with the cultural-behavioral elements of the "host" society. If the circumstances of the transplantation of New World Blacks met one or both of these conditions, then it is highly likely that an African orientation was sustained. (1980:327)

The history I have outlined in the preceding chapters seems to contradict these seemingly necessary requirements. In the Cuban cities and countryside the Afro-Cubans, slave and free, while for the most part isolated from the dominant stratum of whites and the peculiar class-based culture common in that stratum, were not insulated from all cultural interaction with other whites. Afro-Cubans contributed to creating and Africanizing the creole culture into which each new shipment of enslaved Africans had to assimilate and into which each new free black, mulatto, and white generation was born. A lot of it they shaped from below. Furthermore, for the early Cuban santeros exiled in the United States, the initial situation was not only that they were isolated from cultural interactions with the alien mainland society but that, initially, they did not have a religious sanctuary to fall back upon either. This they had to create. The Orisha-Voodooists were impelled toward the African religion, not because they were or felt isolated from the dominant culture in almost all its forms but rather because they sensed that they were drowning in it and wanted out. Their path to further isolation wound through a period of exposure to an African alternative via Santeria. At the same time, it cannot be denied from the record of that same history that many behavioral expressions of the carriers of this indigenous African philosophy in the New World do come into conflict, sometimes openly, with the cultural-behavioral elements of the host society. The banning of culturally distinctive African participation in the Cuban carnivals, the suppression of the Afro-Cuban cabildos, the postindependence persecutions, and the ambivalent relationship that persisted between Cuban Santeria and the ruling socialist government all attest to conflicts with the host society. To a much lesser degree the same thing holds true in the United States, particularly in relation to the sacrifice of animals (see Brandon 1990a).

The West African religious tradition with which we are concerned was transplanted and seems not to have met the conditions Nobles described; and yet it has survived anyway, so we are left with the same questions as before. While we certainly cannot give definitive answers to these questions and may in some cases be forced to speculate, we can at least present some new data related to these problems and try to place that data into a framework different from what has been proposed so far by many previous investigators of Afro-Cuban religion and thus provoke, and possibly orient, future research in a somewhat different direction.

In this section we approach these questions—how could the African tradition have been maintained and what mechanisms and circumstances allowed it to be maintained?—from the vantage point of collective memory. Since we have treated circumstances in detail in earlier chapters, we will be much more concerned with mechanisms than with circumstances. Our orientation is essentially as follows.

Culture can be regarded as a form of information. Informational resources can accumulate and can be distorted, transmitted or lost over time, and managed. Management of the available informational resources involves a system through which the culture manages itself. This self-management includes determining how information is distributed, transmitted, and stored. The cultural information defining a system or maintaining its distinctiveness must be transmitted intergenerationally, and in order to be transmitted and persist it must be remembered. There are four major types of information storage through which individuals, groups, and societies remember: personal memory, cognitive memory, habit memory (or bodily incorporation), and social or collective memory. The mechanisms through which these forms of memory are transmitted collectively are interpersonal linkages, strategies for memory encoding, performance, and strategies of repetition.

Though social or collective memory is the least investigated of the forms of information storage, it is difficult to conceive of either the content of the individualized forms of memory, the persistence of individual and social identities, or longstanding and widespread cultural traditions persisting without it or something like it. The classic treatment is that of Maurice Halbwachs in *The Collective Memory* (1980). Recent treatments of social or collective memory particularly germane to my argument are Bastide's chapter on the subject in his monograph on Afro-Brazilian religions (1978a), Michel Laguerre's treatment of the evolution and transmission of medical traditions in Afro-Caribbean folk medicine (1987), and Phillip Connerton's general theoretical study, *How Societies Remember* (1989). Connerton's work has been particularly influential on the treatment that follows.

It is Connerton who distinguishes the four kinds of memory: personal memory, cognitive memory, habit memory, and social or collective memory. His typology of memory will serve as a useful starting point, after which we will begin to apply it to the problem at hand: the mechanisms underlying the continuity of Yoruba religion in Cuba.

Personal memory refers to an individual's ability to recall events from his or her own life history. Persons in possession of personal memory can recall events from their own past, and when the events are successfully evoked they come located in a context, the context in which the persons, places, things, and events gained their meaning. Personal memory is also concerned with the self that was involved in the past events as well as the self that is recalling these events in the present. It is in relation to the self that we recognize in personal memory both a distance and a continuity.

We can recall an image from our past, but we cannot live the past differently; we cannot alter it in any way that would affect what we have become. The pastness of these images seems irrevocable, the images themselves veiled, the time distant. Yet there is continuity to the self in personal memory as well. A sense of continuity with our own past experiences exists because the self who experienced the events in the past is the same self who remembers them in the present.

Because of personal memory we are able to have a coherent sense of identity and a persisting sense of self. With the aid of personal memory we gain the ability to relate consistently to other people and even to conceive of them as having identities like our own. Our past personal history is a very significant source for our conception of who we are in the present, yet a great portion of our conception of ourselves and our knowledge of ourselves is fashioned by how we view, now, what we have done in the past. Our evaluations of our personal past also condition what we see as our possibilities for the future.

Cognitive memory is the form of memory that allows us to remember the meanings of words, recite a line of poetry or a song lyric unaided, and recall narratives such as jokes and stories. Schemas and models of the environment, like the mental map of a city or neighborhood we use when giving directions to someone who is lost, are stored in cognitive memory, as are such statements of abstract relationships as mathematical equations. Our ability to recall instructions for properly carrying out any procedure (whether it is a recipe or a line of reasoning) and our ability to remember what the outcome should be (a good meal or logical truth) are other examples of cognitive memory.

For cognitive memory it is not necessary that the object of memory itself be something that is past. Cognitive memory does not require that the object of memory be past; it only requires that the object of memory was encountered, experienced, or learned in the past. Information summoned from cognitive memory arrives relatively detached from personal memory. The person need not be able to recall anything about the episodes of learning or their context to retain and use the information.

Out of the stream of all our previous activities, consciously and unconsciously we shape isolated physical and cognitive acts into a large number of coordinated sequences of acts which form practices of some kind. Riding a bike, writing one's name on a piece of paper, greeting a person by shaking hands, playing a melody on a musical instrument, reading a book, and speaking one's own native tongue in ordinary conversation are common everyday examples of such practices. Once we initiate a particular practice we call up, en bloc, the numerous individual behaviors which compose it; these acts form a stream in which each behavior or thought follows the next almost automatically. Our ability to retain these practices in readiness and to execute them when needed is what we mean by the term *habit memory* (Connerton 1989:94). In habit memory the difference between knowing, doing, and remembering almost evaporates because demonstrating possession of a specific habit memory requires the capacity to reproduce a particular performance and to do it, more or less effectively, whenever the need arises. Habit memory is concerned not with facts but with actions, not with the cognitive knowledge of rules or codes but with the ability to exercise mental and physical skills.

We often may not be able to recall how we acquired the specific knowledge or skill or where or when we acquired it. Lack of use or lack of practice may put us in the position where we are not even sure that we have acquired a knowledge or skill or still remember it. Only when we find ourselves in situations like this are we forced to make the additional effort to use conscious recollection as a guide to what was formerly an habitual act or performance. In this case the only way we can recognize for ourselves or demonstrate to others that we actually do remember the skill is to try and perform it. Habit memory, then, is not the same as a ready knowledge of codes, rules, maps, or procedures; nor is it simply an addition to cognitive memory. It seems almost to be a substrate for the practical use of the contents of cognitive memory because the trajectory of repeated, consistent, successful, and convincing performances of the rules, codes, maps, and procedures requires it.

Philosophers such as Henri Bergson and Bertrand Russell considered personal and cognitive memory as "true" or "knowledge" memory and distinguished it from habit acquired through past experience. They attempted to separate mental acquisitions from bodily ones and privileged the mental while regarding the body as inferior. For them memory had to be a cognitive act to be of any philosophical significance, and this decisively excludes habit. Yet habit is an intrusive feature of our mental life and is often present where at first sight it appears not to be. It is especially difficult to separate cognition and habit or motor memory in the realm of culture, where it is clear that both cognitive acquisition and bodily incorporation are avenues for culture learning. Herskovits recognized this:

> If we assume that culture is learned, it becomes apparent that the enculturative experience, the cultural expression of the learning-conditioning process, is so effective in shaping thought and behavior that the major portion of the response-patterns of the individual tend to be automatic rather than reasoned. In this sense, then, cultural stability derives from the fact that so much of socially sanctioned behavior lodges on a psychological plane *below the level of consciousness*. It is only when these automatic responses—which, it should be recognized, may include overt or implicit reactions—are challenged, that emotional and thought processes are called into play. In terms of cultural dynamics,

the analysis of these deeply rooted, automatic, enculturated behavior patterns affords a relatively neglected lead to an understanding of cultural change. It is precisely here that the broad historic controls of the Afroamerican field have the greatest significance. For they permit the assessment of data in terms that make it possible to determine not only which aspects of culture run most deeply beneath the level of consciousness, but how deviations from behavior patterns of earlier periods are the reflection of differing degrees of intensity of exposure and reconditioning—in this case to various types of non-African cultural conventions.

Motor habits of all kinds must be placed high on the list of cultural elements that can be profitably studied from this point of view. (1969:147; my emphasis)

We have asked how individuals preserve and rediscover memories and have found some clues in the concepts of personal, cognitive, and habit memory. We now need to ask how societies and social groups do these same things. It is quite evident that they do, because the content of individual memory goes far beyond one's own personal experiences to *social or collective memory.* The ideas of John M. Roberts on the self-management of cultures and culture as information are helpful here.

According to Roberts, "it is possible to regard all culture as information and to view any single culture as an 'information economy' in which information is received or created, stored, retrieved, transmitted, utilized and even lost. . . . Since no single person can command the entire cultural resources of a tribe, or for that matter, even maintain his own cultural control indefinitely, culture must always be stored in some sort of group" (1964:440, 438–439). It seems to me that assistance from and access to the memories or cultural information of a group is one of the barest preconditions for the existence and persistence of culture and social life as well as a sense of personal or group identity.

Social groups help individuals remember. Society tests our memory for personal information, for cognitive data, and places demands on our skills, but it also provides help for us when we cannot recall something. Other people often help us reconstitute our own past experiences, and our own experience comes to encompass images of the experiences of other people which they have conveyed to us from their memories. Collective memory is part of a group's way of managing and storing its own information. The idea of an individual memory totally separate from social memory is an abstraction almost devoid of meaning. Individuals' memories exist and are maintained in a social and cultural context. Every recollection, however personal it may be, exists in relationship with the whole material and moral life of the societies of which we are part (or of which we have been part) and with ideas which many other people around us also hold. Through membership in a social group—particularly kinship, religious, and class affiliations—individuals are able to acquire, to localize, and to recall their memories. "Every type of group, however, whether it be a secret society, a craft guild, a war party, a children's play group, and so on, serves as a storage unit" (Roberts 1964:440).

While we can assume that there is a theoretical limit to the amount of information any one individual or combination of individuals can learn and remember, it is probably true, also, that no individual receives as much instruction, possesses as much information, or has amassed as large a memory bank as the individual can possibly absorb. The fact that transmission usually takes place in a cultural context further limits the actual capabilities for the storage of information. In practice, transmission in cultural context involves selecting particular information, channeling it to specific groups of individuals, and articulating both the groups of individuals and the information in such a way that the memories and experiences conveyed to them are stored and can continue to be transmitted. This may mean that the information becomes (at least potentially) available to all members or that, while the information remains in the group's store of collective memory, certain groups of people have access to it while others do not.

The vehicle of collective memory consists of a group of human beings linked through communication. This network of human communication, though, is always being punctured: disease strikes people and renders them uncommunicative. Members of the group leave the network and go to a place beyond regular contact. Worse still, they may withhold memory willingly or become truly unable to remember. Finally and inevitably, each generation is winnowed by death.

The fact that a social group endures beyond the life span of any single individual member does not ensure that it is able to "remember" in common or that it will be able to do so in the future. The main means of replacing the disappearing nodes in the web is through socializing children and adults before the older members die. Older members of the group must transmit their mental representations of the past to the younger members. Only in this way will the two generations even have the opportunity to share a common image and representation of the group's past; only by repeating this process with every generation does the group actually come to feel and think of itself as possessing and sharing a common past. A group's failing memories and disappearing elders may be partially replaced also by adding individuals from other groups and by continuing to socialize them. Much of tradition as well as collective memory resolves, then, into acts of person-to-person communication. One of the lifelines of collective memory is a continually renewed chain of person-to-person transmission within institutions and persisting social networks. If this is the case then the description of the storage pattern of a society is essentially a description of the formal, informal, explicit, implicit, individual, and group roles (Roberts 1964:441).

The ideas of individual and collective memory provide only tentative clues to the formation of Santeria and other Afro-Cuban religions during the colonial period and the postindependence era. While these ideas help us to look for and reveal the ways through which the Afro-Cuban slaves and their descendants reconstituted the religious experiences of their old religious communities, they also bring into relief a number of problems. It is some of these clues and problems that we now turn to explore.

Many local cult groups existed in the Yoruba territories. Many were simply local religious groups whose deities might not have been venerated anywhere else in Nigeria. Other deities, however, were widely worshiped throughout the whole area but institutionalized as local groups and individual priests in their communities. The hierarchy of Yoruba religious authorities really began at the family level, where the family head carried out religious functions on behalf of the people residing in his compound. Corresponding officials existed at the level of the ward, the town or village quarter, and for the village or town as a whole at public shrines. Especially in the period before the Owu and Egba wars, it was probably family heads and quarter-level and village-level priests who were brought to the Americas. During the Owu and Egba wars, though, entire villages and towns, and hence entire priesthoods, were enslaved. The higher-level temple organization charged with the veneration of the most widely spread deities and those most closely connected with kingship were centered in the capitals and in the courts. It is possible that priests and priestesses from these temples were not enslaved and traded across the Atlantic, but this is by no means certain. It was inevitable that some priesthoods would not appear in Cuba. Their priests or priestesses were not enslaved or there were not sufficient numbers of devotees of the particular orisha. Perhaps groups of specialists and devotees tried to organize themselves into a priesthood of purely local significance but were unsuccessful. Maybe the personnel were there but their knowledge was too limited, so that the worship of that particular deity died with them. In the earliest period of slave importation, priests or devotees may well have perished without either biological or spiritual descendants.

The lone Yoruba slave priest or priestess was only able to reconstruct that part of the collective memory which he or she had experienced and that part of the religious knowledge and experience that had been communicated to him or her by other people in Africa. This did not encompass the totality of the African ethnic group's experience. Probably not even all of the priest's personal past remained accessible because the environment was so different; there were no Yoruba compatriots, and there was little opportunity to put the knowledge to use in the service of others (Laguerre 1987:16). One probable exception to this is ancestor veneration, the cult of the dead.

In Yoruba territories the ancestor cult was called Egungun. The Yoruba scholar S. O. Babayemi, an Egungun lineage member and participant in Egungun ritual since childhood, has described the social and spatial contexts in which the Egungun are venerated in Nigeria.

In Africa, the worship of Egungun has historically been linked with family lineages. These Egungun function either individually in the interest of their particular families or collectively in the interests of the community. When they function collectively they transcend family and lineage alignments. When necessary, Egungun are invoked individually or collectively on the graves of ancestors (oju orori), the family shrines (ile run) or the community grove (igbale). The ancestors were invited to physically visit the earth through masquerades referred to as Egungun or Ara Orun (inhabitants of heaven). Many community Egungun led their communities in wars or performed other social, political and ritual functions. (1980:1–4, 25)

Mintz and Price have suggested that among Africans in diaspora cognatic descent groups evolved their particular form in order to maximize the number of people participating in ancestor rites (1976:35). Such groups probably came into existence early in the history of slave importation, and in the plantations and cities of the Caribbean they would have had few tasks they could perform other than ancestral rites. Since cognatic descent groups include all the ancestors of a person and all the person's descendants, even lone Yoruba males who never formed families could participate in their rites. Unless they were reinforced by continuous imports of fellow ethnics, one would expect that any ethnic basis restricting participation in the descent group ancestral rites would become attenuated through time and successive generations of interracial and interethnic mating. Even in the absence of fellow Yorubas, then, Yoruba people would have participated in and maintained the ancestral rites of the cognatic descent groups because of the central role the ancestors played in shaping the ongoing life of the community and the individual lives of community members.

In the situation where there were many other Yorubas, the role of maintaining the habits and the images of past religious experience was probably largely performed by adult women, older men, healers, and diviners. Adult women, whether or not they were priestesses before importation, passed the lore on in the course of child care and rearing. Conscientious older men took on the role of keepers of family and cult traditions. Healers and diviners on the plantations and in the cities could function as religious specialists who worked on behalf of their own relatives and friends and on behalf of others to give guidance, to advise, heal, and settle disputes within the slave community. All of them, adult women, adult males, healers, and diviners, were in a position to transmit their memory to a younger generation.

The survival of the cult of the dead into the present day attests to the importance of ancestors in every African ethnic group. Beyond that it points to the centrality of kinship for Africans. Newly imported Africans on the plantations and in the cities of the Caribbean, despite their far-flung origins, would have shared some quite broadly defined conceptions concerning kinship. Among all the enslaved Africans there would have been no question about the centrality of kinship, of the importance of kinship for defining the individual's place in society and structuring relationships with other people. The ideas of unilineal descent, of the perpetuity of the lineage, its eternal nature as an entity stretching back into the remote past and forward into an undefined future of descendants, would have been universal or almost so; so would the idea of the continuing relationship of the living to the dead and the relationship of the ancestors to specific pieces of ground. For most Yorubas in most places, the ancestral cult became less elaborate, shrinking in significance. In the orisha cults that would later form in Brazil and Cuba, the functions of mutual aid, cooperative work, and communal authority remained but were restricted to the charmed circle of the religious community and the initiated. But even in areas where cult groups devoted to the orisha never reformed, the ancient economy of prestations, counterprestations, and gifts directed at the ancestral dead remained.

In Cuba the clans and lineages of former times took on a double reality. The ancestors ceased to have a communitywide cult group; their veneration became solely domestic. At the same time devotees applied the idiom of ritual kinship from the religious fraternities to ancestor veneration. This figures prominently in ritual. Today, devotees who are priests or priestesses have a group of ritual ancestors as well as ancestors by blood and marriage. These ritual, fictive ancestors include the people who initiated them into the priesthood and the initiators' ritual ancestors going as far back and extending as far out as the priest or priestess knows. Any important ceremony opens with an invocation in which the presiding santera has the person for whom it is being performed recite a genealogy of all these ancestors, familial and ritual alike.

The important Yoruba cult groups did not arrive in Cuba all at once. Some among the people reformed their old priesthoods and cult groups at whatever level they knew them, and they continued the process as people who possessed memory of other Yoruba cult groups entered Cuba. Small groups served as the instruments of this process, scanning the information bank of each other's memories to retrieve salient information and always to store it as well. As we shall see, in some cities and rural areas in Cuba these groups may have formed councils which apparently had some authority.

For most communities, especially in an early period when a few of the deities received veneration or had a priesthood, a council like this might have been quite small. A fairly small number of knowledgeable people could pull together different sources of information and present differing points of view. Furthermore each council member could draw on the resources of his or her own kin and other groups. Because information from the devotees of a larger number of deities had to be scanned and assimilated, the council probably had to become larger and draw on still wider resources of memory. After the end of the slave trade, when no more Yorubas were being imported to Cuba, the fund of available resources of collective memory had to expand to include members of other African ethnic groups, people of mixed African ancestry who may have also belonged to other ethnic groups involved in a similar collective efforts, and probably some creole whites who had been exposed to Lucumi religion.

Santeria has integrated the separate cults of the Yoruba orisha into a single comprehensive structure which has itself evolved and changed over time. The cult groups and priesthoods that were known at any specific time and place in Cuba were influenced by the arrival of new ones. We can see this in the case of the santo Ozain, the orisha of herbs and medicines.

Santero Nicolas Anagarica makes some interesting comments about the arrival of Ozain in Cuba. Although I have no way to substantiate the accuracy of his statements, they do throw an interesting light on the issues of collective memory and inter-African syncretism. Angarica describes Ozain as an immigrant, a straggling arrival on the Cuban scene. As important as Ozain is as a healer and guardian of the powers of herbs and medicines in both Yoruba religion and in Santeria, it seems there was a long period of time when he was not known in Cuba.

> This deity comes from the Mandingas. This deity left his territory because of war and other reasons; as other prisoners were imported so were they. Just like the Takuas, the Magino and other peoples, it happened that they brought thousands of Lucumis to Cuba; it was they who made Ozain speak here as he had in Africa.
>
> Ozain came to light when there was formed a Confederation of Council of the orisha; before this conference only Inle was known.
>
> Inle preceded Ozain in what was actually Ozain's work, being known till then as the greatest expert on herbs. Before all the Olochas [santeras] knew Ozain, Inle was the god of medicine, medications and all medicinal substances. When Ozain finally arrived on these shores, Inle had to take a second place with regard to herbs. (Angarica n.d.; my translation)

Possibly what occurred is that a Mandinga with a particularly impressive knowledge of Ozain's lore arrived in Cuba and was able to plant anew Ozain's worship to the detriment of Inle (and Inle's priests). It is impossible to tell when this happened from Anagarica's statement, but whenever it was, Santeria was being practiced in a form that depended much less on Ozain's knowledge of herbs and plants than is now the case. Ozain priests in Nigeria are not simply skilled herbalists; there is also a theatrical aspect to their role in that they allow the deity Ozain to speak to human beings by means of their training as ventriloquists (Thompson 1975). It is significant that Anagarica states that while it was a Mandinga who brought Ozain into Santeria, it was the Lucumi who made Ozain speak. According to Anagarica, Ozain "came to light" at a council of santeros, a gathering through which collective memory was shaped and renewed. Once there was someone who could practice Ozain's work and once that person was accepted, his or her Mandinga origin became irrelevant. The origin was not erased from the collective memory because there were still Mandingas in Cuba, but what this Mandinga brought to the Lucumi became defined as Lucumi and entered the tradition of Lucumi religion.

In another example we can see the opposite kind of situation, one in which the status of the new information has to be changed in order to make it fit into a preexisting religious structure. Thomas Chappel has produced evidence to show that the present veneration of twins as deities in Yoruba territories is the result of the reversal of an earlier practice of twin infanticide. Chappel's research and interviews with high-ranking Yoruba priests led him to the conclusion that the Yoruba practice of twin infanticide was transformed into a cult of twin veneration some time between 1750 and 1850 (1974:250). The statues of the Ibeji, a little pair of wood carvings which the mothers of deceased twins carried and cared for, changed from being representations of the souls of dead twins into being orisha. If Chappel's dates are right, a Yoruba cult devoted to the veneration of the twins could not have arrived in Cuba before 1750. In Nigeria the twin statues continued to be kept by women who had borne twins and lost one or both of them, but the veneration did not develop a priesthood. In Cuba, however, possession of the Ibeji carvings, or the religious dolls that eventually replaced them, ceased to be solely the prerogative of mothers who had lost twins. Lucumi also received the carvings if they were one of a set of twins whose brother or sister had died (Anagarica n.d.:55). This was not the end of the transformation, however. In Cuba the Ibeji, now deities, developed a priesthood, and images of the twin deities were incorporated into the hierarchy of initiation rites. In his description of the Ibeji, Anagarica notes correctly that in Africa there were no Ibeji priests. He then goes on to say that in Cuba there weren't any Ibeji priests being initiated until about two generations before himself, roughly the 1890s through 1910 or so. At that point there was an Ibeji priesthood where there had not been one before and there was also knowledge which Ibeji priests had which was not there before (55). The Ibeji priesthood could not be "remembered" or "come to light" the way Ozain's did because it did not already exist, yet now it is considered just as "traditional" as any of the other priesthoods.

The councils made their decisions on the basis of the informational resources available to them at the time and in line with their own goals and intentions. Early on they had set a basic orientation in which the extant knowledge and memory of all the available orisha cult groups and priesthoods were to be housed within a single hierarchically organized structure. The intended and unintended consequences of their decisions modified the social contexts in which future action took place. Their decisions affected how new information from previously unknown Yoruba priesthoods would be institutionalized. In this instance continuity represented a repeated process of recollecting and rebuilding in line with traditional social, cultural, and religious goals. What this yielded was a subtle mutual transformation of social structures and individual action. Placing Ozain in the pantheon and creating the Ibeji priesthood were conscious decisions. Once it was decided that they should be included, they were put into a social structural context that had already been created to perpetuate other knowledge. Roberts has written of situations like this that "such decisions themselves often change the informational resources available to a group and modify the goals" (1964:442). It should also be seen that such decisions may also be conservative, i.e., they may reshape the information received in order to maintain goals rather than modify them.

Two aspects of memory concern us at this point: the code that represents information and the mechanism that preserves it. The code is the set of conventions governing how concepts, actions, and experiential states are communicated by using sense data which are understood as standing for culturally recognized experiences or things. In essence, these are the rules prescribing the processes by which sense data become signs, indices, and symbols. The code, then, determines how we represent the information being stored in memory. The mechanism, on the other hand, is the process or technique by which memory preserves the information. Mechanisms of persistence are not solely mental or cognitive but are also physical and include performance, various forms of individual and collective repetition, bodily incorporation, and the materialization of concepts. The two aspects are independent of each other, and neither the code nor the mechanism is the information. The sensory data may be derived from natural phenomena, man-made objects, or the external appearance and internal states of human beings. The code also governs how the relationships formed between sensory states and culturally recognized experiences are ordered and transformed into articulate expressions of meaning.

Experimental psychologists have concentrated their efforts on studying three dimensions of memory encoding: semantic encoding, verbal encoding, and visual encoding. The semantic code can be likened to a library catalogue which lists books by subject and author and assigns each book a location in the library according to a prearranged system of numbers so that it may be found easily. This dimension of encoding is semantic because memories are seen as being organized hierarchically by topic. The categories in which memories are organized derive from the world view of the person and the society and culture in which they grow up and the logical relationships which that culture teaches the person to see in the world around them. It is this world view and these logical relationships which integrate the subject slots and categories of memory into a single system and make semantic encoding the dominant dimension for the encoding of memories. The verbal code contains all the conventions and procedures governing how memory states are apprehended and communicated verbally. Verbal encoding determines how we represent linguistically, both to ourselves and to other people, the information stored in memory. The third dimension is the encoding of memory through meaningful visual stimuli. Visual perceptions may be translated easily into mental images, and concrete, visible objects are encoded twice in memory, once in terms of visual coding (mental imagery) but also linguistically (as verbal expression). For this reason concrete objects and information which can be seen and visually encoded are retained much better than abstract items having no visible form or a very remote symbolic relationship to the objects involved.

Santeria ritual and mythology are two aspects of its religious tradition: the tradition of stereotyped action (ritual) and the tradition of stereotyped narrative (myth) (Bastide 1978a:240). Myths are the master narratives, the key stories which verbally represent key symbols, persons, events, and relationships. These stories are told and reflected upon and utilized in the solution of personal problems. They convey an image of the remote past or another world, even as each word of the story itself vanishes. Santeria mythology then can be regarded as a collective form of personal and cognitive memory which maintains to a greater or lesser degree not only the stories from or referring to former times but also the world view, the logic, the procedures and schemas, the resolutions, conundrums, and contradictions as well. Ritual, however, is not a telling or a text. It is the performance of a world, its entities, powers, and relations.

Regarding Santeria ritual as cultural performance amplifies our discussion of memory in several ways. The use in Santeria rituals of speech and song, along with such nonverbal media as dance, acting out, graphic and plastic arts, and instrumental music, drastically increases the types of sensory data that have to be encoded in memory. Santeria ritual is an "orchestration of media," to use Victor Turner's phrase, not transmission through a single medium (1986:23–24). Furthermore, regarding Santeria ritual as performance forces us to realize that all four types of memory—personal, cognitive, habit, and social or collective—are involved.

The body of narratives told in the course of divination rites is probably the major repository of myths in Santeria. These myths and stories are part of the special religious technology of the diviners. Diviners in the New World apply the myths as paradigms for the diagnosis and solution of human problems much as their African counterparts do (Brandon 1983: 247–263; Bascom 1952, 1969a). Through the stories they hold up contemporary problems to mythical comparison and prescribe rituals according to mythical precedent.

Ifa divination derives its name from the deity that speaks through this oracle, Orunmila. Orunmila is said to "own" Ifa divination, and the priests of Orunmila, the babalawo, are said to be his children. Therefore when Ifa speaks it speaks with the voice of Orunmila, an orisha whose name means "only heaven knows the means of salvation" or "only heaven can effect deliverance" (Idowu 1962:75). Orunmila, unlike the other orisha, never manifests as a human body in possession, so the only way to hear his voice is by consulting his oracle and his priests.

In Nigeria Yorubas use two methods of divining Ifa: the *ikin*, or kola nut, method and the divining chain. Both methods were used in Cuba and both are now used in New York (Bascom 1980; Brandon 1983:247). In Yorubaland the ikin were a set of sixteen Guinea palm or kola nuts. In Cuba the ikin were small seedlike nuts or tiny coconuts which were known as "coconuts of Ifa." In Cuba, and now in the United States, the divining chain is by far the more frequently used technique. The diviner inserts eight pieces of gourd, mango seeds, tortoise shell, or brass between the segments of the chain, then holds the chain in the middle so that each of the eight objects that render the outcomes of the divination can fall "open" or "closed" independently of the others. There are, then, sixteen possible outcomes for each half of the divining chain, with a total of 256 (sixteen times sixteen) possible outcomes for one throw. The complete divining apparatus includes a divining board on which the diviner spreads a powder in which he marks the outcomes of his divinatory casts. Each outcome has a name, a graphic representation, and a set of verses, stories, and prescriptions connected with it which it is the job of the diviner to have at his command. Since divination is seen as a means of receiving communication from the orisha, in this case Orunmila, the outcomes are what "Ifa says." After the divination outcome is revealed, everything else is either prescribed or dependent on the particular lore a specific diviner has stored in memory. All this is a nearly exact reproduction of Yoruba practices.

The Ifa diviner tells the client a myth or story explaining how someone in the past had a similar problem and what was done about it, then gives a set of instructions for the client to follow, usually involving a ritual and a sacrifice of some kind. Stories embodying themes of the outcome follow. Not all of the characters in these stories are orisha. Many are diviners or clients, and in some cases even the named outcomes have become personified as mythological characters (see Bascom 1952:174). The situations in the stories revolve around fundamental problems of living in society, problems which are sometimes complicated by the malevolent magical practices of friends and enemies. They also contain historical and geographical information. These stories tell not only of people who sacrificed and followed what "Ifa said"—these people succeeded, prospered, and got what they desired—but also of those who did not follow the advice of the oracle—these people failed, destroyed themselves and others, or drove what they needed even further from them.

Through Ifa a complex, tense, or obscure situation is transformed into a precedent—a category of problems with which the diviner and the orisha already know how to deal—and into the form of a system of specified obligations between humans and the orisha cast as propitiations, exchanges, atonements, thanks offerings, purifications, and protective measures.

In Santeria divination in Cuba and the United States, the names of the outcomes, the divination technique, most of the objects used, even the order in which the divination outcomes are learned point to an unmistakable African and, more specifically, Yoruba origin, as do the names of the deities who appear in the stories and the place names that are evoked (Brandon 1983:253–255; Bascom 1952). It cannot be ignored, though, that at the same time as the ritual aspects of divination show great and specific continuities with African tradition, there is a part of the mythology and lore of the diviners (what Ifa says) which shows the imprint of the Cuban experience, particularly in reference to African ethnic groups with which it is extremely unlike that Yorubas had any contact in their home territories but certainly encountered in Cuba. If we approach Santeria divination ritual not as a type of symbolic representation but rather as a kind of stereotyped performance, what contrasts it with myth is that myth seems to have a reservoir of possibility on which variations can be played, while Ifa divination ritual does not permit such variation.

The Ifa divination ritual appears to have been held more tenaciously and been sustained in traditional form over longer periods of time than its mythology. In Santeria divination, ritual action seems to define a broad channel for the more variable and more rapidly changing elements of myth. But the divination ritual does not really interact with the myths the diviner tells, except to impose upon them some very general constraints which follow from the nature of the outcomes to which the myths are attached and the use of these narratives as paradigms and exemplars of problems and problem solving. The interpretation of the diviner's narrative tradition is conditioned both by its traditional content and the contemporary situations of clients. The continuity of these myths, then, is in the hands of the diviners, for it is they who must apply them to contemporary problems.

In an earlier period anthropologists used to emphasize the conservative, integrating, and stabilizing roles of social and religious rituals. Contemporary anthropologists are just as likely to see ritual performances and cultural media as throwing light on the ways in which cultural themes and values are communicated as well as on processes of social and cultural change (Singer 1972:77). Ritual performances, however, are not simple reflections of culture nor direct unmediated expressions of culture change either. As Turner has suggested, cultural performances may themselves be active agencies of change. Through cultural performances a culture achieves a separate vision of itself and may create a canvas on which it paints a picture of what life would be like if people could change how they lived with each other or even the very nature of their own individual lives (1986:24).

Turner has a predilection for viewing ritual and performance as agents of change. This pushes him to deny that rituals which appear to create an image of society "as it is" are a dominant form within the genre; rather it is those performances which create an image of society "as it is not" (whether that image is of a future state, a remote past, a distant place, or another world) which he seems to see as dominant, especially rites of passage which are examples par execllence of ritual as transformation. I would prefer not to prejudge the issue and to leave it up to observation to see which of these tendencies predominates in any particular case. Indeed in any particular case there may be conflict or disagreement even among the participants about just what is occurring. Furthermore, a ritual performance may also be a target of change rather than an agent of change. Such a change in ritual, emanating from outside causes, may be an accommodation to present circumstances which allows a better preservation of an image or practice from the past, whether that image or practice has changed or not. Certainly the case of Ifa divination, with its combination of continuity in ritual and both continuity and change in myth, is complex and amibivalent. It deserves much further study but appears to me to be essentially conservative.

To get a better understanding of collective memory we will have to study acts that transfer memory and keep the images memory contains circulating within the group, for it is these acts that make it possible for a tradition to persist and for a group to have a common memory. Among them are what Connerton has called "types of repetition" or "rhetorics of reenactment" (1989:39,67). I view these as strategic acts of transfer which must be repeated over and over again or which determine the character of acts that must be repeated over and over again and directs them along a certain course. These strategies of repetition are not peculiar to the subject matter of this book and can be found in the present as well as in the past. In the following paragraphs I will examine three of the strategies found in Santeria: calendrical repetition, in the form of commemorative ceremonies for the saints; verbal repetition, through which the use of Lucumi as a sacred ritual language conditions communication between humans and the orisha; and gestural repetition as it relates to ritual dance and ceremonial spirit possession. Incorporating cultural memory into habitual patterns of social interaction, movement, and body postures, as well as materializing abstract religious concepts by creating icons, are other acts of transfer and memory keeping which we will examine later.

Commemorative festivals or ceremonies articulate times, values, persons, and events spotlighted for communal attention. The calendar of saint's day festivities in Santeria represents not so much a continuation of the African worship as a repetition of the accommodation and coalescence of the Catholic and Lucumi institutions (see Table 4). They are repetitive performances and take on the characteristics of ritual time which is itself indefinitely repeatable. In the ritual period for this year's commemorative festival or ceremony the same religious acts and ritual procedures are performed and the same personages and representations appear as last year or a decade ago. Each commemorative is made to appear, in that which is considered significant, as an exact reproduction of a past one, indeed all past ones. On the calendrically fixed day of each performance the participants find themselves brought back into the same time as before, when the same rites were being enacted and the same heroes and events celebrated. It is the result of several transpositions.

First there was the decisive break in mentality in which the festivals honoring the orisha were removed from a time oriented toward the unfolding

TABLE 4. The Afro-Catholic Sacred Calender of Santeria Saints' Days

Orisha's Name	Celebration Date	Saint's Name
Ogun	June 29	Peter
Yemaya	September 7 and 9	Our Lady of Regla
Ochun	September 8 and 12	Our Lady of Charity of Cobre
Obatala	September 24	Our Lady of Mercies
Ibeji	September 26(?) and January 6	Cosma and Demian
Orunmila (Ifa)	October 4	Francis of Assisi
Chango	December 4	Barbara
Babaluaiye	December 17	Lazarus

of sequences of natural and cosmic processes and social events and transposed into a calendrical frame of reference, one of equal and undifferentiated time units. The calendar puts beside the structure of sacred time, formed out of all the periods repeatedly marked off for specific and notable commemorative ceremonies, the structure of a profane time that occurs between these intervals. Despite the tendency of the calendar to make one day like the next, the sacred and profane times are not reducible to one another. Each day may belong to two different orders of time, the day on which events take place in the world and the day of remembrance on which one celebrates the memory of some past person or event from a sacred mythic history.

The commemorative ceremony shifts the community into ritual time, but that time itself is split and remains on two contiguous but nonidentical planes. At the same time as the African-style commemoration is linked to and correlated with the public Catholic processions, mass attendance, and feasting and takes advantage of the heightened ritual activity, santeros temporally differentiate their worship within this larger movement into a sacred ritual time.

Not all santeras coordinate their African-style drum-dance celebrations honoring the orisha precisely in accord with the Cuban Catholic calendar, as shown in table 4. There arises a kind of temporal aura surrounding the Catholic saints' days which allows Santeria to establish a relationship of correspondence with them which nonetheless remains bivalent. For santeros these two commemorative feasts have never entirely merged. The Christian and African celebrations never take place at the same time, and one never substitutes for the other. They refer to contiguous and intersecting but nonidentical pasts. The full dual complex of celebrations reflects and commemorates this intersection. If the saint is properly celebrated by a Sunday morning mass at church and a public religious procession, the orisha comes down to earth the night before at a devotee's home or in a rented hall to receive its homage of drums, dancing, and food. Both the calendar and this peculiar rhetoric of repetition are a zone of compromise.

The repetition of this dual religious calendar, among other things, continues, commemorates, and repeats this prototypical divided moment of accommodation.

Verbal encoding determines how we represent linguistically, both to ourselves and to other people, the information stored in memory. Santeria structures many recurrent ritual contexts in such a way that participants are compelled to use Lucumi, a verbal code which is archaic and very different from their ordinary language. The differing contexts in which the two codes are used signal a distinction between sacred and profane language and marks one language, the sacred one, as the medium for addressing deities, spirits as well as humans, and the other for everything else. The compulsive repetition of a sacred and archaic tongue has a raison d'être as long as rites refer back to some prized earlier period, and there is a special authority given to texts transmitted in this code. Such texts have to be seen as true in a way in which translations of the same texts into another language would not be true. They also need to be seen as having been transmitted without error. Since neither Santeria nor its parent Yoruba religion is a revealed religion with a sacred book, the motive for use of the archaic code in Santeria is not fidelity to a revelator or an original pronouncement or text which itself has divine authority; rather it resides in a kind of residual ethnic factor in which, among other things, the Yoruba deities and ancestors are expected to like and heed best requests that are addressed to them in their own native tongue.

Lucumi has not been the object of a great deal of investigation. At one time it was thought to be a pidgin. Cuban Lucumi speakers considered it to be Yoruba or a combination of a number of Yoruba dialects. In Bascom's Cuban studies he always referred to it as Yoruba, and he was the first scientist to assert that it was genetically related to Yoruba. In 1953 linguist David Olmstead tested Bascom's assertion by undertaking a comparison of Yoruba and Lucumi texts which he collected in Nigeria and Cuba, respectively. He used a comparative method of investigating phonemic correspondences in cognate items. While Olmstead was able to show that the great majority of the phonemes of Lucumi also occur in Yoruba, only 48.5 percent of the words in his Lucumi texts were indubitable Yoruba cognates. Nevertheless, a great number of terms were very plausibly identical to or clearly related to Yoruba words in both sound and meaning. Some of the phonemic differences were clearly traceable to the influence of the Spanish language. Lucumi also differs from Yoruba in its use of pitch and stress and how pitch and stress combine to indicate differences in meaning. Some Lucumi words and phrases are neither Yoruba nor derived from Spanish. These forms might well be traceable to other West African languages, possibly to the Kwa group (to which Yoruba also belongs) and particularly to Ewe or Fon. Even in New York there are a few old santeros who are said to be conversant with Fon and who, within the context of Santeria, perform minor rites that, according to my informants, derive ultimately from Dahomey. These unexplained forms might also have originated in Yoruba dialects with which Olmstead was unfamiliar, and there is also the possibility of some form of drift or linguistic innovation within Cuba itself.

Surely acquisition of the Lucumi language in adolescence or adulthood within the context of a secret and suppressed cult group represents a rather abnormal learning situation. Despite the fact that some older santeros regard praying to the orisha in a language other than Lucumi as sacrilege, knowledge of Lucumi in Cuba was, in fact, very unevenly distributed. As Bascom points out,

> Some knew very little despite long associations with the cult; but others knew very much indeed, and some could converse fluently in the Yoruba language. Some had learned Yoruba as children; others had studied it in the cults, often from Spanish-Yoruba vocabularies laboriously copied by hand in notebooks. (1972:13)

The numerous glossaries in publications by santeros are perhaps a reflection of their notebooks and of the means by which they have acquired the language. Another source of instruction today comes from commercially available recordings of the religious songs in Lucumi. These recordings, furthermore, serve as a means of diffusing the religion's lore. Pronunciation and spelling of Lucumi are far from uniform. This shows up tellingly on recordings of the liturgical songs where the song leader and the chorus pronounce the same words differently or where the differences in pronunciation within the chorus render their Lucumi responses indistinct.

In the United States the situation is even more atypical. Most devotees I spoke with do not know or understand the language and cannot converse in it. Even many priests know no more Lucumi than what is contained in the religious songs, the names of the deities, and the Mojuba prayer, if that. For most devotees the only context in which they use Lucumi is at bembes and toques when they sing songs in Lucumi, and these are learned through participating at the ceremonies and imitating others.

In the current situation Lucumi could well become a highly conservative, restricted, magical language used in ritual but no longer understood by devotees. Indeed many devotees do not understand the meanings of the songs they sing. Believers consider the question of whether all the participants in the rite understand the Lucumi words to be secondary because their incomprehension of the Lucumi words does not affect the efficacy of the rituals. It is more important that the code be used, and used correctly, than that it be understood by all involved. The invocations, prayers, and songs in Lucumi have the same ritual value as the pantomimic dances in which the body becomes a hieroglyph that calls down the African gods and the same ritual value as the meticulous energy that uncoils from drum heads vibrating at the correct rhythms, and they achieve the same effects, communication with the African powers and commanding the presence of the deities among the humans on earth. These are all recurrent, repeatable performances whose sacredness resides in the perception of their continuity with African tradition and in the sense that they have come down from the past virtually unchanged.

The absence of mythic narrative in these ceremonies is related to the density of nonverbal symbols in them, symbols having mythical associations. Dance steps and gestures, songs, drum rhythms, symbolic objects and color symbolism all convey mental images related to the particular orisha. The most frequent group rites are bembes. Bembes are drum dances which are at once functional and festive. They mark some important event in the religious life of a devotee or priestess or celebrate a particular orisha (Brandon 1983:436–73; Murphy 1988; Gleason 1975).

Furthermore, bembes really consist of two major parts. The first part is the calling of the orisha; the second is their presence. Through spirit possession the orisha come down into the ceremony and the devotees are lifted up into the mythical realm, where they can have encounters with the deities. According to Ortiz, in Cuba these dances had a vivid theatrical quality and constituted a kind of dance-drama distinctly reminiscent of Yoruba possessions in which deities would enact a variety of scenes with onlookers (1959; also see Verger 1969). The myth was not told but enacted.

> These pantomimic dances, their gestures, steps, costumes and symbols are as carefully planned as ballet. . . . Their allegorical movements are so stylized that the uninitiated are unable to understand them without interpretation. In fact, these religious dances of the Yoruba are much more than ballets, for there is always singing as well, and in some cases the poetry of the songs is like a mythological parable which the faithful hear and which they find represented in the pantomime of the dance. (Oritz 1959:261)

This tight-knit complex of song, dance, and ritual gesture kept the mental images associated with the different orisha available for the devotees who could get the assistance of older people to help them understand the mythological meaning of what they were seeing.

In some instances, though, people possessed by the orisha actually interact with each other to bring about some result or to enact some facet of mythology. The most vivid example I observed was in 1979 at a Cuban Santeria house in New York during a bembe for a newly initiated Ochun priest. The orisha Yemaya, Ochun, and Oya are considered to be sisters, and the appearance of all three at this bembe was hoped for as a particularly auspicious event that would augur well for the career of the new initiate. At the time these notes begin there were three people on the dance floor who were already possessed, one by Yemaya and two by Ochun. They then set out to bring an Oya priestess into the possession state so that all three of the sisters would be there. The whole thing was done in dance.

> Oya (priestess)—a dark Cuban woman—had been dancing previously—began to jerk—once, then, again—resuming normal motion as if nothing had hap-

pened—then jerked again—begins to dance, jerks as if stung again—looks stunned—a woman removes her collares, then another removes her head-wrap—Rita (the head priestess) objects to the removal of the head-covering in Oya's colors but it is too late—it's already done.

Those who have already tranced (Ochuns 1 and 2 and Yemaya 1) move in on her, smiling, (dancing) with arms extended as if inviting her to come with them. She backs up but there is a circle of people holding her in. . . . After this she tranced strongly and began to dance with abandon, sweating and moving nearer the center of the dance area. (From my field notes, November 11, 1979)

What had occurred was that the goddesses, people who were already possessed, were inviting the Oya priestess to join them in the possessed state, to become a goddess herself. By removing her beads and headwrap and forming a circle behind her, the onlookers prepared her for that transition. What was recognized in the dance was transmitted to her through it, and finally through the dance it was realized, too, when she entered the center of the dance area in possession, miming the deity. Thus the mythological triumvirate was completed.

The image of the African past held and recited in Santeria's mythology is conveyed, sustained, and reinforced in its ritual performances. This means that what is collectively remembered in ceremonies celebrating the orisha, commemorating the ancestors, and so forth is more than the collective equivalent of personal or cognitive memory contained in the mythology. Santeria ritual demands not only that participants be competent to execute the performance but that they become physically and emotionally involved for the ceremony to work for them. The ceremony must be persuasive, so participants must not only know what to do and how to do it; they must also be physically habituated to the actions, they must have internalized in their bodies certain habits and ways of responding for the ceremonies to work. To the degree that these habits and ways of responding have been passed on from the earlier African tradition and continue to be learned as part of socialization into the religion, they are a component of social or collective memory and religious tradition, as well as being examples of the kind of motor habit memory Herskovits referred to. Not unlike habit memory, ritual requires the capacity of the group to reproduce particular performances by participating in them at social settings whenever the need for them arises. Ritual performances, like habit memories, have their full reality only as practice, but in the case of rituals these are practices set within the ongoing processes of social life. When an entire repertoire of physically habituated motor responses and ways of responding, such as religious dance and ceremonial spirit possession, are modeled on and perpetuate an earlier African tradition, the effect of calling them up is, among other things, to recreate the past and participate in it.

What was most important for the transmission of the African tradition was the preservation of intact versions of the ancestral institutions—or reinterpreted or even reified versions of these institutions—alongside a particular kind of interpersonal etiquette, a way relations between people could be structured that would allow these memories to have a life. Versions of the ancestral institutions include the idiom of the religious brotherhood expressed in Lucumi and Spanish kin terms, the models of marriages and brotherhood that exist in the myths of the orisha, the parent-child relationship that exists between the devotee and their priest or priestess, and the parent-child relationship that exists between the priests and their orisha. Kinship, marriage, and descent as metaphors for the relations among the orisha and the devotees continue an image of the former African social structure in a form which is recognizable to people in the present day but which also has a different character and symbolism from what surrounded it in the larger society. Part of that character and symbolism is preserved and given in etiquette.

The importance of etiquette is not to be slighted. As one astute observer has noted,

> Africans pay a great deal of attention to social formalities, to etiquette, to status differences, and to institutional procedures and roles because these conventions stand as the foundation of their community life, thus providing a framework to help them know what is happening and to get into it. . . . Africans use ritualized social arrangements to externalize and "objectify" their sense of a relationship because, if a relationship is meaningful to them, the recognition one person gives another must be visible outside their own personal involvement. For example, in many African societies, a gift is obligatory as just such a token of recognition that people have become involved or have done something together, a display that acknowledges one person's participation in another's life and often initiates reciprocal responsibilities. Formalities provide a means of setting people's involvements into patterns of communication which have precedents and continuity and which thus extend meaning. (Chernoff 1979:161)

African patterns of symbolizing social relationships are not only embodiments of memory but carriers of it. Two forms of etiquette that reinforce mental images and collective memory of the African past are ceremonial gift exchanges and prostrations. Both call up mental images related to two important Yoruba cultural values: reciprocity and hierarchy.

In Santeria etiquette is expressed in the ceremonial gift exchanges which were, and remain, an important aspect of some rituals. Every year the santeros are supposed to have a celebration of the anniversary of the day on which they completed their initiation into the priesthood. All their godchildren attend and bring symbolic gifts, including small amounts of money. (The amounts are ritually specified, thus turning them into religious symbols.) Other appropriate gifts are rum, five small white candles, and a coconut. All are laid on the floor in front of the orisha shrine as offerings to the santos and the santera. Everyone receives a countergift of fruits and cake from the santera to take home at the end of the celebration. This is a clear example of reciprocal gift exchange.

Sacrifice is another. The entire procedure of sacrifice is embedded within a metaphor of gift giving, or gift exchange as an expression of reciprocity between the human and spiritual worlds rather than as material exchange or as self-denial. Humans depend on the orisha; the orisha depend on human beings. Halifax and Weidman, students of Santeria in Miami, also found this to be the case.

> It [sacrifice] represents an act of obeisance. But, because of Cuban patterns of gift-giving, it also puts the recipient, i.e. the orisha, in a position of indebtedness. The individual is, in effect, "buying" power, a fact which may be reflected by greater confidence in subsequent relationships and activities. (1973:327)

It is only in a very remote sense that Halifax and Weidman's metaphor of buying power is correct, however, but it is still significant. There is always the danger that such exchanges will come to be interpreted just as they describe. This becomes a penetration of the present into the past, an interpretation in which, as many santeras say now, "the santos do nothing without a fee." Some santeros who decry the penetration of commercial values see the old values as best expressed by the attitude "I give to you that you may give to me" or "If I give this thing to you, I will always have it to give." Sacrifice, offering, and the exchange of symbolic objects provide a bridge through which ashe passes back and forth between this world and the other and between people on earth.

Among the Yoruba prostrations were a traditional means of showing recognition of seniority and superior status. D'Avenzac describes prostration in a religious context as the somatic as opposed to the verbal statement of prayer or communication with the deity (1967:276). Prostration is a generalized form of bodily action in Yoruba territories up to the present day. It can even be observed among Yoruba immigrants in the United States in private or domestic contexts where tradition is stressed. On a recent trip to Nigeria I saw a variety of forms of bodily obeisance, from full body prostrations to kneeling and curtsies, all as forms of respect offered to those in noble, senior, or other superior positions.

Prostration has been retained in Santeria as a means of indicating ritual kinship and differences in rank (Brandon 1983:480–82). The godparent-godchild relationship is the crucial relationship in Santeria. The godparent supervises the godchild's growth and development in the religion, schedules and performs subsequent initiations, and advises by means of the different oracles. The difference in status between the two is symbolized by greetings. Upon entry to the godparent's residence the godchild must go to the godparent's orisha shrine and prostrate before it on a straw mat. The godparent utters a verbal greeting and helps the godchild up. The godchild may then greet the godparent. Helping the godchild up is called "raising." Santeras do not raise those who do not bear a ritual kinship relationship to them. The godparent is always the first priest the godchild

"Primitive" Fashion	"Modern" Fashion
Earth *(abode of the ancestors, source of food)*	Floor Table
Legs, buttocks, feet *touch* Earth	Feet *touch* floor
Bowl *touches* Earth	Bowl *touches* table

FIGURE 4. Etiquette, food, and the ancestors, a transposition of collective memory. Left, eating in traditional ("primitive") fashion and completing the circuit; right, eating in "modern" fashion and completing the circuit.

greets upon entering a room, by prostrating before the priest just as before an orisha shrine. In public places and non-Santeria contexts the greeting may be modified from a full bodily prostration to a greeting in which the person bends over and touches the ground in front of the godparent's feet.

Within the prostration, then, is embedded an image of kinship and hierarchy which is signified by being performed as human movement. In prostration one does not simply state or indicate submission or inferior status; one actually becomes physically lower and hence also symbolically and socially lowered. All these messages are incorporated into a single comprehensive bodily performance.

One of the most intriguing examples of this kind, and one which also involves some religious and ecological symbolism, came to light when a Puerto Rican santera explained to me a piece of dinner etiquette. The Santeria house to which she belonged, a very traditional and well-respected one among the Cubans of New York, had a number of rules around meal taking which were explained to me by harking back to still older nonverbal behaviors. "When eating, your feet should touch the floor," she said. "As for the plates and bowls on the table, never pick them up and dish your food out of them. This is ungrateful. Take your dish over to them and, leaving them where they are [i.e., on the table], take the food from them." From further questioning I found that this etiquette was related to traditional Yoruba habits concerning eating sitting down on the earth. "Primitive" fashion, she called it, without disdain (see figure 4). Eating this way is still done in many Santeria houses on certain ceremonial occasions, and in very conservative houses new priests and priestesses take their meals seated on floor mats for a year after initiation (Brandon 1983:434).

What seems to have occurred here is a symbolic transfer of some of the motor habits, meanings, and symbolism related to the earth to the floor and table. Since the earth is conceived as being the abiding place of the ancestors and the source of all food and nourishment, the symbolic connection between humans and the earth and between humans and their ancestors requires that one maintain physical contact with the earth itself to complete and maintain an endless circuit which ceaselessly recycles the living and the dead and sustains them both. In a Western urban environment where one eats inside a house most of the time, the floor comes to take on the meanings formerly associated with the earth. Since devotees follow the European custom and eat most of their meals seated in chairs, the rule of etiquette forces them to maintain contact with the earth with the only remaining vehicle for it, their feet.

Not all the meanings related to the earth have been transferred to the floor. Just as the floor is *like* the earth, so is the table *like* the earth. This is why you don't pick up the bowls but go to them instead and get what you need. To pick up the bowls and plates containing food is to separate them from the earth and take full possession of them as yours, as human property. Doing this is void of reciprocity. It only takes; it turns the food into a mere thing; it is, in a word, "ungrateful." To go to the plates and bowls, however, is to state and recognize your dependence on the earth as source, to be in contact with the earth and to show gratitude. A complete circuit, to use an electronic metaphor, is maintained between the earth, the food, and the eater which in turn makes the meal complete.

The significance of this whole complex of meanings linking food, the ancestors, and the living was summed up aptly for me by the comments of another priestess. "When people die their bodies go into the earth; their bodies feed the grass; the cows eat the grass; and we eat the cows. That's how it is." The meal, once regulated and performed with the proper etiquette, becomes a religious act and, under changed circumstances, an embodiment of the African past.

The Yoruba speak of orisha shrines and altars as being "the faces of the gods." They are the most accessible, the most permanent, and the most controllable visage which the orisha present to humans. The ritual technique for creating a minimal shrine is simple and straightforward. A contemporary Yoruba devotee of the orisha Ogun, the late I. A. Ogunwa, described it succinctly. "When a shrine is called Ogun, it is Ogun. It becomes Ogun once you have placed two pieces of iron together and poured oil on it. The shrine needs food to be active. Then you can offer prayers to it. As soon as it is put together it stays Ogun, and will be Ogun forever after. By dismantling the iron, one takes Ogun away" (quoted in Barnes 1980:37). One did not have to be a priest to create a shrine. What was important was naming the shrine, the spatial relationships of the appropriate symbolic objects, (in Ogunwa's case, two pieces of iron, since Ogun is the orisha of iron), and offering food and prayers.

We have already seen that Lucumi plantation slaves were able to fashion altar images and statuary out of wood and clay and that they marked the walls of their barracks with signs understood only by initiates (Montejo 1968). The faces of the gods could be shaped out of mundane things and might well have gone unnoticed. Temporary or permanent shrines, since they were small collections of common objects imbued with invisible powers through invocation, herbs, and sacrifice, could be erected in the fields or even in the barracoons. Still, it is unlikely that large collections of such objects were ever allowed to accumulate in one place on Cuban plantations during the slavery era unless they were very well hidden.

Just as the rural slave priests and devotees from the different cult groups probably practiced their cultic rituals independently of each other in the beginning, so were the faces of the different orisha probably spatially separated. Where they all came together was in the city and in the countryside, later, after the abolition of slavery. In Early Santeria the sacred emblems which would have been separated and spread throughout a Yoruba community or the entire Yoruba territories were concentrated, compressed, and juxtaposed to each other within a single altar. The presence of these shrines in the homes of santeras means that their homes are capable of becoming temples at any time. Creating these altars was possible because the individual orisha altars were collections of portable objects that could be assembled and disassembled and placed beside other altars to create a single comprehensive spatial context. Doing this was the spatial equivalent of the corresponding social structural decision to integrate the separate orisha cult groups into a single religious sect. At the same time, in the postslavery rural areas and in the western Cuban cities, these orisha altars and shrines began to take on some of the characteristics of other folk Catholic altars, for keeping home altars was one of the major practices of Cuban folk Catholics as well as church Catholics, spiritists, and the adherents of other Afro-Cuban religions. The Santeria shrine became a parallel to this altar-keeping tradition, one of a set of ethnic and class variations on this nearly universal Cuban religious practice. Santeria altars are at once material culture, historical records, and forms of popular art. There is a visible symbolism which evokes mental images of the orisha, but there is also a hidden symbolism which evokes not only a mental image but also a power, ashe, which by its very nature is invisible and has no mental image of its own. Hence Santeria shrines consist simultaneously of the exposed and the concealed, the visible and the hidden.

The visible symbolism represented in plate 11 has its origins in myths, ritual prescriptions, and dreams. The color symbolism is ritually prescribed and is related to the corresponding colors of each of the santos. Numerous attributes of the orisha serve as symbols for them in the shrine. These originate in myth and spill over into ritual, particularly the ritual dress which the deities assume once they have possessed a devotee. While attempting to portray the characteristics of the deities according to their ancient mythical models, santeras have had to work with what was readily available to them. Many of the shrine objects are bought and manufactured objects which were not created to symbolize the santos. The objects have to be taken out of another context, often a nonreligious one, and put into the religious context of the orisha shrine. Brass and copper crowns are used to denote royalty, not the beaded headdress traditional for Yoruba kings. Miniature oars and miniature ships' steering wheels evoke the image of the sea goddess Yemaya. Ogun requires railroad spikes, European-style anvils, and iron pistols and pots.

Both the tradition of stereotyped narrative (myth) and the tradition of stereotyped action (ritual) are storehouses of mental images and concepts intended to be spoken, remembered, and acted out. All the variety of altar symbolism is an extension of ancient images already contained in the mythology and ritual in interaction with the ecology and technology of the new environment. The relationship between the concept in the mind and the sense image (whether present or remembered) is intrinsic. They are two sides of the same coin, but the relation between the sense image and an object in the external world is always symbolic, metaphorical, and to a greater or lesser extent arbitrary (Leach 1976:19; Fernandez 1974:120; Bucyznska-Garewicz 1979:253). Mythology and ritual provide a set of templates, guidelines, or exemplars, however, from which conventions can be extrapolated to cover new instances and to generate new practices. Mental images of the orisha derived from the mythology and ritual were projected onto objects from the new environment which could be made to contain and reinforce the images from memory by representing them externally in a visible material form that was continually perceptible. Believers attempted to preserve these images and memory collectively by recreating religious icons or by taking mundane objects, placing them in the appropriate spatial context, then designating them as religious icons pointing toward the orisha and distinguishing one orisha from another (see Ojo 1979:336–39). In the process they also incorporated new objects into the altars on the provision that they were in consonance with the already existing symbolism or personal characteristics of the deities as represented in mythology and ritual experience. These objects, then, could become signs pointing to the presence and existence of the orisha once they became stabilized by convention and habitual use. Any arbitrary association that is repeated consistently over a long period begins to appear to be an intrinsic part of the symbolism which may have always been there. The visible, the changed and changing face of the gods, embraces materials from scattered sources. It is an accumulation of symbolic objects of remembrance and tradition, African and Cuban, religious and secular. Put into the space of the shrine or altar, the objects acquire religious significance and through placing the objects in the shrine, personal experiences have religious significance conferred upon them. In some shrines Catholic symbolism seems outwardly fused with, yet inwardly separated from, symbols regarded as

African. In all cases, however, new symbols are embraced as long as they can be reconciled and fulfill a function in the old system of belief and in the social situation of the time.

Now that all of the orisha, symbolized by porcelain tureens, are contained in a single space, they are not simply placed next to each other but stacked up in a hierarchy in which Obatala, father of all the orisha, is topmost and Yemaya, their mother, just below him. When the shrine is in use and in effect becomes an altar, all the appropriate orisha objects are removed from the shelves that usually house them and are placed on the floor so as to be in contact with the earth (see plates 11 and 12). The santera puts a straw mat in front of the altar so that devotees may prostrate there (see plate 12). This is done on all important religious occasions. In ceremonies or altars erected for a particular orisha, the order of precedence which is shown by elevation may be altered. The change of spatial position signals the specific kind of altar involved. Such is the case in plate 12, which is not a general altar but a throne erected specifically for Yemaya (Our Lady of Regla), something which is revealed also by the presence of the crowned black female doll, the chromolithograph, and the blue cloth covering the large tureen constituting and containing Yemaya's witnessing objects. If the photograph reproduced here were in color it would be easy to recognize the cloth-covered tureens flanking the central one as belonging to Obatala and Ochun because of the color symbolism involved.

Despite the attention and expense lavished on this external visage, ultimately all the visual symbolism is but decoration, the accumulation of the efforts of generations of devotees to represent in a semi-public fashion the faces of the santos. The visible symbolism is an accommodation to external circumstances and an extension of the symbolism of sources of power that remain hidden and invisible. The sources of this hidden power are concealed within the tureens: a set of stones bathed in an herbal infusion and sacrificial blood. It is in this nexus of stones, herbs, and blood that the orisha reside; it is here that their powers are concentrated and are available to humans; it is here that humans gain some control over the ashe of the santos. What is concealed here is not only the ashe but also those elements of Santeria which are least compatible with either official or folk Catholicism yet represent the union and condensation of the whole array of powers encompassed within the Yoruba cosmological system. The stones serve, then, as a powerful symbolic link to the African past. According to believers, the most powerful stones are those brought from Africa, and some African slaves brought to Cuba concealed such stones in their stomachs (Bascom 1950:523). No one possesses such stones anymore but the stones in the priests' orisha shrines are connected with Africa nonetheless once they have been baptized in the African fashion, that is, "fed" with herbs and with blood from sacrificed animals.

Bascom, who studied Yoruba culture in Nigeria as well as in Cuba, noted a difference between the two regions in the ritual emphasis placed

on stones and herbs. To him, stones and herbs seemed to be more central
to religion, more focal, in Cuba.

> On the basis of my own field work among the Yoruba, stones (or *imponri*),
> blood, and herbs do not seem to assume the same importance that they hold in
> the minds of Jovellanos worshipers. The mythology or theology of the gods, the
> prayers and verbal formulae, and the rituals themselves seem of equal, if not
> greater importance. . . . The focal elements of Cuban santeria [the stones, herbs
> and blood] may not represent a carry-over of the focus of West African religion,
> but a shift in emphasis which has occurred as a result of culture contact. In this
> instance, acculturation would have resulted, not in a coalescence of beliefs, such
> as is represented by the syncretism of African deities and Catholic saints, the
> use of plaster images, chromolithographs, candles, and holy water, or the rec-
> itation of the Lord's Prayer and Hail Mary in santeria rituals, but a shift in the
> opposite direction. The present evidence is largely negative, but this interpre-
> tration is at least plausible. (1950:526–27)

Bascom's Cuban research was brief, three months in the summer of 1948,
and his descriptions of Santeria ritual seem to be about the more extreme
Catholic-oriented end of the continuum. (I have never seen a recitation of
the Lord's Prayer or Hail Mary in any of the Santeria ceremonies and rituals I have attended.) In the light of the material presented earlier in this
chapter and of the history detailed in previous chapters, I believe that in
Santeria the evidence of a "shift in the opposite direction" from syncretism
with Catholicism is no longer largely negative and is quite plausible, especially given the veil of secrecy and hiddenness which surrounds the stones.

In Nigeria the secrecy of some religious knowledge was conventional
and gave the different priests distinctive types of powers. This was the secrecy that separated the family of descendants of one orisha from those of
another and separated the laity from the priesthood. Secrecy assured that
the potentially lethal power which the truth was thought to possess would
be under responsible care and control, for truth had life-destroying as well
as life-enhancing powers. While it was not intended that religious truths
would be kept secret perpetually, it was recognized that revealing them involved control of their possibly deadly effects so that their life-giving effects
could be released (Buckley 1976:418–20). In the plantations and cities of
Cuba this became a secrecy that protected the sons and daughters of the
orisha from the slave master and the police.

What we seem to have here is continuity at one level in the midst of
change on another. At the same time as there is an emphasis on elements
defined in the present context as prototypically African, these elements are
also kept hidden for a number of reasons: for fear of persecution or disapproval, for the protection of the things themselves, and because of the
African convention of secrecy that attends the esoteric truths of religion.
Secrecy and hiddenness, too, can be forms of emphasis. The stones, blood,
and herbs remain hidden, concealed in the place where the strong powers

reside, more powerful and more truthful because they are hidden. They are maintained and transmitted as part of the collective memory accessible to all santeros. Knowingly or unknowingly they are a jealously guarded focus marking differences between Santeria and Catholicism and emphasizing the continuity of African religious traditions.

The memory of an African, then, was part of a web of collective memory that spread throughout an African ethnic group. The uprooting of the person from African soil, the purgatory of the Middle Passage, and the casting down as a slave in the Americas did not obliterate individual memories, but there was a decisive break, an abyss, that separated the old community in Africa from the new slave community. The cultural resources of any group never remain constant. When the innovations of individuals become acceptable to the group, when knowledge diffuses from one group or location to another, when people migrate between the city and the countryside, and when there are significant demographic shifts in the population, the cultural resources of a group are affected. Normally any group would want to pursue a two-sided strategy of self-management in which it added to its informational resources while conserving the resources it already had. Internal problems of gaps and breakdowns in the transmission process virtually guarantee that there will be some changes in cultural resources over time. Many changes in the cultural resources of a group, though, are the result of conscious decisions by individuals and organized collections of individuals within the group. Some changes in cultural resources may even be the result of decisions made by people outside the group (Roberts 1964:442). A variety of external forces promoted the disintegration of African religious consciousness; other external forces promoted the transformation of that consciousness into Catholicism; but there was an internal process at work, too, that militated against a total reconstruction. I do not wish to make a case for a pristine, frozen kind of continuity. That simply is not the case. The African religious system could not be reconstructed in its original form because memory of it was reshaped by the activities and experiences of later generations of Afro-Cubans, slave and free, in the diverse contexts of Cuban society in which they found themselves. Here we begin to encroach on the problem of Afro-Catholic syncretism in Santeria. What I have tried to do is to suggest some ways in which the continuity of the tradition may have been accomplished and to show how the reconstruction of the Yoruba religious system in Cuba was not only an individual accomplishment but a collective one as well.

Problems of Syncretism

The traditional models for anthropological research have been oriented toward the study of relatively simple, relatively isolated, small-scale "primitive" societies on one hand and marginal, nationally based, culturally distinctive ethnic groups on the other. Anthropologists could carry out studies of these groups with the assumption that for each of them there was but a single culture. To assume that these monocultural societies and groups were culturally uniform as well was entirely consistent with that point of view and projected an ideal of cultural purity that became enshrined in the form of a temporal and methodological fiction, the ethnographic present. Multicultural societies and the kinds of events and situations I have described in previous chapters could only be seen as somewhat exceptional cases, culturally impure because they are tainted by contact between cultures and by the odor of history. For this reason the study of culture contact and syncretism has remained a comparatively undeveloped aspect of anthropological research and theory.

The history of Western religious polemic also reveals an intellectual predilection for purist and elitist philosophies. Syncretic religions, such as Santeria, certainly look bad in the midst of the emphasis on credal purity and religious exclusiveness that has dominated the history of Western religions. In the center of religious battles over doctrine, interpretation, and ritual, the syncretist is a traitor, someone whose loyalty and faith are questionable. From this point of view the best that can be said about syncretism is that it is an effort of would-be peacemakers to reconcile conflicting religious traditions by wishful thinking. Syncretism is unity at the expense of truth and is inevitably superficial because what bothers syncretists is not truth but religious conflict. The worst that can be said is that syncretism is evidence of insincerity, confusion, and ambivalence. Syncretism is corrupt and lacking in doctrinal integrity. The believers are confused and do not realize that they participate in different religions. In their confusion syncretists distort and impoverish religious tradition. Such objections to syncretic religion tell more about the terms of Western religious debates than about religious phenomena themselves.

The Western religionist's assumption that religious groups must have clear doctrinal boundaries and mutually exclusive memberships parallels anthropological assumptions about culture and society. Yet cultural struggle and the fusion and separation of peoples and civilizations are part of the whole of human history. Continuity and discontinuity, persistence and disruption, survival, disintegration, and death mark the path of the history I have tried to trace, scouring the dominant and subordinate, the oppressor and the oppressed. In the Americas, Amerindian, African, Asian, and European peoples were brought together under an economic system dominated and controlled by Europeans. Intact preservation of the lifeways of the homeland was not possible for any of these peoples. Nowhere have their traditions continued to exist without change. Slavery, conquest, and colonialism favored neither the calm dissolution of cultural differences nor the formation of homogeneous monocultural societies. Syncretism in this context is emblematic of oppression, change, youthfulness, and cultural impurity.

Explanation of change of this type involves three separate problems. The first, the transition problem, is to find the route by which one stage of a change has evolved from an earlier one. Second is the embedding problem: what is the matrix of social and cultural behavior in which the change is being carried? Solving this problem shows that the change being studied is linked to other cultural changes going on in the system and that, cumulatively, they all possess a common direction. It is also concerned with relationships between the changed cultural feature and social, economic, demographic, or ecological changes. The evaluation problem is the last of the three. It involves the discovery of the subjective (or latent) correlates of the objective (or manifest) changes that have taken place. Solving this problem involves obtaining statements of the social and cultural significance of the changed form. It implies that at some point the change was part of an issue that rose into consciousness. At some point people consciously accepted, resisted, negotiated, accommodated, or promoted the changed feature.

We can look at syncretism as a state or as a process. If we look at Santeria, which has been described as syncretic, in terms of how its particular components or attributes are systematically related to each other—the embedding problem—we are viewing it in terms of a specific state or condition. I will not attempt to do this here. Alternatively, we can look at syncretism as a gradual process that develops over time and through a number of stages that can be distinguished from each other—the transition and evaluation problems. Here we will be concerned mainly with syncretism as a process. While the two perspectives of state and process are not inherently irreconcilable, bringing them together has proved to be one of the knottiest problems of the social sciences, cultural studies, and history.

Syncretism is accomplished, first of all, by reconciling ideas which do not conflict with each other. Yet fusion of the totality of distinct religious systems is very unlikely and is certainly too rigid a criterion for assessing the cultural integrity of the new religious tradition. Syncretism is always selective. The idea, then, that syncretism in Santeria represents an unresolved conflict, a failed synthesis between African religion and Christianity, is something that needs to be taken seriously. But conflict for whom? In what circumstances or contexts?

Conflict and contradiction, even when recognized as such, can persist as normal experience for relatively long periods of time. Social and material conflicts can become embodied in ongoing patterns of ritual symbolism, politics, or how people organize themselves to do work. Conflicting ideas, though, can only be reconciled by redefining the reality to which they refer.

We see this most readily with words, in dictionaries which trace the changes in meaning that words have undergone. When changes in the meanings of words and ideas occur, the meanings and associations they previously had do not simply vanish. For at least some people the old meanings remain the primary ones, the only ones which are truly correct. For others the old meaning becomes one of an array of possible alternative meanings. And for others the old and the new meanings are fused under a broader conception. For all of them knowledge of the appropriate context in which the idea, word, or representation can occur is crucial. The same applies to syncretism, in which the reality to which an image, word, or gesture refers becomes redefined while the same word, image, or gesture continues to be used. This creates a situation in which the important and fundamental cultural categories people use become at once semantically rich and internally inconsistent.

Cultural systems using such categories can persist over long periods. Most of the postcolonial world and all multiethnic or multiracial societies are in this situation, a situation in which the ideological, ethnic, racial, and economic conflicts which exist within a highly differentiated cultural system are all expressed by a common set of symbols and concepts. Since the conflicts are real and the concepts, symbols, representations, and categories are continually being contested and redefined, they are always incompletely synthesized.

The roots of this cultural system in Cuba are in the period 1492–1760, when the Cuban population was small yet very diverse and atomized. The Spanish conquest of Cuba was the crucible in which Amerindian, African, and European influences, objects, and ideas began to interweave. A parallel intermingling took place on the biological level, and a subtle and elaborate racial terminology evolved in which an ideology of "pure" types gave way to a graded racial continuum only partially related to skin color and ancestry. A relatively widespread yet mixed creole culture and a system of racial relations that functioned without either fixed color lines or group endogamy emerged out of this period. The creole culture continued to evolve by absorbing elements from Spanish, Islamic, West and Central African, and Amerindian sources. But a set of distinctions gradually arose siting the main cultural groups and trends in the society between two poles: Spanish and African.

When, in the period of the mid-eighteenth-century sugar boom, immigration (largely black) became the order of the day, the newcomers were absorbed into a national culture and system of racial and ethnic relations that was already set and coherent. The culture and system of racial and ethnic relations later came to include populations from Haiti, Jamaica, China, and the Yucatan Peninsula. Incorporating diverse groups into a starkly yet fluidly class-structured society produced a great deal of cultural variation. Nonetheless the creole culture continued to be seen as poised between the poles of Africa and Spain. Whether in the form of political divisions, economic inequality and poverty, ethnic group stereotypes, or racial and religious hostility, difference and division became fundamental in the structure of Cuban society. Though under severe strain at times, both the

Spanish-oriented but internally syncretic creole culture and the graded socioracial continuum have survived up to today. In a society like Cuba where the cultural traditions of the Africans could neither be continued entirely intact nor smoothly integrated into a harmonious national culture what evolved was an intersystem or cultural continuum (Drummond 1980:353).

In a cultural continuum the differences in thought and behavior derive from a shared pool of ideology, history, myth, and experience. But people relate to this shared pool differently because of their place in society and because of their place on the continuum. Thus these differences can be used as a way for people to represent themselves to others and to themselves. Into this shared pool fall racial and ethnic concepts, stereotypes, and images, the relationships between symbols and economic and political power on one hand and tradition and self-identity on the other. The reality of the intersystem then is the bridges or transformations necessary to get from one end of the intersystem to the other. It is from this perspective that we will look at what happened when African and European religions encountered each other in Cuba and produced Santeria. In such a situation the systematic nature of culture must be located in the relationships which, through a series of gradations or transformations, and situational adjustments, link one intersystem with another (ibid.:370).

In the course of sketching the history of Santeria I tried to describe the stages through which Santeria seems to have developed. The stages around which I organized the history constitute the developmental continuum of Yoruba-Santeria illustrated in figure 5: the network of Aja-area Yoruba-dominated religious traditions brought to Cuba, what I have called Lucumi religion or Early Santeria, an ethnically exclusive religion containing African as opposed to strictly Yoruba elements and elements of Cuban folk Catholicism; and the fusion of the earlier African and Catholic elements with healing-oriented Espiritismo which came to be Santeria as it persists today. In the Cuban context Yoruba religion, Early Santeria, and Santeria all developed under the dominance and hegemony of official Catholicism and the colonial and metropolitan governments which exerted continuous pressure until the Cuban Revolution and served as exemplars toward which people were to aspire. What have been dubbed Santerismo and Orisha-Voodoo came into existence in the United States under the dominance and hegemony of a secular democratic political ideology and an advanced monopoly capitalist state.

The different phases or religions I refer to as Yoruba religion, Early Santeria—Lucumi religion, Santeria, Santerismo, and Orisha-Voodoo can be seen as the path by which a single "ethnicity" was transformed over time. In this passage through time, aspects of the old ethnic identity were deleted, reified, or generalized in response to the logic of historical situations and events. Along this path the "ethnicity" absorbed a wide diversity of cultural elements and many individuals of non-Yoruba origin. These ac-

Developmental Continuum		Location	Form of Hegemony
	Yoruba religion	Aja area West Africa	Feudal-like, monarchical regimes; religious hegemony
	Yoruba religion	Cuba	Colonial dominance; hegemony of official Spanish Catholicism
	Lucumi religion (Early Santeria)	Cuba	Colonial dominance; hegemony of official Spanish Catholicism
	Santeria	Cuba	Since 1960s dominance of socialist hegemony
	Santeria	USA	Dominance of secular capitalist hegemony
	Santerismo	USA	Dominance of secular capitalist hegemony
	Orisha-Voodoo	USA	Dominance of secular capitalist hegemony

FIGURE 5. The developmental continuum of which Santeria forms a part, correlated with location and dominant hegemonic form. The arrow indicates the variant forms which the tradition has evolved. Forms higher up in the figure are usually earlier in time but are not necessarily replaced by those evolving later, even in the same location.

cidents of heritage and birth were made coherent by coalescing them into a unique socioreligious category and what members came to think of as a distinct and unchanging heritage. Of all the tributaries, only the Yoruba tended to be remembered as ancestral; all innovation and change were fitted into it.

It is useful to look at the cultural continuum as having two levels of structure, external and internal. As we shall see, the internal variation within the continuum contributes some of its most important characteristics and gives rise to a number of situations that seem confusing, contradictory, and anomalous but which are also very common.

Let's take the instance where the creole cultural continuum emerges out of the contact of populations from two systems. The cultural continuum which forms between the two systems thus has two poles. Using Yoruba religion (Y) and Catholicism (C) as examples, the external structure is simple and looks like this:

Y   YC   C

Y	YC			C	*External*
Y	YC	C	C	C	*Internal*
Y	Y	YC	C	C	
Y	Y	C	CY	C	

FIGURE 6. Model of the restructuring continuum of Early Santeria–Lucumi religion. Y = Yoruba religion, C = Catholicism. The shaded area encloses the range of variation of Early Santeria.

Between Yoruba religion and Catholicism there emerges a third system (YC) which contains elements of both. While, for the sake of the clarity in this example, it is justifiable to assume that both Yoruba religion and Catholicism were culturally uniform, we know that this was not the case. Within each of the religious traditions there were internal differences, but for the time being we will assume that they are not relevant because they affect neither the perceived "Yorubaness" of Yoruba religion, the "Catholicness" of the Catholic religion, nor the continuum that evolves between the two. We cannot assume, however, that YC is culturally uniform. People assimilated and retained Yoruba religion and Catholicism in different ways and at different rates as well as within different social and ecological situations so that there inevitably arose a range of variation between Y and C. In figure 6 YC encloses this range, and this range of variations is YC's internal structure. In some areas of the internal structure of YC, Y dominates. In others, C does. In still others, Y and C have equal influence and might actually be fused, while in still other areas Y or C might exist alone. However, neither Y nor C occurs exclusively in this area of the structural continuum and, overall, YC is a mixture of Ys and Cs unlike the ends of the continuum which are uniform. If we take the internal structure of YC into account, our previous example looks like figure 6 and represents the continuum at the stage of Lucumi religion–Early Santeria.

In the situation where there are several cultural sources, the level of heterogeneity increases tremendously. Below I have added Espiritismo to the previous amalgam and represent the situation at the stage of Santeria in prerevolutionay Cuba. The cultural continuum becomes slightly more complex externally as variant forms develop between the two old external poles and the new pole (E) as well as with the preexisting variant YC.

$$Y \qquad YC \qquad C$$
$$YE \qquad YCE \qquad CE$$
$$E$$

The internal structure, however, would be even more complicated (see figure 7). If we combine the developmental continuum (the sequence of

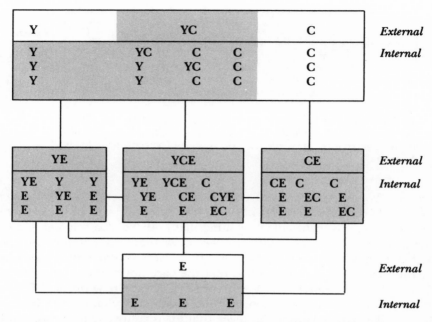

FIGURE 7. Model of the restructuring continuum of Santeria in prerevolutionary Cuba. Shaded areas indicate the continuum of variation occurring between the three poles of Yoruba religion (Y), Catholicism (C), and Espiritismo (E).

stages) with the simplified version of the structural continuum which was renovated at each stage of the process, we get some idea of the actual complexity and variety of religious practice that must have existed on the ground. Here we restrict ourselves to the Cuban situation.

We can see that succeeding stages need not entirely eliminate earlier ones and that at each stage of the development of Santeria there is a renovation of the structural continuum that was the product of the previous stage (figure 8). This differentiation in the realm of religion I take to be symptomatic of the highly differentiated cultural system that existed in Cuba.

Any cultural continuum is identified by arbitrary boundaries that break up the series of intermediate forms. The boundaries can be of many types. Often they are part of a more general system of differences related to behavior, belief, physical features, social status, or ancestry by which the population is divided into categories of religious, ethnic, racial, or other social groups. These differences can be lifted out and shown as representations of the groups because they derive their meaning from a repository of popular images and myths as well as the personal experiences of individuals and

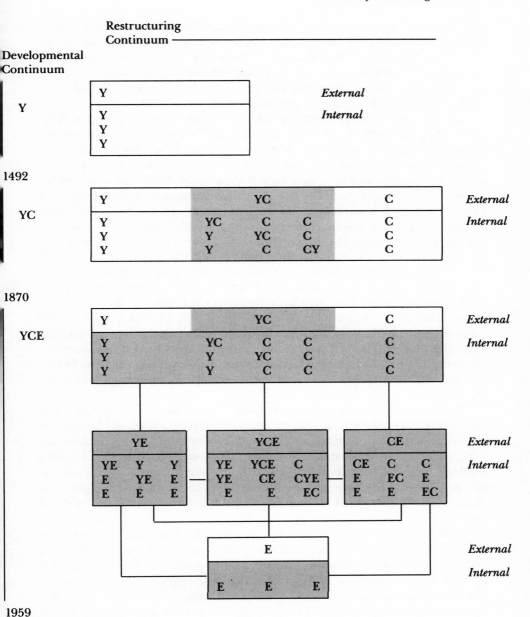

FIGURE 8. A processual model of the cultural continuum (or intersystem) of Santería in Cuba.

the historical knowledge of the various groups. The content of such ethnic, religious, or racial stereotypes varies from case to case and may well change over time. In the case of Cubans of African ancestry, the stigma of slave status and African origin lay stamped onto the skin and the memory of free and slave alike. Powerful images clustered around these physical and social differences were the legacy of generations of Afro-Cubans.

At the same time as prerevolutionary Cuban creole religious culture was highly differentiated, there was but a small number of common concepts and images in which that differentiation could be expressed because of the hegemony of the state and the union of the state with Roman Catholicism. Groups within Cuban society assimilated the hegemonic culture at different rates and in different ways. These groups are distinct from each other, but they are also linked. Yoruba religion was preserved in the urban cabildos, possibly in the maroon communities, and among rural slaves, but the guided syncretism the church hoped to foster was most evident in the cabildos. In slave quarters in the countryside, where the priests rarely tread, there was a more diffuse Catholic influence emanating from the creole culture as much as or more than from the church or priests.

Despite the fact that they assimilated Catholicism in different ways, most Cubans were prepared to assert that they were Catholics and behaved as Catholics did. This did not mean that they all necessarily agreed on what Catholics did or didn't do but rather that the category of Catholic was a meaningful one by which they distinguished and described religious behavior and was both compulsory and commonplace in the prerevolutionary period.

We have seen that in Cuba many people regarded themselves as Catholic even if they didn't go to church, if they practiced a form of Catholicism different from what went on in church, and even if they practiced in a way which the church condemned. For many the crucial incident cementing a Catholic religious identity was infant baptism. Moreover, as the population of Cuba grew and became more diverse, so did the number of religious influences, even though official Roman Catholicism remained dominant and hegemonic.

Folk Catholics, church Catholics, people who practiced the different African religions at home and went to church, people who practiced mixed Afro-Catholic rites exclusively, as well as those who went to church and practiced Espiritismo, or Afro-Catholic-Spiritist religion, all claimed to be Catholic. The semantic content of the term *Catholic* thus became both rich and internally inconsistent. What it meant to be Catholic in Cuban creole culture was in a continuous process of redefinition through time.

If we take only a few of the social and cultural differences that were relevant during the development of Lucumi religion and correlate them with probable religious practice, we get the diagram in figure 9, period 1. The four groups are the Spanish-born governing elite (the peninsulares), the white creoles born on the island, and two groups of Afro-Cubans, the Lucumi and a putative group of other African nations. At the same time as the four groups are differentiated in terms of nativity and ethnicity, they are linked by being included under Catholicism; this was the hegemonic intention all along. However, in terms of the internal structure of each group they are at once linked to the others but also differentiated from them. Lucumis and Spanish peninsulares both considered themselves Catholic, but the peninsulares were supposed to be church Catholics while Lucumi practiced varying mixtures of Yoruba religion and folk Catholicism, or possibly one or the other alone. This was the situation in period 1, Lucumi religion–Early Santeria. With the advent of Espiritismo some of the spiritists include themselves as Catholics and some people who already think of themselves as Catholics continue to do so even if they also practice Espiritismo, so the internal diversity accumulates even further (period 2). Nonetheless, the term *Catholic* remains a meaningful category of religious identity for all the groups even if it does not have the same meaning for everyone or apply to the same cultural content when people at different points on the continuum make use of it.

The acceptance of Catholic terms as the idiom in which distinctions could be made that applied to all the groups was intended to unite them. At some level it did. Hence a series of bridges can be constructed across at least four religious systems at different points. The saints' images were only the most obvious cultural key to this set of bridges because they were a central symbol for adherence to Catholicism and because of the imposition of the saints' images as representations of social as well as spiritual powers. We have previously noted the difference between folk Catholic and official interpretations of the nature of sainthood. These differences did not mean that folk Catholics at home and priests at church necessarily used very different images to represent the saints. They did not. One could go from official Catholicism to a folk Catholicism which need not be mixed with either spiritism or African influences (although it might be), through Espiritismo, and over to Santeria and even other Afro-Cuban religions by a series of bridges and transformations. These would be provided in part by varying interpretations of the cult of saints. From this perspective folk Catholicism, Santeria, and Espiritismo look like uninstitutionalized saint cults parallel to the cult of saints in the hegemonic Roman Catholic religious institution.

In light of the foregoing discussion of the role of common concepts, it would not be inappropriate to argue that any talk of syncretism is irrelevant, that syncretism is really a product of the outside observer's knowledge of history and of his or her relationship to the religion under study. The concept of syncretism is irrelevant to insiders and is not a factor in their religious consciousness.

Syncretism is a concept of the historian and anthropologist, not of the believer who has no scientific or historical interest in his religion. Yet some version of the idea is inherent in the statements and intuitions of believers

Period 1. Lucumi Religion–Early Santeria

Catholic										
Spanish	Creoles		Lucumi				Other African nations			
C	C	F	F	FY	YF	Y	F	FX	XF	X

Period 2. Santeria

Catholic														
Spanish	Creoles				Lucumi						Other African nations			
C	C	P	F	H	H	HFY	HYF	YHF	FY	YF	Y	H	FX	HX	HFX	X

FIGURE 9. The meaning of *Catholic* at two periods of the developmental continuum. Y = Yoruba religion, C = official Catholicism, F = folk Catholicism, P = philosophical spiritism (the *cientificos*), H = mystical, healing oriented spiritism, X = palo, Congolese religion. When letters appear in combination they appear in decreasing order of cultural influence. For example, in FY folk Catholic influences are more prevalent than Yoruba ones, while in YF the opposite is true.

who do have such an interest and constitutes a folk science and body of distinctions and observations on which we must draw. Believers may make distinctions among religious traditions and syncretized elements of them in relation to a collective memory in which making these distinctions has become traditional and stereotyped and if there exist, in the present, distinct social contexts or institutions to which believers can refer them. It might be that the actual content of these categories, contexts, and social institutions need not be the same as they were in the past as long as their relationship to each other is the same, i.e., as long as they occupy similar positions in the structure of ideas and social life as they did in previous periods.

While it is often stated that syncretists, and by implication, Santeria devotees, do not know that they are practicing two religions, it cannot be said that Santeria adherents do not make a distinction between Catholicism and the African religions. At least some do, and there is evidence for this.

Lazaro Benedi Rodriguez, who had been active as a diviner before the Cuban Revolution and was involved in both Santeria and Palo, was interviewed in 1969 by members of the team led by Oscar Lewis which produced *Living the Revolution*. He clearly does not identify the African and Catholic religions but distinguishes them.

> I've had many arguments with Catholics and with believers in the African religion, and have never been able to come to an agreement with any of them.

There are those who say that the African religion is a myth, a dream, a means of exploiting the ignorance of others, a web of deceit. But I, and all believers, have faith because we've had proof. It's exactly the same in the case of Catholicism. Men pick and choose among its teachings, and in the end each does what is most convenient for him. (Quoted in Lewis, Lewis, and Rigdon 1977:130–131)

Benedi was not alone. Francesca Muniz, despite the fact that she referred to the deities of Santeria as the saints in a passage quoted earlier, distinguished "her religion" from church Catholicism on the basis of the statues and images found in the church.

In my religion, the only things that are like the statues [of the Roman Catholic Church] are the Elegua. There are other stones, and each has a name. We don't have images and statues or pictures like the Church has. Things are symbolically represented by colors and stones, but not by things which could have been made by man. I don't know why it's that way. (Quoted in Butterworth. 1980:88)

Muniz's comment is significant also because it indicated in a general way the point on the continuum of Santeria practice from which she is viewing the Catholic Church and indicating what she sees as important differences. She can distinguish Santeria from church Catholicism in terms of the use of statues and images. Other Santeria devotees, however, might not be able to make the distinction in the same way as she does because they do use the Catholic images in their religious practices.

Estaban Montejo, who was a slave in the 1860s, gives the most detailed and extended example of these distinctions which I have found. On the plantation where he grew up and from which he escaped, there were three religions. He was able to distinguish them readily, and so were other slaves.

The African gods are different, though they resemble the others, the priest's gods. They are more powerful and less adorned. Right now if you were to go to a Catholic church you would not see apples, stones or cock's feathers. But this is the first thing you see in an African house. The African is cruder. I knew of two African religions in the barracoons: the Lucumi and the Congolese. . . . The Congolese used the dead and snakes for their religious rites. They called the dead nkise and the snakes emboba. They prepared big pots called nganga which would walk about and all, and that was where the secret of their spells lay. *All the Congolese had these pots for mayombe. . . .*

The Congolese were more involved with witchcraft than the Lucumi who had more to do with the saints and with God. . . . The difference between the Congolese and the Lucumi was that the former solved problems while the latter told the future. This they did with diloggunes, which are round white shells from Africa with mystery inside. . . .

The other religion was the Catholic one. This was introduced by the priests, but nothing in the world would induce them to enter the slaves' quarters. They were fastidious people, with a solemn air which did not fit the barracoons—so

solemn that there were Negroes who took everything they said literally. This
had a bad effect on them. *They read the catechism and read it to the others with all the*
words and prayers. . . .The fact is I never learned that doctrine because I could
not understand a thing about it. *I don't think the household slaves did either although,*
being so refined and well treated, they all made out that they were Christian. . . .There
was no love lost between the Congolese magic-men and the Congolese Christians, each of who thought they were good and the others wicked. *This still goes*
on in Cuba. The Lucumi and the Congolese did not get on either; it went back
to the difference between saints and witchcraft. (Montejo 1968:33–37)

In skeletal form, here are some of the more salient attributes and distinctions Montejo made:

Lucumi	*Congolese*	*Catholic*
African	African	Catholic
religion	religion	religion
saints, gods, and God	the dead	the priest's gods
saints	witchcraft	———
crude	crude	refined
more powerful	more powerful	less powerful
divination	magic	?
shells	pots	?
field slaves	field slaves	house slaves, priests
rebellious	cowardly	fastidious
disliked cane	hardworkers	house work, no
cutting	at cane	cane cutting
	cutting	well treated

Montejo equated gods and saints and linked the saints with Lucumi religion rather than with Catholicism. For him the saints and the orisha may
be the same powerful spiritual beings, but neither of them have anything to
do with the teachings of Catholicism (of which he claims to understand
nothing). It would be a mistake to view these distinctions as referring solely
to the historical origins of the religions. These distinctions were important
because they stood in a relationship to groups that made up the contemporary world in which he lived. There were still people who identified
themselves as Congolese and there was still a Catholic Church with priests.
("This still goes on in Cuba.") Montejo also made use of a number of stereotyped images (rebellious Lucumis, cowardly Congolese, and fastidous
white priests; field slaves as African religious devotees with Catholicism as
a religion for the house slaves and priests). With stereotyped images such as
these he was able to distinguish the three religions and to give them different placements within the social and cultural world of the Cuban sugar
plantation as seen from the point of view of a field slave.

At least two things are clear from the words of these three devotees
(Benedi, Muniz, and Montejo). The first is that at least some devotees see

a difference between Santeria and official Catholicism and can say what the difference is within an idiom dominated by Catholic terminology and symbolism. That very same hegemonic symbolism can be used to distinguish one religious form from another. This seems clear enough. The second thing is that those who make this distinction do not all make it in the same way or with the same means. None of them give any evidence that they think they are practicing two religions, one African and one European. Indeed they seem to identify themselves primarily, if not solely, with a religion they regard as African, or at least one which is not official Catholicism. While this may not be true of all Cuban devotees and priests, it is certainly true of some of them. If they are able to distinguish one from the other, in whatever terms, it is not too far-fetched to think that they might also be able to tell when they overlap.

Individuals might know quite well where they lie along the continuum in terms of what they see as the relevant stereotypical characteristics of other groups. They might also be aware of all or much of the range of behavior or belief which the continuum allows. They may not imitate the behavior of other groups. Then on the other hand they might do so, as LePage describes in relation to the creole linguistic continuum.

> Each individual creates the systems for his verbal behavior so that they resemble the group or groups with which from time to time he may wish to be identified, to the extent that: (a) he can identify the groups (b) he has both opportunity and ability to observe and analyse their behavioral systems (c) his motivation is sufficiently strong to impel him to choose, and to adapt his behavior accordingly (d) he is able to do so. (Le Page et al. 1974)

Much depends upon the nature of the relationships between the groups and the contexts in which members of the groups typically encounter each other. Classification of a slice of behavior as Catholic (or Santeria or Espiritismo) depends on who is doing the classifying and where the behavior is taking place. Events, behaviors, and situations drift back and forth between stereotyped images of the ends of the continuum, and the content of ethnic or religious stereotypes varies from case to case. People appear to be following multiple but incompatible rules, but their behavior is still systematic and closely related to particular situations and contexts. The intersystem brought into prominence when, for example, Palo and Santeria are the focus is different from that created when Santeria and Espiritismo or regla de ocha and church Catholicism are the focus. Raymond Smith, using the creole language analogy again, describes a situation strikingly like that which confronts us.

> Different concepts are used in different contexts by the same people; the meaning of a given usage has to be interpreted in its context of use. The situation has been likened to the 'post-creole speech continuum' (DeCamp 1971) where a particular speaker commands a certain range of the continuum of linguistic

variation, deploying speech abilities in different ways depending on the context (Drummond 1980). This leads to the question of whether the contexts themselves fall into any kind of pattern, bringing us back to class and racial group variation by another, though perhaps more rewarding, route. (Smith 1988:39)

In a situation like this the question "What religion is this person practicing?" needs to be answered within a framework that gives due recognition to the internal variation of the cultural system as a whole and the characteristic way in which people divide it up and classify it in terms of religion. Ambivalence and a kind of false consciousness combine to deny importance to Catholic or African customs as such. The actual origins are not seen as that important and in many cases are not known anyway. The customs are honored not in their absence but only after they have been redefined and reconstituted as "Catholic" or "African." If the relevant distinction is between Catholic and African religion, then it doesn't matter if, objectively, the "African" religion contains Catholic elements, is not traceable to a single, pure ethnic source, and differs considerably from any presumed African prototype. In the context of segmenting the continuum between these two stereotyped poles Catholic and African, some part of it will be defined and constituted as "African" in line with the polar stereotype and regardless of what other content may be there.

The kind of situation that results from this is illustrated in figures 10 and 11. Figure 10 represents hypothethical divisions and classifications of the Cuban religious continuum into Catholic and African as seen from the points of view of two persons who are encountering each other (encounter A). In response to the question "Who are the real Catholics?" the two persons in this encounter disagree. The two can be imagined to be facing each other with their different respective classifications of the same religious continuum and projecting their classifications out into the world and onto other people. One person applies the term *Catholic* extremely broadly, while the other views only those who who do not mix their Catholicism with any form of African religion as being real Catholics. In figure 11, there is a similar encounter involving another pair of hypothetical classifications of the Cuban religious continuum into Catholic and African (encounter B). The two persons in this encounter disagree in a way different from those in the previous encounter. They can be imagined to be answering the question "Who are the practitioners of African religion?" In the more general context of the inclusive self-identification as Catholic, as we saw before, the "African" becomes "Catholic" and different attributes are relevant. In these kinds of situations only some attributes are considered relevant by each of the parties and even those might not be consistent in different contexts. Ethnic-racial identity needs to be seen as a process of taking up or learning parts of a rich repertoire of beliefs about what is involved in being African, Lucumi, Cuban, white, "in the religion," etc.

The creole cultural continuum, therefore, contains no invariant properties and no uniform rules. The society and culture are continuously in

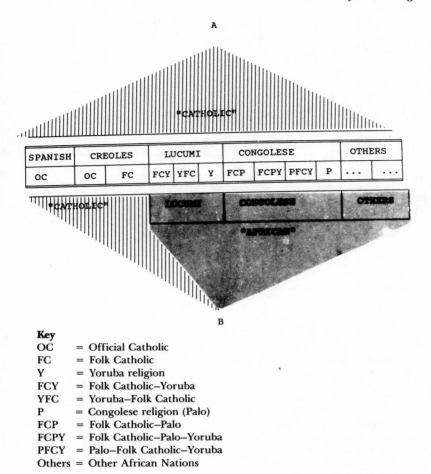

Key

OC	=	Official Catholic
FC	=	Folk Catholic
Y	=	Yoruba religion
FCY	=	Folk Catholic–Yoruba
YFC	=	Yoruba–Folk Catholic
P	=	Congolese religion (Palo)
FCP	=	Folk Catholic–Palo
FCPY	=	Folk Catholic–Palo–Yoruba
PFCY	=	Palo–Folk Catholic–Yoruba
Others	=	Other African Nations

FIGURE 10. Redefinition through encounter A. Two people encounter each other and respond to the question "Who are the
real Catholics?" by projecting their classification onto the continuum. Lines designate "Catholic," and the solid gray area designates "African."

the process of definition, constantly defining and redefining themselves
through the encounters of groups and individuals. Over time some areas of
the continuum may become more densely populated than others, i.e.,
more of the cultural practice of more people may occur in that area than
was previously the case. The content of the stereotypes may alter while
their place in the overall scheme remains unchanged. (It can be argued
that this is what happened to the stereotype of the Cuban black during
Afro-Cubanism.) Part of the continuum may become empty because the
carriers of it have died out. The content of one category may be redefined

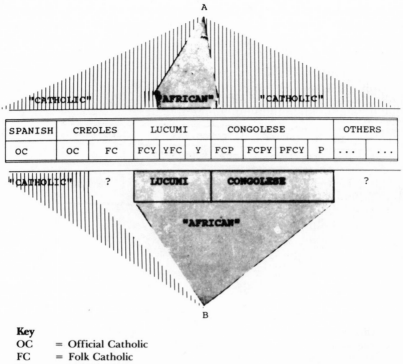

Key
OC   = Official Catholic
FC   = Folk Catholic
Y   = Yoruba religion
FCY   = Folk Catholic–Yoruba
YFC   = Yoruba–Folk Catholic
P   = Congolese religion (Palo)
FCP   = Folk Catholic–Palo
FCPY = Folk Catholic–Palo–Yoruba
PFCY = Palo–Folk Catholic–Yoruba
Other = Other African Nations

FIGURE 11. Redefinition through encounter B. Two people encounter each other and respond to the question "Who are the
practitioners of African religion?" by projecting their classification onto the continuum. Lines designate "Catholic," solid gray
area designates "African," and "?" designates the category "not
classified" or "not known."

and reconstituted as being part of another. On this basis alone the content
of the cultural continuum cannot be considered to be fixed. But the category structure, the boundaries drawn around the groups and structuring
their relationships, can persist over long periods, even while the range of
meanings and the specific meanings of the categories can shift and become
an arena of conflict, contest, and control in the process of defining per-

sonal, group, and national identities. The intersystem, then, is the result of, and also a means for, the efforts of peoples in a multiethnic or multiracial class society to define themselves vis-à-vis one another.

The statement that syncretists do not know that they are practicing two religions or have confused the two may be true for some people after the syncretism has reached a certain stage and become a fait accompli, but it cannot be said that this is necessarily true for those who are actually creating and carrying out the process. This is best seen in the transitions which must inevitably occur between the periods of the developmental continuum. In the transitions between periods, borrowing does not go unnoticed because not everyone agrees with introducing new materials into the religious tradition. Furthermore there is always a more or less prolonged period in which the old forms and the new coexist. While it may be assumed that something like this occurred in the transition from Yoruba religion to Lucumi religion–Early Santeria, there is not much evidence to demonstrate that this was so. For the later transition from Lucumi religion–Early Santeria to Santeria following the infusion of Kardecan spiritism, we have some data. These are the observations of Lydia Cabrera from her fieldwork in Cuba in the late 1940s and early 1950s and her quotations from santeros and devotees of the time (Cabrera 1971). We focus here not only on Cabrera's observations and her informants' observations and distinctions but also on Cabrera's own distinctions, for these were part of the context in which the observations were taking place.

Cabrera was not surprised that Cuban blacks should pick up on Espiritismo. She attributed its spread among the Afro-Cuban population to what she felt was the ease with which blacks went into the trance state. For her, falling with the saint, i.e., being possessed by one of the Yoruba deities, was not much different from the trances of the spiritist mediums. One of her informants also saw things this way.

> It is astonishing the facility with which our negroes fall with the saint, that is to say, into trance. Nothing is more logical, then, that espiritismo, multiplying its centros all over the island, should count thousands and thousands of believers and thousands and thousands of mediums among them. One cannot assume, however, a weakening of the faith in the Orishas nor desertion of the cults of African origin; espiritismo marches hand in hand with them, tightly united, in spite of its pretensions of spirituality . . . of "spiritual advance, of light, of faith and progress." Many babalawos, oluos, babalochas, mamalochas, mayomberos, villumberos, kimbiseros, now have spiritualist spirits and are also espiritista mediums. As one priestess of Santeria — who works the spirits and manifests Cachita–Mama Cache–the Virgin of Cobre in alternation with the spirit of a Congolese slave — said to me: "Ocha or palo. Doesn't it come to the same thing? Spirit, no more! Doesn't one fall into trance with the saint as well as the dead? In religion everything is the thing of the dead. The dead become saints." Saints and spirits are daily visitors in the houses of the Cuban people. "Espiritismo! Bah! In Africa, the same, the dead spoke. This is not new." (29)

Cabrera's informant made several distinctions which gave her a perception of what was new in Espiritismo and what was not, while at the same time differentiating it from the Afro-Cuban religions. The Yoruba-derived regla de ocha (Santeria) and the Congo-Angola-derived palo mayombe are essentially the same thing to her. Both deal with spirit. As far as she is concerned, communication with the dead is the core of both religions. Insofar as Espiritismo was communication with the dead, it was nothing new. Even insofar as Espiritismo was communication with the dead through possession, it was not new. However, the idea on which she could hang this identity and see spiritism as the same as the African religions was that the dead become the saints (orisha), an idea which was by no means shared by all spiritists. For the Africans this idea remained connected with the tradition of ancestor veneration. For other spiritists, such as the white and creole científicos and those whose practice, while more mystical and healing oriented, did not contain much admixture of African belief, such an idea was not true and did not make sense. Accession to sainthood (as they understood it) was by no means automatic; it was the work of many lifetimes, much faith, much charity, and spiritual development through a long chain of reincarnations and tests.

Cabrera also noted that the influence of Espiritismo did not weaken the African cults or lead people to desert them. Instead some adherents of the African religions added the spirits peculiar to Espiritismo to their own pantheons as additional sources of power and worked simultaneously as spiritist mediums and in the cult groups to which they already belonged. The loftier "pretensions" of Espiritismo, its self-image as a progressive, advanced form of religion, a higher form of spirituality than the Catholic Church (and the African religions, for that matter), do not seem to have kept it from being embraced by believers in the African religions.

Like the informant quoted by Cabrera, some people saw nothing new in Espiritismo. They were free to see it as simply another form of what they already knew about. In that case they could ignore it, look into and investigate it, or even embrace it as one of a range of equally legitimate nonexclusive religious or spiritual practices, one that was not African or connected with a specific African heritage or ancestry.

Other Afro-Cubans, however, could grant to Espiritismo its claims of superiority. For such people Espiritismo represented a kind of upward mobility in the hierarchy of spiritual practices, an upward mobility which compensated for their inability to rise in the class system or which possibly accompanied that mobility. In this way one moved upward and away from the African traditions but did not sever one's links entirely. In the trance one was inhabited by the Cuban-grounded African elders, the slaves come through the freeman to heal, and it was the free descendant who bore the task of elevating the slave's spirit from heathen darkness, through progress, and finally to the light of a spiritualist science. It is not only people who can move upward on the status ladder; it is possible for practices to do so, too. Furthermore the spiritist table became a context in which the black medium could work with white mediums as an equal. Cabrera's comments on the color of the mediums have the aroma of the residual racism we find even in liberal Cuban intellectuals of this period. Along with the recurrent comments on "the African nature" and "our negroes" that appear in her observations, in this passage we must also note her suspicion that the white mediums who manifested African spirits might not be as white as they looked or as they claimed to be.

> What is interesting is that the majority of the spirits that manifest themselves through so many mediums of color, and through supposedly white mediums, are spirits of tribal blacks, of African slaves, royal Congolese or angungas, all "disencarnated" during the time of the slave trade and expressing themselves like bozales, raw Africans straight off the boats. They call themselves Taito Jose, Na Francisco, Ta Lorenzo Lucumi, Juan Mandinga, el Mina, el Ganga, el Macua. These beings, who are very advanced in their spiritual evolution and very high and luminous in space, also cure with herbs and sticks, in addition to vases of water, "vases of presence or assistance." In their consultations they prescribe the same as the babalocha or the mayombero. The repertory of cleansings, baths, ebbos, remedies doesn't differ one bit and, like them, they prepare talismans and amulets.

Here we see the residual suspicion of a racist society in which nonetheless there had still been interracial mating for four hundred years and in which family lines not only got darker but got lighter as well. What seems to have struck Cabrera particularly, though, and made her question the racial background of the physically white spiritist mediums was, first, the context in which they were practicing —spiritist tables that included black mediums — and second, the character and attributes of the spirits they received. These spirits were blacks for the most part, and slaves, the lowest of the low, and a presence from the past. In the context of these spiritist meetings, some of them had Spanish names with either African relationship terms tacked on in front or African ethnic group names tacked on behind. They were creole products. The other black spirits were stereotypical ciphers standing for whole African ethnic groups. Though these were considered very advanced in their spiritual evolution and very high spirits, they expressed themselves according to the Cuban stereotype of the bozales, raw, un-Christianized blacks who had just emerged from the holds of the slave ships. Yet they were not base, primitive, or barbaric but luminous. In the back of Cabrera's mind, it would seem, was the idea that if the white mediums were really white they wouldn't have been incarnating these African spirits and elevating them to a superior status and that their ability and willingness to do so indicated something about their biological ancestry. Their presence in the context and what they were doing there made the whole thing anomalous. The only way to bring it into line was to leave open a possibility that would redefine the situation and bring it into line with the racial organization of other contexts: the possibility that the white mediums were really black mediums.

Cabrera notes the emphasis on healing which separates this form of spiritism from the spiritism of the científicos. But she also notes that these spiritists prescribed the same kinds of remedies as Santeria and Paleria practitioners. I believe that this locates the particular kind of spiritism with which she was dealing within a range of spiritist practice which included spiritists who did not prescribe in the same way as santeros and paleros did but also were not científicos. There was a variety of spiritisms at this time, not just one.

Just as the spread of Espiritismo did not separate most of its Afro-Cuban adherents from the African religions they belonged to, Espiritismo did not separate most of them from Catholicism either. Official Catholicism remained exemplary even after the popularity and status of Espiritismo grew to the point where some believers came to regard the spiritist seance as equivalent to mass and likened it to the official rite performed by Catholic priests. The spiritist session thus became *la misa espiritual* (the spiritual mass), just as the bembe drum-dance earlier had been called *la misa africana* (the African mass).

> This "spiritual mass," in which one gives light to the disencarnated soul that is still in darkness, though widespread, does not annul in any way the Catholic mass for putting a soul to rest: "first, the dead asks for mass." . . . And this cannot be set aside or disregarded. . . . The spiritual mass consists in offerings of flowers and vigils —"the flowers attract the spirits" — and in invoking the deceased with the end of knowing its wishes and fulfilling them, to help if it is confused, and to elevate it if it was a conceited being on earth, something "slowing down its immaterial evolution." In effect one assembles various mediums around a table on which are placed bouquets of flowers and glasses (vessels) of perfumed water (Pompey lotion and Florida water). Not only do the self-styled professional mediums readily fall to the floor in trance but so do the relatives and friends of the disappeared one, as do invited guests and curious people who, attracted to those spiritist sessions "in which many spirits come down," often attend without invitation. In these spiritist sessions appears, as in all that concerns the religiosity of our negroes, the immutable African nature (heart). (62)

Just as there were spiritist mediums who prescribed like santeros — a lot of them probably were santeros, or were mediums who learned the techniques from santeros at these sessions — so were there santeros who objected to some aspects of spiritism and thought that they had no business being in the context of Santeria's practices. These issues seem to have arisen with particular force in reference to divination, ancestor veneration, and funeral rites.

When a santero died, the cabildo to which he belonged sponsored two Catholic funeral masses at a church, one nine days after death and a second a year later on the anniversary of the death. There was also a separate African funeral rite. This was called Itutu. In this ritual a santero invoked the dead person and divined his will through cowrie shells, the Ifa priest's divining chain, or the casting of fig leaves (Brandon 1983). By the time Espiritismo assumed prominence among santeros, the practice of having the African Itutu funeral rite done parallel with the two Catholic masses had become the orthodoxy and tradition. After Espiritismo appeared on the scene there arose differences of opinion among the mass of Santeria devotees and priests concerning the status of the spiritual mass as a death rite.

Some spiritist santeros evidently were at once so taken with Espiritismo and so distant from the Catholic Church that they would substitute the misa espiritual for the misa católica. This was never orthodox and, as Cabrera indicated, the Catholic mass for the dead could not be set aside or disregarded. The implication is that those who did this were no longer practicing Santeria or any of the African-based religions — they were doing something else. What Cabrera did not address directly was whether there were some mediums who used the misa espiritual to replace the Itutu instead. Evidently there were, for at the spiritist masses held after the deaths of santeros sometimes the spirit of the dead priest would come down into the ceremony and protest the innovation.

> Notwithstanding the favor that spiritual masses enjoy, one finds cases where some "brothers from space," who are conservatives, recalcitrants and intractable reactionaries, present themselves at the sessions. Although they [the mediums and relatives] call them in the spiritual mass, they demand to speak their sufferings by means of the shells, through Ifa or they speak through the same saint in the head of some "son" [orisha devotee] that they don't want the spiritual mass but rather "the real one, the one with fundamento (foundation)." (63)

These spirits of the dead protested against the spiritual mass as not being real, as being without foundation, without roots in the traditional practice of the cabildos. They protested against the attempt to supplant the divination devices of the Santeria priesthood with the spiritist medium's body and trance state. In the context of the African Itutu the will of the dead African priests had been known through the Yoruba divination techniques; in the context of the spiritist seance these devices had no place. Others felt the same about the changes that spiritism-oriented santeros were introducing to the ancestor shrines that devotees kept in their homes. Some people evidently regarded the spiritual mass and the spiritist's white table as equivalent to or as a substitute for the ancestor shrines which devotees of Lucumi religion kept in their homes. Cabrera quotes an elderly devotee, a living "recalcitrant," who was witnessing the spiritist fashion wash over the Lucumi tradition of the earlier period and simply decided to practice as she always had.

"The spiritual mass is fashionable. Good . . . I always set up for my dead by setting out for them the food they like most in a little corner in the toilet. That is
where they eat and are thus content," one of my old acquaintances says to me,
concluding philosophically, *"Mine have not come into the fashion of those that give
them light in space* [the spiritists]. *I light them a little oil lamp and that is enough for
them."* (62–63; my emphasis)

The two forms of the rites to the dead coexisted at least for the period
that the struggle between them went on. When the new form became traditional, some houses and religious families continued to use it. Others
continued to practice as they had before; they either came in line with the
new practices as time went by, or they continued in their old ways and contributed to the structural continuum of Santeria practice existing at later
points in time. There was no rupture between these two phases, no total
break or gap between the Cuban contexts involved. Such a total break or
gap would have been the result of repeated transformations which were
massive, very generalized, and extremely rapid. This does not seem to have
been the case, for approximately ninety years after Espiritismo was introduced to the island and at least fifty years after it probably began to seriously affect Santeria, it had not eradicated the preexisting forms of that
religion. Collective memory records no such rupture because there was
none.

In the course of this argument I have taken the concept of syncretism
apart, "deconstructed" it. But this deconstruction has had an unfortunate
consequence. Once the concept of syncretism has been taken apart in this
way, it cannot be put back together again. The pieces are no longer there.
Instead of lying about like the scattered pieces of a jigsaw puzzle, these
pieces have dissolved into thin air. This points up a very important fact:
from the perspective of process it may well be that there is nothing distinctive about syncretism and that what has drawn our attention to it is our
own knowledge of the history of the phenomena we are investigating, a
certain stance toward the societies involved, and what we see as the significant cultural differences between the interacting traditions. It is much as if
we were to observe someone pour two beakers of water each of which contained a different food coloring into a common vat and assumed that the
major factor governing the process by which the two waters mixed was the
difference in food coloring rather than diffusion, which would be operating whether the waters were the same color, were uncolored, or differed in
some other property unrelated to color, such as temperature or viscosity.
From this there flows another observation, that there is nothing distinctive
about so-called syncretic religions, i.e., from the point of view of process.
But far from pushing the study of these "impure" religions further to the
margins, this observation brings them to the forefront of study. It just
points up the pervasiveness of culture change in the modern and postmod-
ern world, its importance as a ubiquitous and fundamental phenomenon

in the contemporary world and the recent past. It also points up the selectiveness of borrowing, the reality of intention in borrowing, and the differing effects that borrowed elements exert on the recipient traditions.

Rather than resolving the problems of syncretism we have come in a roundabout fashion to the conclusion that the concept of syncretism is a problem for history and anthropology, a problem which cannot be resolved but only dissolved. In my opinion the concept of syncretism is a black box concept. The black box contains a number of processes which when illuminated turn the box white. In every black box there are two boxes trying to get out. Here, one concerns processes and the other states. I believe that processes are the more fundamental of the two. Whenever the innards of the black box become illuminated, some of the box dissolves. I believe that the concept of syncretism will dissolve into the study of cultural and social processes and the effects of problem solving and manipulation, decision-making, ecology, and creativity in relation to social and historical contexts, that it will yield to tools that can handle variation, rapid change, and context dependence.

It is my belief that these facts have, or ought to have, profound implications for theory and method in the study of sociocultural phenomena. Any significant and continuing sociocultural phenomenon results from the interaction of a number of processes operating over different time spans and defined by different time boundaries. In such a multicultural continuum or intersystem, much behavior is situation-bound, and it is necessary to conceive culture in terms of levels of organization in relation to specific contexts.

> There are different role-expectations that go with different social relationships and different social situations. Each of these different expectations constitutes a different culture to be learned. Because such cultures are situation bound and thus ordered with respect to other situation-bound cultures, we may choose to think of them as subcultures or microcultures, reserving the term "culture" for the larger, ordered system of which these are a part; in this sense, culture ceases to refer to a generic phenomenon of study and refers instead only to some level of organization of that phenomenon. (Goodenough: 1978:82)

The most comprehensive meaning of a continuing sociocultural phenomenon may also require the realization that it exists in relation to multiple spatial and geographical contexts, from the microspace of an individual room to local, regional, or even global relationships shaping the thoughts, behaviors, and self-concepts of the people involved in it.

The different phases or religions I refer to as Yoruba religion, Early Santeria–Lucumi religion, Santeria, Santerismo, and Orisha-Voodoo can be seen as the path by which a single "ethnicity" was transformed over time. We have seen that ethnicity—as a calculus of cultural differences and as a structural principle—may be important long before a group can be said to have become incorporated within a complex modern society as one "ethnic group" among others. (This was the case in Africa among the Yoruba and between them and their neighbors.) The story I have told shows that symbols of ethnicity can be used to survive the invasion of a stronger, technologically superior civilization and, even in that situation, can be used to further a dominated group's own interests. In this passage through time, aspects of old ethnic identities were deleted, reified, or generalized in response to the logic of historical situations and events. Along this path Lucumi ethnicity, formerly the crux of Yoruba religion, absorbed a wide diversity of cultural influences and many individuals of non-Yoruba origin. These accidents of heritage and birth were made coherent by coalescing them into a unique socioreligious category and what members came to think of as a distinct and unchanging heritage. Our story has also described the price of taking this path and the ambiguities of the results.

What makes a people "particular" is the group's own perception of a distinct cultural heritage and the relationship that obtains between what are seen as significant elements of its cultural heritage and what are seen as distinctive elements of the cultural heritages of other groups with which it interacts. Much of this perception is worked out through means of stereotypical images of the interacting groups. These stereotypes are an objective reality affecting how people view themselves and how they view others, and they are elements in a popular anthropology, a folk calculus of significant cultural differences which is often endowed with mythic force and intensity. This particularity is in a continuous dialogue with notions of foreignness. Notions of otherness and exoticism are not the monopoly of popular stereotypes but are also present in the social, cultural, and historical sciences. The construction of the Other as the object of history and of anthropological research is dependent on global patterns of domination and on local and regional resistance to that domination. For no one has this been truer than for Africans and their descendants. Whether in the colonial mother country or the colony, the "big house" or the slave barracks, the centers of international domination or their peripheral reaches, a European model of culture, civilization, and human nature held sway in which the African was always found wanting.

The concept of ethnicity and the notion of tradition go together. Tradition is the preserved or invented heritage that makes ethnicity socially useful. Tradition represents the legacy of the past, but it is also an ongoing process. The fact that some groups can sincerely declare that they are doing what they have always done often masks the fact that one of the most important characteristics of some of these groups has been their ability to adapt to rapid change. This apparent contradiction is often resolved by a fiction.

Many or most cultures create a useful but peculiar fiction about time. In this fiction the essential story line is always "the old ways are best." But present experience sometimes objects to fiction. It says, "The old ways are from the old days. People do not live in those days anymore; they live in the present." Still, it is possible for people to have it both ways if they are willing to accept both the present and the past as best. Inside the story line "the old ways are best" it is easier for people to accept the present as best if they think it is old. It fits the story line better. In this way people can say that they are doing what they have always done even if they are not. This is possible because whether or not they are actually doing what they did at a previous point in time does not affect what they say about their relationship to their own past. It is the relationship to their own past which is at issue, and the main effort is not only to make both the past and the present "best" but to keep the past and present aligned, like two mirrors facing each other.

Today a quivering, invisible web connects all human societies; this web is so sensitive that an event occurring on its most inaccessible node can send a tremor through the whole world. These tremors do not come from contemporary events alone. We now know more about the history of the world than was ever possible to know before. There is simply more history than there used to be, and it continues to accumulate and become more accessible. An historical event that affected only a small number of people when it occurred can have massive consequences visible today in widely separated regions of the world. Whatever happened to some people in the past affects virtually all people today.

A series of little-known wars among Africans affected trade agreements with Europeans and caromed through the massive trade in slaves which formed a foundation for the economic, cultural, and political development of Europe and the Americas. Africans, Amerindians, and Europeans met in specific places and situations, ports of call where their three civilizations flowed into each other without abandoning assumptions of foreignness and difference. Each had an orientation toward the world into which it had to fit the others and endow them with meaning. These assumed meanings shaped the realities of contact and were shaped by those realities. This skein of assumed, interdependent, and deformed meanings was the matrix for the creole culture of conquest and colonization. Spanish priests "christened" sugar plantations with the names of Catholic saints, while Afro-Cubans carried out rites "baptizing" ceramic tureens and iron pots with African and Spanish names; upper-class white Cubans went to African medicine men for a witchcraft they could insert into their own demonology and in the process made the medicine men witches; the military gleam of unsheathed swords flashed at the elevation of the communion host while the priest's unintelligible Latin droned on; Africans danced funerals in front of a Virgin Mary that had black skin, a silk dress, and scarifications; white mediums cured clients with tobacco smoke (which they took to be an Indian practice) while smoking cigars to draw near the spirits of Congolese slaves. The practical affairs of colonial life—making sugar and profits, synthesizing religious traditions, plotting elite sorcery, uniting state and church, death, healing and sickness—were also dramatic enactments, fantastic new rituals of conquest staged under a mythos of fear, power, and race.

The attempts of the Africans to preserve and adapt their religious traditions affected not only themselves and their masters and descendants but to some degree music, art, dance, and literature around the world. Now, with the immigration of their descendants and people influenced by them to the United States, their influence has left the margins of the third world and entered the contemporary center of a world capitalism whose development has conditioned most of its recent history. Here it has influenced the beliefs and traditions of other recent immigrants who adopted the religion as one means among others for dealing with their own alienation, sickness, and dissatisfaction, and it has influenced the native African-descended people who, finding the tradition scarred by the ravages of history, tried to return to the African source and turn what had become a religious category back into an ethnic group.

It used to be that time receded from us in a straight line. The past was behind us, the future ahead of us, the present at our feet. This is no longer true. The straight line leading to the past has bent back on itself. The past is no longer a single, bounded entity and the present often requires multiple descriptions, as if we were looking at the same object under different lights (Bateson 1979, 1982). We now feel past events in a new way because the effects of history have come back to haunt us. As we take one step toward the future we walk into the effects of the past on the present.

History has caught up with us. More important, the effects of history have caught up with us. These effects are not paper-and-pencil ghosts or shadows that bend over a guilty conscience. This relationship to history is not simply an effect in the world of ideas. It is a concrete historical and material reality involving the migration of "marginal" peoples and their integration into the centers of domination, while these centers themselves have expanded out into the so-called third world via slavery and contract labor, international trade and multinational corporations, foreign aid, mass communications, and tourism. These effects and relationships are people who walk the streets of cities they do not know, people whose lives and heritages are witness to a past studded with brutalities, complicity, envy, and courage.

For some people history is a nightmare. The cumulation of historical knowledge renders the world of the past increasingly foreign, irrational, and corrupt, and the need to break with that world becomes ever more compelling. Karl Marx spoke for them when he wrote that "men make their own history, but they do not make it as they please . . . but under circumstances directly encountered, given and transmitted from the past. The tradition of all the dead generations weighs like a nightmare on the brain of the living" (1963:15). For others, perhaps the majority of the world's peoples, history is one means of awakening from a nightmarish present. They have been on the receiving end of history and, to quote Richard

Wright, "the ultimate effect of white Europe upon Asia and Africa was to cast millions into a kind of spiritual void; I maintain that it suffused their lives with a sense of meaninglessness. I argue that it was not merely physical suffering or economic deprivation that has set over a billion and a half colored people in violent political motion. . . . The dynamic concept of a spiritual void that must be filled, a void created by a thoughtless and brutal impact of the West upon a billion and a half people, is more powerful than the concept of class conflict, and more universal" (1957:34–35). For that billion and a half people, the past becomes ever more necessary and familiar; it is the foundation on which they build a reappraisal of both the present and the future. Needless to say, I cannot predict to which group the reader belongs, but I can hope that this work will be of some benefit, for

> someone in each era must make clear the facts with utter disregard to his own wish and desire and belief. What we have got to know, as far as possible, are the things that actually happened in the world . . . the historian has no right, posing as a scientist to conceal or distort facts; and until we distinguish between the two functions of the chronicler of human action, we are going to render it easy for a muddled world out of sheer ignorance to make the same mistake ten times over. (Du Bois 1969:722)

Bibliography

Abbot, Rev. Abiel
1971 (1829) Letters Written in the Interior of Cuba. Books for Libraries Press, Freeport, N.Y.
Abercrombie, N., Stephen Hill, and Bryan Turner
1984 The Dominant Ideology Thesis. 2d ed. Allen and Unwin, London.
Adedeji, Joel
1972 Folklore and Yoruba Drama: Obatala as a Case Study. In African Folklore, ed. R. Dorson, Indiana University Press, Bloomington, 321–40.
Adefunmi I, Oba Osejiman Adelabu
1981 U.S.A.: Building a Community, Caribe 4, no. 4 (Fall-Winter), 10–12.
1982 Olorisha, a Guide Book into Yoruba Religion. Great Benin Books, Oyotunji Village, Sheldon, S.C.
Aguirre, Benigno
1976 Differential Migration of Cuban Social Races. Latin American Research Review, no. 11, 103–24.
Aimes, H. H.
1905 African Institutions in America. Journal of American Folklore 18, 15–32.
1967 A History of Slavery in Cuba: 1511–1868. Octagon Books, New York.
Ajayi, J. F. A., and R. Smith
1964 Yoruba Warfare in the Nineteenth Century. Cambridge University Press, London.
Akinjobin, I. A.
1966 The Oyo Empire in the Eighteenth Century—a Reassessment. Journal of the Historical Society of Nigeria 3, no. 3, 449–60.
1967 Dahomey and Its Neighbors, 1708–1818. Cambridge University Press, New York.
1972 Dahomey and Yoruba in the Nineteenth Century. In Africa in the Nineteenth and Twentieth Centuries, ed. J. C. Anene and G. Brown, Humanities Press, New York, 255–69.
Anene, J. C.
1972 The Peoples of Benin, the Niger Delta, Congo, and Angola in the Nineteenth Century. In Africa in the Nineteenth and Twentieth Centuries, ed. J. C. Anene and G. Brown, Humanities Press, New York, 270–91.
Angarica, Nicolas Valentin
1955? Manual de Oriate, religión Lucumi. Cuba.
Anonymous
1950 A Dictionary of the Yoruba Language. Oxford University Press, London.
Arguelles, Lourdes
1982 The U.S. National Security State: The CIA and Cuban Emigre Terrorism. Race and Class 23, no. 4, 287–304.
Argyle, W. J.
1966 The Fon of Dahomey. Clarendon Press, Oxford.
Ascarte, E. D.
1970 The Influence of Exile on the Psychopathology of Cuban Patients. Paper presented at the Seventy-eighth Annual Meeting of the American Psychological Association, Miami, Sept. 3–10.

Atkins, Edwin F.
1926   Sixty Years in Cuba. Privately printed by Riverside Press, Cambridge.
Babayemi, S. O.
1980   Egungun among the Oyo Yoruba. Ibadan.
Barber, Karin
1981   How Man Makes God in West Africa: Yoruba Attitudes toward the
              Orisha. Africa 51, no. 3, 724–45.
Barnes, Sandra T.
1980   Ogun: An Old God for a New Age. Institute for the Study of Human
              Issues Occasional Paper in Social Change no. 3. Philadelphia.
Barros, J. de
1552   Da Asia. Lisbon.
Bascom, William
1942   The Principle of Seniority in the Social Structure of the Yoruba.
              American Anthropologist 44, 37–46.
1944   The Sociological Role of the Yoruba Cult Group. American Anthro-
              pologist 46 (January), Memoir no. 63.
1950   The Focus of Cuban Santeria. Southwestern Journal of Anthropol-
              ogy 6, no. 1, 64–68.
1951   Social Status, Wealth and Individual Differences among the Yoruba.
              American Anthropologist 53, 490–506.
1952   Two Forms of Afro-Cuban Divination. Proceedings of the Twenty-
              fourth Congress of Americanists, vol. 1, 196–99.
1960   Yoruba Concepts of the Soul. In Man and Cultures: International
              Congress of Anthropological and Ethnological Sciences of 1956,
              ed. A. F. C. Wallace, University of Pennsylvania Press, Philadel-
              phia, 401–10.
1969a   Ifa Divination: Communication between Gods and Men in West Af-
              rica. Indiana University Press, Bloomington.
1969b   The Yoruba of South Western Nigeria. Holt, Rinehart and Winston,
              New York.
1972   Shango in the New World. Occasional Publication of the African and
              Afro-American Institute, no. 4, University of Texas, Austin.
1980   Sixteen Cowries: Yoruba Divination from Africa to the New World.
              Indiana University Press, Bloomington.
Bastide, Roger
1971   African Civilizations in the New World. Harper and Row, New York.
1978a   The African Religions of Brazil. Trans. Helen Sebba. Johns Hopkins
              University Press, Baltimore.
1978b   O Candomblé da Bahia (Rite Nago). Brasiliana 313. Companhia Ed-
              itora Nacional, São Paulo.
Bateson, Gregory
1979   Mind and Nature. Dutton, New York
1982   Difference, Double Description and the Interactive Designation of
              Self. In Studies in Symbolism and Communication, ed. F. A. Han-
              son, University of Kansas Publications in Anthropology 14, 3–8.
Bercerra, Berta, and Juan Comas
1957   La obra escrita de don Fernando Ortiz. Revista Interamericana de
              Bibliografia, no. 7, 347–71.
Bergson, Henri
1911   Matter and Memory. Allen and Unwin, London.
Bermudez, Armando Andres
1967   Notas para la historia del espiritismo en Cuba. Etnología y Folklore,
              no. 4, 5–22.

1968   La expansion del "Espiritismo del Cordon." Etnología y Folklore, no.
                5, 5–32.
Booth, David
1973   Neighborhood Committees and Popular Courts in the Social Trans-
                formation of Cuba. Ph.D. diss., University of Surrey.
Borello, Mary Ann, and Elizabeth Mathias
1977   Botanicas: Puerto Rican Folk Pharmacies. In Natural History 86, no.
                7 (Aug.–Sept.), 65–73.
Bosman, William
1967/1701   A New and Accurate Description of the Coast of Guinea. Ed. J. R.
                Willis, J. D. Fage, and R. E. Bradbury. London.
Boswell, Thomas D., and Curtis, James R.
1984   The Cuban American Experience: Culture, Images, and Perspec-
                tives. Bowman and Allanheld.
Bradbury, R. E.
1957   The Benin Kingdom and the Edo-Speaking Peoples of Southwestern
                Nigeria. International African Institute, London.
1964   The Historical Uses of Comparative Ethnography with Special Ref-
                erence to Benin and Yoruba. In The Historian in Tropical Africa,
                ed. Vansina, Maury, and Thomas, Oxford University Press, Lon-
                don, 145–64.
1973   Benin Studies. Oxford University Press, London.
Bram, Joseph
1958   Spirits, Mediums and Believers in Contemporary Puerto Rico.
                Transactions of the New York Academy of Sciences 20, 340–47.
Brandon, George
1980   Santeria, Black Nationalism and Orisha-Voodoo. Paper presented at
                Rutgers University Latin American Institute Conference on Intra-
                hemispheric Migration. Oct. 31, New Brunswick, N.J.
1983   The Dead Sell Memories: An Anthropological Study of the Santeria
                of New York. Ph.D. diss., Rutgers University, New Brunswick, N.J.
1990a   Sacrificial Practices in Santeria, an African-Cuban Religion in the
                United States. In Africanisms in American Culture, ed. Joseph
                Holloway, Indiana University Press, Bloomington, 119–47.
1990b   African Religious Influences in Cuba, Puerto Rico and Hispaniola.
                Journal of Caribbean Studies 7, nos. 2 and 3 (Winter-Spring),
                201–32.
Brown, Diana DeG.
1986   Umbanda: Religion and Politics in Urban Brazil. Studies in Cultural
                Anthropology no. 7, UMI Research Press, Ann Arbor, Mich.
Brown, Diana DeG., and Garrison, Vivian
1981   Popular Religions, Identity and Mental Health Implications for Car-
                ibbean Immigrants in Metropolitan New York and New Jersey.
                MS.
Buckley, Anthony
1976   The Secret—an Idea in Yoruba Medicinal Thought. In Social An-
                thropology and Medicine, ed. J. B. Louden, Academic Press,
                396–421.
Buczynska-Garewicz, Hanna
1979   Peirce's Method of Triadic Analysis of Signs. Semiotica 26, nos. 3-4,
                251–59.
Bustamante, J. A.
1968   Cultural Factors in Hysterias with Schizophrenic Clinical Picture. In-
                ternational Journal of Social Psychiatry 14, no. 2, 113–18.

Butterworth, Douglas
1980   The People of Buena Ventura: Relocation of Slum Dwellers in Post-
            revolutionary Cuba. University of Illinois Press, Urbana.
Cabrera, Lydia
1959   La sociedad secreta Abakwa Narrado por viejo adeptos. Ediciones
            C. R., Havana.
1971   El Monte. Colección Chichereku en Exilo, Miami.
1973   La laguna sagrada de San Joaquín. Ediciones Madrid, La Hay.
1977   La regla Kimbisa del Santo Cristo de Buen Viaje. Colección Chich-
            ereku en Exilo, Miami.
1979   Reglas de Congo, Palo Monte–Mayombe. Miami.
Cadamosto, Alvise
1937   The Voyages of Cadamosto and Other Documents. Trans. and ed.
            G. R. Crone. London.
Calvo, Lino Novas
1932   La luna de los nanigos. Revista de Occidente, no. 35 (January),
            85–105.
Cancio, Felix
1981   Cuba and Venezuela: Religious Communities in the Americas. Car-
            ibe 5, no. 4 (Fall-Winter), 9–10.
Carpentier, Alejo
1933   Écue-Yamba-O: Historia afrocubana. Editorial España, Madrid.
1946   La Música en Cuba. Fondo de Cultura Económica, Mexico City.
Castellanos, Isabel Mercedes
1976   The Use of Language in Afrocuban Religion. Ph.d. diss., George-
            town University, Washington, D.C.
Castellanos, Jorge, and Isabel Castellanos
1987   The Geographic, Ethnologic and Linguistic Roots of Cuban Blacks.
            Cuban Studies 17, 95–110.
Chappel, T. J. H.
1974   The Yoruba Cult of Twins in Historical Perspective. Africa 44, no. 3,
            250–65.
Chernoff, John Miller
1979   African Rhythm and Sensibility. University of Chicago Press,
            Chicago.
Clapp, Steven
1966   A Reporter at Large: African Theological Archministry. MS.,
            Schomburg Collection, New York.
Cohn, Sandra
1973   Two Essays on Ethnic Identity and the Yoruba of Harlem: Essay I:
            Ethnic Identity in New York. Essay II: Ethnic Identity in the
            South. Master's paper. Columbia University, New York.
Cole, Johnetta B.
1980   Race toward Equality: The Impact of the Cuban Revolution in Rac-
            ism. Black Scholar 11, no. 8 (Nov.-Dec.), 2–24.
Communist Party of Cuba
1971   Declaration of the First National Congress on Education and Cul-
            ture in Cuba: Religion. Havana, April 30. Vertical File, Center for
            Cuban Studies, New York.
1975   Resolution of the First Communist Party of Cuba on Religion. Ver-
            tical File, Center for Cuban Studies, New York.
Connerton, Paul
1989   How Societies Remember. Cambridge University Press, New York.

Corwin, Arthur
1967   Spain and the Abolition of Slavery in Cuba. University of Texas
              Press, Austin.
Courlander, Harold
1944   Abakwa Meeting in Guanabocoa. Journal of Negro History 24, no. 4,
              462–63.
1975   A Treasury of African Folklore. Crown, New York.
Cox, Oliver C.
1970   Caste, Class and Race. Monthly Review Press, New York.
Crahan, Margaret
1979   Salvation through Christ or Marx—Religion in Revolutionary Cuba.
              Journal of Inter-American Studies and World Affairs 21, no. 1
              (Feb.), 156–84.
Curtin, Philip
1969   The Atlantic Slave Trade: A Census. University of Wisconsin Press,
              Madison.
1971   The Slave Trade and the Atlantic Basin: Intercontinental Perspec-
              tives. In Key Issues in the Afro-American Experience, ed. Hug-
              gins, Kilson, and Fox, Harcourt, Brace and Jovanovich, New York,
              74–93.
D'Avenzac, Marie Armond
1967/1845   The Land and the People of Ijebu. In Africa Remembered, ed.
              Philip Curtin, 223–288.
Davey, Richard
1898   Cuba Past and Present. Scribners, New York.
De la Riva, Francisco Perez
1973   Cuban Palenques. In Maroon Societies, ed. Richard Price, Double-
              day, Garden City, N.Y., 49–59.
Dennett, R.
1960   Nigerian Studies on the Religious and Political Systems of the
              Yoruba. Macmillan.
Dillard, J. L.
1973   Black Names. Mouton, The Hague.
Dominguez, Jorge
1978   Cuba: Order and Revolution. Harvard University Press, Cambridge,
              Mass.
Drake, St. Claire
1975   The African Diaspora in Pan-African Perspective. Black Scholar 7,
              no. 1 (Sept.), 2–13.
Du Bois, W. E. B.
1969/1935   Black Reconstruction in America 1860–1880. World Publishing,
              Cleveland.
Drummond, Lee
1980   The Cultural Continuum: A Theory of Intersystems. Man 15, no. 2,
              352–74.
Eades, J. S.
1980   The Yoruba Today. Cambridge University Press, New York.
Eblen, Jack Ericson
1975   On the Natural Increase of Slave Populations: The Example of the
              Cuban Black Population, 1775-1900. In Race and Slavery in the
              Western Hemisphere, ed. Engerman and Genovese, 211–48.
              Princeton University Press, Princeton, N.J.

Echevarria, Roberto
1977   Alejo Carpentier: Pilgrim at Home. Cornell University Press, Ithaca,
            N.Y.
Egharevba, J. U.
1936   Benin.
1972/1951   Benin. Kraus Reprints, Nendeln.
Ellis, A. B.
1894   The Yoruba-Speaking Peoples of the Slave Coast of West Africa.
            Chapman and Hall, London.
Eltis, David
1977   The Export of Slaves from Africa, 1821–1843. Journal of Economic
            History 37, no.2, 409–33.
1979   The Direction and Fluctuation of the Transatlantic Slave Trade,
            1821–1843: A revision of the 1845 Parliamentary Paper. In The
            Uncommon Market: Essays in the Economic History of the Atlan-
            tic Slave Trade, ed. Gemery and Hagendorn, New York.
Engerman, Stanley, and Eugene Genevese, eds.
1975   Race and Slavery in the Western Hemisphere—Quantitative Studies.
            Princeton University Press, Princeton, N.J.
Epega, Rev. D. Onadele
N.d. (1938?) The Mystery of the Yoruba Gods. Imole Oluwa Institute, Ode Remo,
            Lagos.
Essien-Udom, E. U.
1970   Black Nationalism: A Search for an Identity in America. University
            of Chicago Press, Chicago.
Fage, J. D.
1969   A History of West Africa. Cambridge University Press, New York.
1983   A History of Africa. Knopf, New York.
Fagen, Richard B.
1968   Cubans in Exile: Disaffection and the Revolution. Stanford Univer-
            sity Press, Stanford, Calif.
Fagg, William
1963   Nigerian Images. Praeger, New York.
Farrow, S. S.
1926   Faith, Fancies and Fetish on Yoruba Paganism. London.
Femia, J.
1975   Hegemony and Consciousness in the Thought of Antonio Gramsci.
            Political Studies 23, no. 1, 29–48.
Feminelli, F. X., and J. S. Quadagno
1978   The Italian-American Family. In Ethnic Families in America, ed.
            Mindell and Habenstein, Elsevier, New York, 61–63.
Fernandes, Valentim
1951   Descriptión de la Ciote occidentale de l'Afrique. Ed. Th. Monod, A.
            Teixeiro da Mota, and R. Mauny Bissau.
Fernandez, James W.
1965   Symbolic Consensus in a Fang Reformative Cult. American Anthro-
            pologist 67, 902–27.
1974   The Mission of Metaphor in Expressive Culture. Current Anthopol-
            ogy 15, no. 2 (June), 119–45.
Fisch, Stanley
1968   Botanicas and Spiritualism in a Metropolis. Milbank Memorial Fund
            Quarterly 43, no. 3, 377–88.
Fitzpatrick, Joseph
1976   The Puerto Rican Family. In Ethnic Families in America, ed. C. Min-
            dell and R. Haberstein, Elsevier, New York, 192–218.

Foner, Phillip
1962   A History of Cuba and Its Relations with the United States. 2 vols.
              International Publishers, New York.
Forde, Daryll
1951   Yoruba-Speaking People of Nigeria. Ethnographic Survey of Africa,
              West Africa, 4. International African Institute, London.
Foster, George M.
1953   Relationships between Spanish and Spanish American Folk Medi-
              cine. Journal of American Folklore 66, 201–17.
1960   Culture and Conquest: America's Spanish Heritage. Viking Publica-
              tions in Anthropology, no. 27. Quadrangle Books, Chicago.
Franco, Jose L.
1973   Maroons and Slave Rebellions in Spanish Territories. In Maroon So-
              cieties, ed. Richard Price, Doubleday, Garden City, N.Y., 35–48.
Fraser, Douglas
1972   The Fish-legged Figure in Benin and Yoruba Art. In African Art and
              Leadership, ed. Fraser and Cole, 261–94.
Fried, Morton
1975   The Notion of Tribe. Cumming, Calif.
Friedman, Robert A.
1982   Making an Abstract World Concrete: Knowledge, Competence and
              Structural Dimensions of Performance among Bata Drummers in
              Santeria. Ph.D. diss., Indiana University, Bloomington.
Frobenius, Leo
1913   The Voice of Africa. Hutchinson, London.
Garrison, Vivian
1977   Doctor, Espiritista or Psychiatrist? Health-Seeking Behavior in a Pu-
              erto Rican Neighborhood of New York City. Medical Anthropol-
              ogy 1, no. 2 (pt. 3), 65–180.
Gates, Skip
1976   Eldridge Cleaver on Cuba. In Yardbird Reader 5, Berkeley, Calif.,
              188–210.
Genovese, Eugene, Ed.
1973   The Slave Economics. 2 vols. John Wiley, New York.
Gleason, Judith
1973   A Recitation of the Ifa Oracle of the Yoruba. Grossman, New York.
1975   Santeria, Bronx. Atheneum, New York.
Gonzalez-Whippler, Migene
1973   Santeria: African Magic in Latin America. Julian Press, New York.
1982   The Santeria Experience. Prentice-Hall, Englewood Cliffs, N.J.
1983   Pancho Mora: Babalawo Supreme and Oracle of Orunla. Latin New
              York 6, no. 9 (Sept.), 27–28.
Goodenough, Ward H.
1978   Multiculturalism as the Normal Human Experience. In Applied An-
              thropology in America, ed. E. M. Eddy and W. L. Partridge, Co-
              lumbia University Press, New York, 79–86.
Graham, James D.
1965   The Slave Trade, Depopulation and Human Sacrifice in Benin His-
              tory. Cahiers d'Etudes Africaines, no. 18, 317–34.
Gramsci, Antonio
1971   Selections from the Prison Notebooks. Ed. and trans. Quintin Hoare
              and G. Nowell Smith. International Publishers, New York.
Granma
1977   There Are No Contradictions between the Aims of Religion and the
              Aims of Socialism. Nov. 20, 1977.

Gregory, Steven
1986   Santeria in New York: A Study in Cultural Resistance. Ph.D. diss.,
               New School for Social Research, New York.
Grossberg, L.
1984   Strategies of Marxist Cultural Interpretation. Critical Studies in
               Mass Communication 1, no. 4, 392–421.
Gudeman, Stephen
1976   Saints, Symbols and Ceremonies. American Ethnologist 3, no. 4
               (Nov.), 709–30.
Guerra y Sanchez, Ramiro, et al.
1952   Historia de la nación cubana. 10 vols. Editorial Historia, Havana.
1964   Sugar and Society in the Caribbean. Yale University Press, New Ha-
               ven, Conn.
Guillen, Nicolas
1969   Fernando Ortiz (1881–1969). Casa de las Americas 10 (July-Aug.),
               6.
Halbwachs, Maurice
1980   The Collective Memory. Trans. Francis and Vida Ditter. Harper and
               Row, New York.
Halifax, Joan, and Hazel Weidman
1973   Religion as a Mediating Institution in Acculturation. In Religion and
               Psychotherapy, ed. R. H. Cox, Charles C. Thomas, Springfield,
               Ill., 319–31.
Hall, Gwendolyn
1971   Social Control in Slave Plantations. Johns Hopkins Studies in Histor-
               ical and Political Science. Johns Hopkins University Press,
               Baltimore.
Hall, Stuart
1985   Signification, Representation, Ideology: Althusser and the Post-
               Structuralist Debates. Critical Studies in Mass Communications 2,
               no. 2, 87–114.
Hannerz, Ula
1974   Ethnicity and Opportunity in America. In Urban Ethnicity, ed. Ab-
               ner Cohen, Tavistock, New York.
Harber, Francis
1980   The Gospel according to Allan Kardec. Theo Gaus, Brooklyn.
Harwood, Alan
1977   RX: Spiritist as Needed: A Study of a Puerto Rican Community Men-
               tal Health Resource. John Wiley, New York.
Helbing, Mark I.
1972   Primitivism and the Harlem Renaissaince. Ph.D. diss., University of
               Minnesota.
Herberg, W.
1956   Protestant-Catholic-Jew. Doubleday, Garden City, N.Y.
Herrera, Rosalia Garcia
1972   Observaciones ethnologías de dos sectas religiosas afrocubanas en
               una communidad lajera, la Guinea. Islas, no. 43 (Sept.-Dec.), 145,
               147–50, 155, 179–80.
Herskovits, Melville J.
1937   African Gods and Catholic Saints. American Anthropologist 39,
               639–43.
1938   Dahomey, an Ancient West African Kingdom. J. J. Augustin, New
               York.

1948   The Contribution of Afro-American Studies to Africanist Research. American Anthropologist 1, no. 1 (pt. 1), 1–10.
1969   Some Psychological Implications of Afro-American Studies. In Acculturation in the Americas, vol. 2, ed. Sol Tax, Proceedings of the Twenty-ninth International Congress of Americanists, University of Chicago Press, 152–60.
Herskovits, M. J., and F. S. Herskovits
1933   Outline of Dahomean Religious Belief. Memoirs of the American Anthropological Association, no. 4.
Hoetink, H.
1973   Slavery and Race Relations in the Americas. Harper and Row, New York.
1985   "Race" and Color in the Caribbean. In Caribbean Contours, ed. Sidney Mintz and Sally Price, Johns Hopkins University Press, Baltimore, 55–84.
Howe, Julia Ward
1969/1890   A Trip to Cuba. Negro Universities Press, New York.
Humboldt, Alexander
1856   The Island of Cuba. Derby and Jackson, New York.
Hunt, Carl M.
1979   Oyotunji Village: The Yoruba Movement in America. University Press, Washington, D.C.
Hunwick, J. O.
1972   The Nineteenth Century Jihads. In Africa in the Nineteenth and Twentieth Centuries, ed. J. C. Anene and G. Brown, Humanities Press, New York, 291–307.
Idowu, E. Bolaji
1962   Olodumare, God in Yoruba Belief. Longman, London.
Jaffe, A. J., Ruth Cullen, and Thomas Boswell
1980   The Changing Demography of Spanish Americans. Academic Press, New York.
Janney, Frank
1981   Alejo Carpentier and his Early Works. Thames Books, London.
Jeffreys, M. D. W.
1956   Some Rules of Directed Culture Change under Roman Catholicism. American Anthropologist 58, no. 4, 721–31.
Johnson, Samuel
1973   The History of the Yorubas. Ed. Dr. O. Johnson. CMS Bookshops, Lagos.
Kardec, Allan
1963   El libro de los espíritus. 9th ed. Editorial Diana, Tlacoquemecatl, Mexico.
1963   El libro de los mediums. 9th ed. Editorial Diana, Tlacoquemecatl, Mexico.
1975   Collection of Selected Prayers (New Devotionary Spiritist). Studium Corp., New York.
Kiple, Kenneth F.
1976   Blacks in Colonial Cuba 1774–1899. Latin American Monographs, 2d ser. Center for Latin American Studies, University of Florida, Tallahassee.
Klein, Herbert
1967   Slavery in the Americas: A Comparative Study of Virginia and Cuba. University of Chicago Press, Chicago.

Knight, Franklin
1970   Slave Society in Cuba in the Nineteenth Century. University of Wisconsin Press, Madison.
1972   Cuba. In Neither Slave nor Free, ed. D. W. Cohen and J. P. Greene, Johns Hopkins University Press, Baltimore, 278–308.
1977a   Origins of Wealth and the Sugar Revolution in Cuba, 1750–1850. Hispanic American Historical Review 57, no. 2, 231–53.
1977b   The Social Structure of Cuban Society in the Nineteenth Century. Annals of the New York Academy of Sciences 292, 259–66.
Koss, Joan
1975   Therapeutic Aspects of Puerto Rican Cult Practices. Psychiatry 38, no. 2, 160–71.
Lachatanere, Romulus
1938   Oh Mio Yemaya! Editorial Arte, Manzanilla, Cuba.
1942   Manual de Santeria. Editorial Caribe, Havana.
Laguerre, Michel
1987   Afro-Caribbean Folk Medicine. Bergin and Garvey, South Hadley.
Law, R. C.
1971   The Constitutional Troubles of Oyo in the Eighteenth Century. Journal of African History 12, no. 1, 25–44.
Lawal, Babatunde
1977   The Living Dead: Art and Immortality among the Yoruba of Nigeria. Africa 47, no. 1, 50–61.
Leach, Edmund
1976   Culture and Communication: The Logic by Which Symbols Are Connected. Cambridge University Press, London.
Lears, T. J. J.
1985   The Concept of Cultural Hegemony: Problems and Possibilities. American Historical Review 90, no. 3, 567–93.
Le Page, Robert, P. Christie, A. J. Weekes, and A. Tabouret-Keller
1974   Sociolinguistic Survey of Multilinguistic Communities, Stage I: British Honduras Survey. The Analysis of Sociolinguistic Data. Language in Society 3, 1–32.
Le Riverend, Julio
1973   Fernando Ortiz y su obra cubana. In Orbito de Fernando Ortiz, ed. Le Riverend, Unión de Escritores y Artistes de Cuba, Havana, 7–51.
Lewis, Oscar, Ruth Lewis, and Susan M. Rigdon
1977   Living the Revolution, an Oral History of Contemporary Cuba: Four Men. University of Illinois Press, Urbana.
Leutz, W. N.
1976   The Informal Community Caregiver: A link between the Health Care System and Local Residents. American Journal of Orthopsychiatry 46, 678–88.
Lloyd, P. C.
1955   The Yoruba Lineage. Africa 25, no. 2, 235–51.
Lombard, J.
1967   The Kingdom of Dahomey. In West African Kingdoms in the Nineteenth Century, ed. Forde and Kaberry, 70–92. Oxford University Press, London.
Lovejoy, Paul
1982   The Volume of the Atlantic Slave Trade: A Synthesis. Journal of African History 23, 473–501.

Lowry, Nelson
1950   Rural Cuba. University of Minnesota Press, Minneapolis.
Lucas, J. Olumide
1948   The Religion of the Yorubas. CMS Bookshops, Lagos.
MacEwan, Arthur
1981   Revolution and Economic Development in Cuba. St. Martin's Press,
            New York.
Macklin, June
1974   Belief, Ritual and Healing: New England Spiritualism and Mexican-
            American Spiritism Compared. In Religious Movements in Con-
            temporary America, ed. Zaretsky and Leone, Princeton University
            Press, Princeton, N.J.
MacGaffey, Wyatt, and Clifford Barnett
1962   Cuba. HRAF Press, New Haven, Conn.
Martinez-Alier, Verena
1974   Marriage, Class and Color in Nineteenth Century Cuba: A Study of
            Racial Attitudes and Sexual Values in a Slave Society. Cambridge
            University Press, London.
Marx, Karl
1963/1852   The Eighteenth Brumaire of Louis Napoleon. International Publish-
            ers, New York.
Maupoil, Bernard
1943   La géomancie a l'ancienne Côte des Esclaves. Travaux et Mémoires
            de l'Institut d'Ethnologie 42.
Mauro, Frederic
1960   Portugal et l'Atlantique (1570–1670). Paris. SEVPEN.
Mauss, Marcel
1972   A General Theory of Magic. Trans. Robert Brain. Routledge and
            Kegan Paul, London and Boston.
Mbiti, John S.
1970   African Religion and Philosophy. Doubleday, Garden City, N.Y.
Mintz, Sidney
1974   Caribbean Transformations. Aldine, Chicago.
Mintz, Sidney, and Richard Price
1976   An Anthropological Perspective on the Afro-American Past. ISHI
            Occasional Paper in Social Change, no. 2. Philadelphia.
Montejo, Esteban
1968   The Autobiography of a Runaway Slave. Ed. Miguel Barnet. Pan-
            theon, New York.
Moore, Carlos
1970   Cuba: The Untold Story, pt. 3. Soulbook 3, no. 2 (Fall), 54–73.
Morales-Dorta, Jose
1976   Puerto Rican Espiritismo: Religion and Psychotherapy. Vantage
            Press, New York.
Moreno Fraginals, Manuel
1976   The Sugar Mill. Trans. Cedric Belfage. Monthly Review Press, New
            York.
1977   Africans in Cuba: A Quantitative Analysis of the African Population
            in the Island of Cuba. Annals of the New York Academy of Sci-
            ences 292, 187–201.
Morton-Williams, Peter
1960a   The Yoruba Ogboni Cult in Oyo. Africa 30, no. 4, 362–74.
1960b   Yoruba Responses to the Fear of Death. Africa 30, no. 1, 34–40.

1964   An Outline of the Cosmology and Cult Organization of the Oyo Yoruba. Africa 34, no. 3, 243–61.

1967   The Yoruba Kingdom of Oyo in the Nineteenth Century. In West African Kingdoms in the Nineteenth Century, ed. D. Forde and P. Kaberry, Oxford University Press, London, 36–69.

Morton-Williams, P., W. Bascom, and E. McClelland

1966   Two Studies of Ifa Divination. Africa 36, no. 1, 406–32.

Mullen, Edward

1987   Los Negros Brujos: A Reexamination of the Text. Cuban Studies, no. 17, 111–32.

Mullings, Leith

1978   Ethnicity and Stratification in the Urban United States. Annals of the New York Academy of Sciences 318, 10–22.

Murphy, E. Jefferson

1972   History of African Civilization. Dell, New York.

Murphy, Joseph

1981   The Ritual System of Cuban Santeria. Ph.D. diss., Temple University, Philadelphia.

1988   Santeria: An African Religion in America. Beacon Press, New York.

Murray, D. R.

1971   Statistics of the Slave Trade to Cuba, 1790–1867. Journal of Latin American Studies 3, no. 2, 131–49.

1980   Odious Commerce: Britain, Spain and the Abolition of the Cuban Slave Trade. Cambridge University Press, London.

Nobles, Wade

1980   African Philosophy: Foundations for a Black Psychology. In Black Psychology, ed. R. Jones, 2d ed., Harper and Row, New York.

Nodal, Roberto

1983   The Social Evolution of the Afro-Cuban Drum. Black Perspective in Music 11, no. 2 (Fall), 157–77.

Ojo, J. R. O.

1976   The Diffusion of Some Yoruba Artifacts and Social Institutions. In Proceedings of the Conference on Yoruba Civilization, ed. I. A. Akinjobin and G. O. Ekemode, University of Nigeria, 364–98.

1979   Semiotic Elements of Yoruba Art and Ritual. Semiotica 28, nos. 3–4, 333–48.

Olmsted, David L.

1953   Comparative Notes on Yoruba and Lucumi. Language 29, no. 2, 157–64.

Ortiz, Antonio Dominguez

1971   The Golden Age of Spain 1516–1659. Basic Books, New York.

Ortiz, Fernando

1914   La filosofía penal de las espiritistas. Revista Bimestre Cubana 9, 30–39, 122–35.

1916   Los negros esclavos. Editorial Revista Bimestre Cubana, Havana.

1920   La fiesta afro-cubana del "Día de Reyes." Revista Bimestre Cubana 25, 5–26.

1921   Los cabildos afro-cubana. Revista Bimestre Cubana 26, 5–39.

1952–1955   Los instrumentos de la música afro-cubana. 5 vols. Dirección de Cultura del Ministerio de Educación, Havana.

1959   Los bailes y el teatro de los negros en el folklore de Cuba. Havana.

1970   Cuban Counterpoint. Vintage Books, New York.

1973   Hampa afro-cubana: Los negros brujos. Ediciones Universal, Miami. Originally published 1906.

Parrinder, G.
1947   Yoruba-Speaking Peoples of Dahomey. Africa 17, no. 2, 122–29.
1949   West African Religion. London.
1962   African Traditional Religion. Harper and Row, New York.
Peel, J. D. Y.
1968   Aladura: A Religious Movement among the Yoruba. Oxford Univer-
            sity Press.
Pellicani, Luciano
1981   Gramsci: An Alternative Communism? Hoover Institution Press,
            Stanford University, Stanford, Calif.
Perez y Mena, Andres
1977   Spiritualism as an Adaptive Mechanism among Puerto Ricans in the
            United States. Cornell Journal of Social Relations 12, no. 2 (Fall),
            125–36.
1982   Socialization by Stages of Development into a Centro Espiritista in
            the South Bronx of New York City. Ed.D. diss., Columbia Univer-
            sity Teachers College.
Philalethes, Demoticus
1856   Yankee Travels though the Island of Cuba. Appleton, New York.
Pike, Ruth
1967   Sevillian Society in the Sixteenth Century: Slave and Freemen. His-
            panic American Historical Review 47, 344–59.
Porter, R. P.
1899   Industrial Cuba. Putnam, New York.
Portes, A.
1969   Dilemmas of a Golden Exile: Integration of Cuban Refugee Families
            in Milwaukee. American Sociological Review 34, 505–18.
Pressel, Esther
1973   Umbanda in São Paolo: Religious Innovation in a Developing Soci-
            ety. In Religion, Altered States of Consciousness and Social
            Change, ed. Erika Bourguignon, 264–318, Ohio State University
            Press, Columbus.
Richardson, Miles, Marta E. Padro, and Barbara Bode
1971   The Image of Christ in Spanish America as a Model for Suffering:
            An Exploratory Note. Journal of Inter-American Studies and
            World Affairs 13, 246–57.
Roberts, John M.
1964   The Self-Management of Cultures. In Explorations in Cultural An-
            thropology, ed. Ward H. Goodenough, McGraw-Hill, New York,
            433–54.
Rogg, Eleanor Meyer, and Rosemary Santana Cooney
1980   Adaptation and Adjustment of Cubans: West New York, New Jersey.
            Monograph no. 5, Hispanic Research Center, Fordham University,
            New York.
Rogler, Lloyd, and August B. Hollingshead
1961   The Puerto Rican Spiritist as Psychiatrist. American Journal of So-
            ciology 67, 17–22.
Rouse, Irving
1963a   The Arawak. In Handbook of South American Indians, ed. Julian
            Steward, Smithsonian Institution Bureau of American Ethnology
            Bulletin 4, no. 143, Cooper Square Publishers, New York, 507–46.
1963b   The Carib. In ibid., 547–65.
Rout, Leslie B.
1976   The African Experience in Spanish America. Cambridge University
            Press, New York.

Rubinstein, D.
1976   Beyond Cultural Barriers: Observations on Emotional Disorders
            among Cuban Immigrants. International Journal of Mental
            Health 5, no. 2, 69–79.
Ruiz, Pedro
1972   Santeros, Botanicas and Mental Health: An Urban View. Transcul-
            tural Psychiatric Research Review 9, 176–77.
Ruiz, Pedro, and Ezra H. Griffith
1977   Hex and Possession: Two Problematic Areas in the Psychiatrist's Ap-
            proach to Religion. In Current Perspectives in Cultural Psychiatry,
            ed. Foulkes et al., Spectrum, New York, 93–102.
Ruiz, Pedro, and John Langrod
1976   The Role of Folk Healers in Community Mental Health Services.
            Mental Health Journal 12, 392–98.
1977   The Ancient Art of Folk Healing: African Influence in a New York
            City Community Mental Health Center. In Traditional Healing:
            New Science or New Colonialism?, ed. Phillip Singer, Conch Mag-
            azine, New York, 80–95.
Rumbaut, R. David, and R. G. Rumbaut
1976   The Family in Exile: Cuban Expatriates in the U.S. American Jour-
            nal of Psychiatry 133, no. 4, 395–99.
Russell, Bertrand
1921   Analysis of Mind. Allen and Unwin, New York.
Russell-Wood, A. J. R.
1974   Black and Mulatto Brotherhoods in Colonial Brazil. Hispanic Amer-
            ican Historical Review 54, 567–602.
Ryder, A. F. C.
1965   A Reconsideration of the Ife-Benin Relationship. Journal of African
            History 6, no. 1, 25–37.
Salgado, Ramona Matos
1974   The Role of the Puerto Rican Spiritist in Helping Puerto Ricans with
            Problems of Family Relations. Ed.D. diss., Columbia University
            Teachers College.
Sanchez, Julio
1978   La religión de los orichas. Colección Estudios Afrocaribenos, Hato
            Rey, Puerto Rico.
Sandoval, Mercedes Cros
1975   La religión afrocubana. Colección Libre Plaza Mayor, Madrid.
1977   Santeria: Afro-Cuban Concepts of Disease and Its Treatment in Mi-
            ami. Journal of Operational Psychiatry 8, no. 2, 52–63.
1979   Santeria as a Mental Health Care System: An Historical Overview.
            Social Science and Medicine 13B, 137–51.
Schwab, William
1955   Kinship and Lineage among the Yoruba. Africa 25, no. 4, 352–74.
Seda Bonilla, E.
1969   Interacción social y personalidad en una communidad en Puerto
            Rico. 2d ed. Ediciones Juan Ponce de Leon, San Juan.
Simpson, George E.
1962   The Shango Cult in Nigeria and Trinidad. American Anthropologist
            64, 1204–19.
1965   The Shango Cult in Trinidad. Institute of Caribbean Studies, Uni-
            versity of Puerto Rico, Río Piedras.
1972   Afro-American Religions and Religious Behavior. Caribbean Studies
            12, no. 2 (July), 5–30.

1973   The Kele (Shango) Cult of St. Lucia. Caribbean Studies 3, no. 3 (Oct.), 110–16.
1978   Black Religions in the New World. Columbia University Press, New York.
1980   Selected Yoruba Rituals: 1964. In Religious Cults of the Caribbean, Caribbean Monograph Series. no. 15, Institute of Caribbean Studies, University of Puerto Rico, Río Piedras, 127–39.
Smith, M. G.
1960   Social and Cultural Pluralism. Annals of the New York Academy of Sciences 83, 763–77.
1969   Some Developments in the Analytic Framework of Pluralism. In Pluralism in Africa, ed. L. Kuper and M. G. Smith, University of California Press, Berkeley.
1971   A Note on Truth, Fact and Tradition in Carriacou. Caribbean Quarterly 17, 134–35.
Smith, Raymond
1988   Kinship and Class in the West Indies: A Genealogical Study of Jamaica and Guyana. Cambridge University Press, New York.
Steiner, Stan
1974   The Island: The Worlds of the Puerto Ricans. Harper and Row, New York.
Talbot, P. A.
1926   Peoples of Southern Nigeria. London.
Thomas, Hugh
1971   Cuba: The Pursuit of Freedom. Harper and Row, New York.
Thompson, Robert Farris
1975   Icons of the Mind: Yoruba Herbalism Arts in Atlantic Perspective. African Arts 8 (April), 52–59, 89–90.
1976   Black Gods and Kings. Indiana University Press, Bloomington.
1983   Flash of the Spirit. Random House, New York.
Trotman, David V.
1976   The Yoruba and Orisha Worship in Trinidad and British Guyana: 1838–1870. African Studies Review 19, no. 2 (Sept.), 1–17.
Turnball, David
1840   Travels in the West: Cuba with Notices of Puerto Rico and the Slave Trade. Longman, London.
Turner, Victor W.
1986   Images and Reflections: Ritual Drama, Carnival, Film and Spectacle in Cultural Performance. The Anthropology of Performance, 21–32, PAJ Publications, New York.
Verger, Pierre
1954   Dieux d'Afrique. Paris.
1957   Notes sur le culte des orisha et vodun. Mémoires de l'Institute François d'Afrique Noire, no. 51, Dakar.
1966   The Yoruba High God—A review of the Sources. Odu 2 (new series), no. 2 (January), 19–40.
1969   Trance and Convention in Nago-Yoruba Spirit Mediumship. In Spirit Mediumship and Society in Africa, ed. Beattie and Middleton, Africana, 50–66.
Wagley, Charles
1957   Plantation-America: A Culture Sphere. In Carribean Studies: A Symposium, ed. Vera Rubin, Institute for Social and Economic Research, University College of the West Indies, Jamaica, 5–13.

Wallace, A. F. C.
1956   Revitalization Movements. American Anthropologist 58 (April), 264–81.
1966   Religion: An Anthropological View. Random House, New York.
Wallace, Caroline
1898   Santiago de Cuba before the War. F. Tennyson Neely.
Webster, J. B., and A. A. Boahen
1967   The Growth of African Civilization: The Revolutionary Years: West Africa since 1800. Longmans, London.
Welti, C. V., and R. Martinez
1981   Forensic Sciences Aspects of Santeria, A Religious Cult of African Origin. Journal of Forensic Sciences 26, no. 3 (July), 506–14.
Westcott, Joan
1962   The Sculpture and Myths of Eshu-Elegba, the Yoruba Trickster. Africa 32, no. 4, 336–53.
Willet, Frank
1967   Ife in the History of West African Sculpture. Thames and Hudson.
Willet, John
1978   Art and Politics in the Weimar Period: The New Sobriety 1917–1933. Pantheon, New York.
Williams, Raymond
1980   Base and Superstructure in Marxist Cultural Theory. Problems of Materialism and Culture, Verso Press, London, 31–49.
World Conference on Orisha
1982   The World Conference on Orisha, a Special Report. Visual Arts Resource Center relating to the Caribbean, New York.
Wright, Irene Aloha
1916   The Early History of Cuba (1492–1586). Macmillan, New York.
1920   Rescates: With Special Reference to Cuba, 1599–1610. Hispanic Review 3, 333–61.
1922   Our Lady of Charity. Hispanic American Historical Review 5, 709–17.
Wright, Richard
1957   White Man Listen! Doubleday, Garden City, N.Y.
Wurdeman, J. G. F.
1844   Notes on Cuba. James Monroe, Boston.
Zahan, Dominique
1979   The Religion, Spirituality and Thought of Traditional Africa. Trans. Kate and Lawrence Martin. University of Chicago Press, Chicago.

Index

GEORGE BRANDON is Associate Professor and
Director of the Program in Sociomedical
Sciences at the Sophie Davis School of
Biomedical Education of the City University
of New York. He is the author of a chapter on
Santeria in *Africanisms in American Culture*
(1990) and of articles in the *Journal of Caribbean
Studies*, the *Journal of Black Studies, Oral History
Review*, and the *Griot*.